# KANURI
# SCHOOLCHILDREN
*Education and Social*
*Mobilization in Nigeria*

**ALAN PESHKIN**

# CASE STUDIES IN
# EDUCATION AND CULTURE

---

*General Editors*

GEORGE *and* LOUISE SPINDLER

*Stanford University*

# KANURI SCHOOLCHILDREN
*Education and Social Mobilization in Nigeria*

## NIGERIA (showing political divisions in 1966)

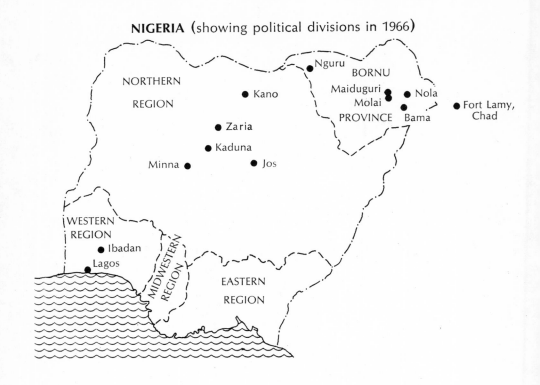

NORTHERN REGION

● Nguru

BORNU

● Kano

Maiduguri ●
Molai ●    ● Nola
PROVINCE    Bama ●

● Fort Lamy, Chad

● Zaria

● Kaduna

Minna ●        ● Jos

WESTERN
REGION

● Ibadan

Lagos ●

MIDWESTERN REGION

EASTERN
REGION

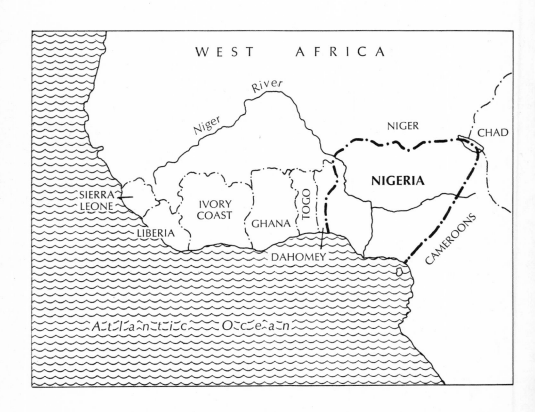

WEST    AFRICA

Niger River

NIGER        CHAD

SIERRA LEONE

IVORY COAST

GHANA    TOGO

NIGERIA

LIBERIA

DAHOMEY

CAMEROONS

Atlantic    Ocean

# KANURI SCHOOLCHILDREN

## *Education and Social Mobilization*

## *in Nigeria*

ALAN PESHKIN
*University of Illinois*

HOLT RINEHART AND WINSTON, INC.
*New York • Chicago • San Francisco • Atlanta
Dallas • Montreal • Toronto • London • Sydney*

Library of Congress Catalog Card Number: 70–163190
ISBN: 0-03-085612-4
Printed in the United States of America
2 3 4 5   059   9 8 7 6 5 4 3 2 1

TO MY PARENTS

*Harriet and Morris Peshkin*
*Evelyn and Simon Rotberg*

# Foreword

## About the Series

This series of case studies in education and culture is designed to bring to students in professional education and in the social sciences the results of direct observation and participation in the educational process in a variety of cultural settings. Individual studies include some devoted to single classrooms, others focus on single schools, some on large communities and their schools; still others report on indigenous cultural transmission where there are no schools at all in the Western sense. Every attempt is made to move beyond the formalistic treatments of educational process to the interaction between the people engaged in educative events, their thinking and feeling, and the content of the educational process in which they are engaged. Each study is basically descriptive in character but since all of them are about education they are also problem oriented. Interpretive generalizations are produced inductively. Some are stated explicitly by the authors of the studies. Others are generated in the reader's mind as hypotheses about education and its environmental relationships.

The cross-cultural emphasis of the series is particularly significant. Education is a cultural process. Each new member of a society or a group must learn to act appropriately as a member and contribute to its maintenance and, occasionally, to its improvement. Education, in every cultural setting, is an instrument for survival. It is also an instrument for adaptation and change. To understand education we must study it as it is—imbedded in the culture of which it is an integral part and which it serves.

When education is studied this way, the generalizations about the relationship between schools and communities, educational and social systems, education and cultural setting that are current in modern educational discussions become meaningful. This series is, therefore, intended for use in courses in comparative and overseas education, social foundations and the sociology of education, international educational development, culture and personality, social psychology, cultural dynamics and cultural transmission, comparative sociology—wherever the interdependency of education and culture, and education and society, is particularly relevant.

We hope these studies will be useful as resources for comparative analyses, and for stimulating thinking and discussion about education that is not confined by one's own cultural experience. Without this exercise of a comparative, transcultural perspective it seems unlikely that we can acquire a clear view of our own educational experience or view education in other cultural settings without ethnocentric bias.

## About the Author

Alan Peshkin studied at the University of Illinois (1948–1954) and the University of Chicago (1957–1962). He taught high school social studies for several years before completing his doctoral research on a project of planned educational change in East Pakistan. After two years of teaching and field work in Bornu, Nigeria, he joined the University of Illinois, where he is Professor of Comparative Education and, until recently, Director of African Studies. His research interests include education in Islamic societies, political socialization, and the effect of schooling on traditional-modern value orientations.

## About the Book

The Kanuri of Bornu, Nigeria, like many peoples with a well-developed traditional culture, are confronted with the necessity of moving decisively into the modern world so heavily influenced in its present shape by an alien system of ideas, values, and technology. In all such movements around the world, education is playing a decisive role in what Alan Peshkin refers to as "social mobilization." That the educational process in these situations is not free of defects and problems is hardly surprising. The nature of the confrontation of old and new can hardly be grasped by the Western reader. It is not merely a difference in content, but in the organization of that content at all levels of thought and perception. In Kanuri society the influence of modern education is being felt, and yet the old cultural system is not falling apart.

Usually the processes of adaptation and change that are set in motion by the confrontation of systems alien to each other are described and analyzed in generalizing and frequently abstract terms. This is not satisfying because it is impossible to appreciate the significant dynamics of such processes without direct observational detail. The author has successfully avoided this difficulty by providing four case studies of Kanuri schoolchildren in school and in their families. These data were collected by twelve Nigerian Kanuri-speaking "observers" trained by the author at Bornu Teacher Training College. The author also provides us with a provocative and thoughtful interpretation of the implications of these case studies taken together. In this way the needs for both detailed observations of situational reality and for abstract generalizing and interpretation are met in this unique book.

We are fortunate in having a case study by Ronald Cohen on the Kanuri of Bornu in the related series Case Studies in Cultural Anthropology. The two studies are decidedly complementary.

George and Louise Spindler
*General Editors*
STANFORD, CALIFORNIA

# Preface

This book is about four Muslim children who attended primary schools in the Nigerian province of Bornu where I was a teacher in a training college. I had come to Bornu as part of a group of educators in a project sponsored by the Ford Foundation and designed to improve teacher education. My students were preparing to be primary school teachers and one of my responsibilities was to supervise their practice teaching. Consequently, during the two years I worked in Bornu Province I had extensive contact with primary schools and their teachers.

Two considerations were particularly important in the decision to study children in the setting of their school and home: First, I hoped to learn what conflict, if any, existed between what children learned at school and at home; and second, I hoped to provide instructional materials which prospective teachers could use in their training colleges and which dealt with Nigerian rather than European children. With at least these notions in mind, I selected four children—two boys and two girls—from two urban and two rural families, and I prepared a case study on each child. My intention was to explore what appeared to be both the short-run and long-run impact of school experiences on children whose parents had not been educated in Western-type schools.

The researcher who conducts cross-cultural studies often faces a dilemma in that his data may be the basis for descriptions and generalizations that are interpretable as uncomplimentary of the persons or institutions studied. If this is the case, the agencies that permitted the investigation may feel grieved that their hospitality was infringed upon. The researcher then may choose to "call his shots" as he sees them, or in deference to his former hosts he may temporize, euphemize, bowdlerize. I do not feel that I did the latter. Nor, in staying true to the data, do I feel that the Kanuri, their schools, or the four families have been presented in uncomplimentary terms. To be sure, some of the parents appeared to be less admirable than others, but only in the ways that some individuals from any group anywhere in the world are less admirable than others. And if Bornu Primary School in Maiduguri appears less effective than Nola Primary School or any other good school anywhere in the world, it must be understood that its problems are known to Nigerian educators and are remediable. Neither the individual nor institutional shortcomings described are any more or less inherent in the Kanuri than in any people. For example, Bintu just happened to be a rude and outspoken child and Bornu Primary School just happened to have some punitive and ineffective teachers.

Furthermore, misunderstandings may result from statements that were true at the time of the study but either are less true or no longer true at the time of publication. To cite a minor example, in Chapter 3 I noted that primary school teachers are not trained to teach science and that students receive virtually no science instruction. From these facts the reader should conclude that science was not emphasized in Bornu's primary schools. Though there was reason to believe that this shortcoming would be corrected in the near future, it was definitely not corrected before the study was completed. Yet it would be much too complicated and confusing to take each such statement that may have become somewhat dated and make it as current as possible. Granted, a reader can make negative inferences about the quality of schooling in Bornu and from such an inference make judgments about educational leadership in Bornu. Because of this possibility, but without intending to offer any apologies (none are needed), I would like to explain that the descriptions of education provided here should be viewed within the following context. At the time of this study, Western-type schooling in Bornu had been emphasized only during the previous five to ten years and hardly touched the lives of most Kanuris. The first postprimary schools were built after independence in 1960. Mounting pressure to catch up to the educationally more advanced southern Nigerians strained regional and provincial resources, both financial and human. Accordingly, the school system in Bornu is new and plagued by all the expected problems of getting started and of meeting substantial quantitative expectations. These problems are not attributable to unwise, shortsighted, or unimaginative leadership; basically it is time that is required for their resolution.

Throughout this book the political terminology used applies to the situation at the time the study was made in April 1966. The then Federal Republic of Nigeria contained four regions (Northern, Eastern, Western, and Midwest), each with its own governor, prime minister, cabinet, and parliament. "Bornu" at this time designated two political entities. It was the name of one of sixteen provinces in Northern Nigeria and, also, of one of five divisions in Bornu Province. Bornu Division was so large that it was almost coterminous with Bornu Province. For this study it is not necessary to keep clear the distinction between the two entities. "Bornu" will be considered synonymous with "Kanuri society," although the division and province contain other tribes. (For a brief but useful historical sketch of Bornu and its kingdom see Cohen 1967:12–32.) And unless otherwise stated, "region" refers to the Northern Region and "province" refers to Bornu Province.

Profound changes have occurred in Nigeria since the political upheavals that began in January 1966. At that time top political and military leaders were assassinated in a coup d'état organized by young military officers seeking a unitary state in place of the federation. The administrative structure of Bornu, and all of Northern Nigeria as well, was reorganized in 1967; six new states were created from the sixteen former northern provinces, and the regional structure was abolished. It should be understood, however, that any reference to the educational or political system relates to circumstances before the coup, circumstances which were in fact the determining ones in shaping the schools as we see them in April 1966. Neither the control and content of education nor the relationship between school and society had been altered in any essential way in the first few months of the "New Nigeria."

The data for the four case studies were provided by the extensive efforts of twelve able young men who were all in training to become primary school teachers. Without their remarkable ability to establish rapport with the four families, there would have been no observations and no study. I am profoundly indebted to "the observers," as they came to be known, and would like to recognize them by name: Baba Machina, Abubukar Sodangi, Harun Abubukar, Ahmed Idris, Ibrahim Abba, Yahaya Gwio Kura, Kalli Geidam, Zarami Geidam, Masu Mohammed, Mai Kachalla, Baba Kadau, and Usman Karagama. I am also indebted to the Bornu Education Authority, particularly Alhaji Kadi, for granting permission to study children in school and to the headmasters who helped select the study children. The children and their families were wonderfully cooperative throughout the four weeks of observation. Needless to say, their willingness and ability to conduct their lives normally under continual scrutiny is the very basis of the entire study. Financial support for the study was provided by the Northern Nigeria Teacher Education Project which in turn was funded by the Ford Foundation. I am especially grateful to Ronald Cohen, Nancy and Louis Brenner, Blair Kling, Barbara Yates, and Josephine and Marvin Knopp for their encouragement and advice; to Walter Feinberg for his helpful critical reading of an early draft; to David Spain for his exceptionally detailed and insightful reading of the manuscript; to Ann Edwards and Marcia Schramm for their patient and painstaking typing of the manuscript; and to Phil Foster and Robert LeVine who generously provided the necessary push for publication. Final expressions of gratitude are properly reserved for the author's family. My wife, Maryann, and children, Nancy, David, and Julie, have contributed in countless ways to the completion of this study.

A. P.

# Main Characters in the Case Studies

NOLA—a village in Bornu Province; 2300 population; a district headquarters.

*Case Study 1*
   Aisa—seven-year-old girl in Class 2 in Nola Primary School.
   Ya Falta—Aisa's mother; housewife and grain seller.
   M. Musa—Aisa's father; grain broker and client of Nola's village head.

*Case Study 2*
   Buba—seventeen-year-old boy in Class 7 in Nola Primary School.
   Zara—Buba's mother; housewife and seller of millet cakes.
   Umar—Buba's father; tanner of hides and skins.


MAIDUGURI—the major city in Bornu Province; administrative, educational, commercial, and transportation center.

*Case Study 3*
   Maliki—thirteen-year-old boy in Class 7 in Bornu Primary School.
   Ya Jalo—Maliki's mother; housewife.
   M. Ahmed Kura—Maliki's father; retired soldier and policeman and now a petty trader.

*Case Study 4*
   Bintu—seven-year-old girl in Class 2 in Bornu Primary School.
   Ya Amina—Bintu's mother; her husband's senior wife.
   M. Zarami Goni—Bintu's father; formerly a religious leader and now engaged in politics.

# Contents

# KANURI SCHOOLCHILDREN

*Education and Social Mobilization in Nigeria*

# 1/Introduction

LTHOUGH WESTERN EDUCATION[1] was introduced in Nigeria early in the colonial period, the Muslim-dominated northern provinces did not welcome it. Education in Koranic schools was much preferred. For decades there was insignificant educational growth in Northern Nigeria except in its largely non-Muslim Middle Belt, a tier of provinces separating Southern Nigeria from Muslim Northern Nigeria.[2] Not until after 1950 did the northernmost provinces strive to expand their school facilities and enrollments. Only for the past twenty years, therefore, have many Muslim families had the choice to send their children to a "white man's school" as well as to a Koranic school or to no school at all.

To Muslims the Koranic school is not a disruptive institution; for hundreds of years it has served, and indeed continues to serve, their religious, social, and intellectual needs. Most communities in the Muslim-majority areas of Northern Nigeria have access to formal Koranic instruction, although most children do not receive it. Girls are not especially encouraged to be educated, and many boys are needed at home to work with their parents. While Koranic education is often associated with the mosque, a child usually studies in a school with a single teacher who instructs a wide age range of pupils. The teacher, forbidden by Islamic tradition to charge fees for teaching the Koran, is compensated by gifts and the labor of his pupils. At the heart of Koranic education is the memorization of the entire Koran, "by which power is gained in this world and reward in the next" (Trimingham 1959:158). Few students achieve this feat. For the majority of Koranic students who do not become teachers, Koranic education is valued as a mark of achievement (as in the case of Maliki's father); they will have memorized many verses and learned to worship properly. For those who become teachers, Koranic instruction is the first stage in a system of education that offers satisfaction measured not only in religious but also in economic terms (as in the case of Bintu's father).

---

[1] *Western education* refers to the type of schooling established during the colonial period based on metropole models. It should be noted that hereafter the terms *education, primary education, primary school, white man's school,* and *schooling* refer to formal Western schooling. Non-Western education, viz., Koranic education, will always be specified as such.

[2] See Coleman 1958:132–145 for a fine elaboration of this point.

1

For the few who become Islamic scholars, their skills in Arabic and in the many branches of Islamic learning enable them to participate in an intellectual life that spans the globe. The main consideration here is that Koranic education is integrally linked to traditional needs and aspirations of the Muslim community which have prevailed virtually intact through the colonial period and, among many families, up to the present time.

The "white man's school," in contrast, represents a break with tradition. Although its students do not invariably desert their family, religion, or community, they do learn skills, acquire knowledge, and develop habits that are outside tradition. For the purposes of this study, a *traditional society* is viewed as one in which the norms and authority of the family, the marketplace, the polity, and religion remain basically unmodified by the rationalizing forces of Western-type education, urbanization, science and technology, politicization, and the value orientations associated with universalism and high need achievement.

Deutsch's concept of *social mobilization* is useful in comprehending the general impact of Western education in traditional societies. He defines the term as a process "in which clusters of old social, economic, and psychological commitments are eroded or broken and people become available for new patterns of socialization and behavior" (Deutsch 1961:494). The reason for discussing social mobilization at this point is to alert the reader to a major conceptual tool used in preparing the concluding chapter. This concept is meant to embrace not only the effects of acquiring new knowledge, new language skills, and a passport to jobs and more formal education, but also the less obvious effects of the school experience.

But what in fact does the primary school do to promote social mobilization? Do teachers consciously profess and reinforce "modern" values and beliefs? Do children return home with alarming tales of what they learned in school? Do parents experience conflict between their efforts and those of the school to educate their children?

In short, if we study what appears to be a confrontation between traditional and modern forces—Muslim Kanuri children, from ordinary homes, attending a primary school, the first generation not to receive Koranic education—what is the result? Do the different socializing environments—home, school, and community—stress different and possibly conflicting values and behavior? In this book the above-mentioned "confrontation" is examined through case studies of four primary school students of the Kanuri tribe, a Muslim group living in Bornu Province, the northeasternmost area of Northern Nigeria. The case studies focus on the socialization of the four children through family, peer, and community associations, but most particularly as it is influenced by schooling. This latter emphasis is in keeping with my interest in education and with my view of it as the most pervasive, nontraditional agency for social mobilization in the lives of the children studied.

This chapter will discuss the methodology employed to organize the case studies, their physical and sociocultural setting, and the nature of the education system attended by the four children.

## PLANNING AND ORGANIZING THE STUDY

Data for the case studies were collected through observations conducted by twelve bilingual Kanuri speakers, all of them my students in the Bornu Training College. Since I cannot speak Kanuri, I had to rely upon these students as participant-observers and to be particularly careful regarding their selection and training. The twelve students were invited to attend a three-week training program. This was a trial period in that the students could leave if they did not like the work, and I could dismiss them if they proved unequal to the tasks of observation. Although the training sessions took place while the students were still in school, the study was conducted during a holiday period. Each observer was paid a salary sufficiently generous to leave no doubt that he was a salaried assistant and not a student fulfilling his training college obligations.

Observations and note taking constituted the basic activities for achieving the ends of phase one. All assignments involved ordinary, everyday situations: a classroom teacher at work, a conversation at the dinner table, prayers at the mosque on Friday, and scenes at the local post office, market, and hospital. Each observer worked individually; he was expected first to observe carefully and then to prepare the fullest possible notes of his observations. I read the notes and made comments. When we met as a group, which we did approximately three times a week, I generalized about the quality and quantity of their writing, intending to convey a clear impression of the desired standard of writing and the precision and comprehensiveness of observation.

During the second phase, the observers worked in the teams organized for the actual study. Each team of three observers was assigned to observe a child of the same age as its child in the actual study. This work, spanning parts of three days, took the observers into the school and the homes of these children. It paralleled in many details their work in the first two weeks of the study: establishing rapport with a family, observing a child for 35 minutes, and preparing notes during a 70-minute break. The end of phase two coincided with that of the school term.

Phase three began with two full days of meetings. General instructions and a detailed description of the four weeks' work had been prepared and distributed to the observers during phase one. A careful examination and discussion of this document constituted the main work of the two days. In addition, some of the situations anticipated during the study were role-played, such as approaching a respected old man for information about the community and explaining the purpose of the study to a teacher who inquires about the work.

The general instructions were a heterogeneous list of suggestions and advice. Specific conditions of work were set forth for the observers. They would work in teams of three; the work would last four full weeks with a day off each week except the last. Working hours during the first two weeks would be from 7:30 A.M. to 7:00 P.M., and during the final two weeks they would last as long as the study child was awake. Each observer would be on duty for 35 minutes, which is usually the length of a class period in the primary school, and break for 70 minutes.

During the first two weeks, when they were not to take notes during their observations, note writing was to be done during the 70-minute break. In the last two weeks, notes were to be taken during the observations, with the break providing an opportunity to relax.

The objectives of the first two weeks were to polish and refine the skills of observation; to resolve unanticipated problems in the mechanics of the study, such as the working of the teams and establishing proper contact with the families and schools; and to assist the observers to develop a flexible concept of the general instructions. The general operating principles were specified, but since they did not cover all contingencies, each team had to learn to think for itself in terms of the study's objectives.

At school, during the first weeks, the observers viewed many different classes in addition to those of the four study children. This was done to accustom as many children as possible to the observers and to eliminate the crowding and staring which visitors to a primary school normally engender. It also helped the study child to accommodate himself to his unusual role. In short, during the first two weeks, the observers did not overexpose themselves to the child or his family; at the same time, they saw them enough to enable them to feel comfortable in the observers' presence.

In addition to observations, time was designated for interviews to be conducted with mother, father, and child. Planned but informal interviews with the child began during the second week and continued throughout the study. This material was used for the introductory section of each case study. A second type of interview was entirely unplanned in the original work schedule. Each team of observers submitted their completed daily notes the morning after they were taken. When the notes revealed incidents that offered promising leads for further inquiry, I instructed the observer to question the persons involved at the earliest opportunity. For example, one observer's notes described a mother who collapsed in her compound, undergoing what was reported to be a fit caused by the sight of a cannibal (see Chapter 3). Because details were scanty and the event could not be adequately reconstructed or viewed within the perspective of her life, the team observing this woman's family was asked to discuss the matter with the woman and with others who saw and knew her. In general, however, the observers recorded only what they saw and heard. They were asked to establish an acceptable presence in the life of the child and his parents but to minimize their interaction with them and, moreover, to make no judgment regarding the importance of one event over another. To be sure, the observers could not record everything that took place before them and their observations certainly were colored by their own perceptions. How this fact affected the study is a most interesting question and though it is not explored here it is worthy of consideration.

Observers were permitted to take notes in the language of their choice, as long as the final set of notes was submitted in English. All the families were of the Kánuri tribe and Kanuri was the language spoken in their homes. School instruc-

---

[3] In Nigeria the term *class* rather than *grade* is used to designate a student's educational level in the primary school.

tion was supposed to be mostly in English in the upper classes,[3] and in English and the vernacular in the lower classes. Most of the time, children speak to each other in Kanuri; the teachers use Kanuri as much as or more than English. Thus, the majority of the conversations required translation into English. In actuality, all notes were taken in English, since using any other language would have increased the observers' work load immensely and would probably have discouraged them from taking the completest notes possible.

The individual observer took notes in his own notebook, with the time and date carefully marked so a team's daily notes could be assembled easily in sequence. I read the four collected sets of notes each day and prepared for each team an individualized comment sheet. Typical comments included requests for clearer handwriting; clarification of uncertain references to persons and events; reworking of poorly translated songs or sayings; or the expansion of descriptions too brief to be understood. In general, the observers were asked to develop further any note which initially was inadequate. The response of the observers to the comment sheet was appended to the original notes. These sheets were essential to feed back my reactions to the observers' work and to reinforce established performance standards.

Throughout the four weeks I made only one brief and formal visit to each family. I expressed appreciation for their cooperation verbally and by means of a small gift, discussed the work of the remaining two weeks, and asked for their questions, comments, and complaints. My role in this investigation was to plan it, establish it, and finally to direct it once it was underway. I conducted none of the interviews and I made none of the observations.

Of the four children studied, Maliki, a Class 7 boy, and Bintu, a Class 2 girl, live in the city of Maiduguri; their rural counterparts are Buba and Aisa who live in the village of Nola.[4] Maiduguri and Nola were selected to see what difference place of residence made in one's response to the agencies of socialization and in the agencies available to socialize. Variability was reduced by identifying children whose parents are alike in several important aspects. All are Muslims of the Kanuri tribe who, except as adults in brief night school programs, have never experienced Western education.

Nola was selected from among hundreds of Bornu villages because of its access to Maiduguri where I lived (due to the paucity of all-season roads, accessibility is an important consideration); and Maiduguri because as the most urban habitat in Bornu it provided the greatest contrast with Nola. Nola Primary School is the only school in Nola. In Maiduguri, Bornu Primary School was chosen on the advice of the Chief Education Officer, without whose cooperation it would have been most difficult to work in any school.

The headmasters of the two schools were requested to identify children who were neither the most nor the least talented in their class and whose fathers could

---

[4] "Nola" is a fictitious name, as are the names of all members of the families, their friends, and the schools attended by the children. Anonymity was assured to the families and the schools. Fictitious names were not adopted for Maiduguri and most other places and persons.

and would live up to the expectations of the study. Both gentlemen were wonderfully patient with my request to find families that fit certain specifications, especially in view of what must have been some doubt about why anyone would plan to have schoolchildren observed for an entire month. I made no attempt to identify average children, families, schools, or communities. In fact, my primary concern was not with typicality, but rather with the difficult problem of identifying four families willing to submit themselves to prolonged and intensive observation. It was indeed an act of faith in my project that they acceded to the anomaly of strangers, guided by "the European," systematically encroaching upon the privacy of their homes.

The families selected were atypical in at least three obvious respects: they willingly participated in the study with no promise of compensation; they had a child in school at a time when most children never even saw a classroom and when many families, preferring Koranic schools, still rejected Western education; and, with one exception, they voluntarily sent their child to school. In the fourth family, the child's uncle enrolled him during his father's absence from the country. Although over the years some of the parents have developed ambivalent feelings toward education, none of them, including our formerly reluctant father, was hostile to it. A relatively different interaction between school and nonschool sources of values and beliefs might have been observed if they had strongly opposed their child's attendance in school.

The product of four weeks' observation of each child and his family was a mass of data requiring organization into a readable and meaningful form. To begin with, the original transcripts were edited to modify Nigerian-English constructions, misspellings, and nongrammatical forms into what, for my purposes, was more satisfactory language. Then the first decision for organizing data involved whether or not to prepare a case study that would span the entire month or, possibly, some shorter period. At the outset of the study the format of a single day was favored, on the order of Lewis' *Five Families* (1962). Subsequent considerations to use a time period covering a few days or to present a child for the period of one month were rejected. These two alternatives were unwieldly, cumbersome, and personally unsatisfactory. A second decision involved the organization of the day. At first, a single day was selected from the many available and presented just as it occurred, using information and events from other days for depth and perspective. This approach proved unpromising because of gaps even in the most carefully observed days. For example, if the school segment of a child's day was adequately illustrative of the school experience, the remainder of the day might be filled with interviews. Or an otherwise suitable day might be flawed by periods during which there was no teacher present and children idly amused themselves. Since I did not intend to present a "slice of life," the capturing of an actual day was not a primary criterion to guide the organizational process. The selection of any day already represents a judgment that it is more useful or more valuable, however these terms are defined. To illustrate the socialization theme it was judged best, accordingly, to prepare a synthetic day which drew on the events and interviews of the entire month. While each case study is in a sense a fictional product, the only truly fictional aspects are the juxtaposition of events from different days and the very brief transitional sections that connect them. Otherwise, the essence of every event is presented faithfully as it appeared in the notes of the observers.

The segments selected from the protocols were meant to document the socialization process. In addition, the following considerations guided the choice of contents for the case studies. First, to establish the setting for each child extra background material was included. Second, to describe fully the impact of education, events from a number of lessons were placed in a single lesson, although the temper of a routine classroom was retained. Third, to convey the importance of elements that repeatedly appeared in the life of a family a special emphasis in the day was provided. For example, I did not mean to highlight religious events, but their frequent appearance in the observation notes argued for their prominence in the case studies. Thus, this stress upon religion helps to portray more accurately the balance of religious elements in the families' lives than would be evident in the straight presentation of an ordinary day. A marriage/divorce theme appears repeatedly in the observation notes[5] and it, too, is emphasized.[6]

Creating a composite day invites criticism from those who value authenticity: such a day did not happen, it can be claimed, even though its component events are true. There are also those who would fault such a day as a fictional product because in staying too close to the data it lacks the quality of a literary work. While both these views have some merit, I must make it clear that the intent of the study was neither to capture the reality of any particular day in the life of a child nor to produce a fictional work. The intent was to examine the phenomenon of socialization under the particular circumstances of a Muslim family's first generation attending a Western-type school. One can study this phenomenon through unstructured or structured interviews, through questionnaires, through taped or written autobiographies. Indeed, there is no single ideal method of pursuing such research, and given ample time and resources all methods would be employed. My preference was to cast a wide net, that is, to place three able Nigerian observers in a position to note virtually everything that happened to a child over a period of one month and to enrich the resulting protocols with interviews and observations of the child's parents. (There was no rationale for the period of

---

[5] Levy makes a similar observation from his interpretation of thematic apperception data on the Kanuri. "Divorce occurs readily; it can be done at home, at court, by proxy. It is so common an experience that people who have not divorced tell stories as casually as those who have. It is a pervasive fact of the environment and constant possibility in inter-personal relations" (1968:14).

[6] Another area of emphasis may have been created inadvertently. During the month the study was conducted the families made many references to education. This may be accounted for as follows. In the course of the four weeks, each parent was interviewed on several occasions regarding his views on education, and in this manner he may have been sensitized to the topic. And the only rationale for the study known to the participating families was that it was being made to help improve the education of primary school teachers. (My position as a teacher in Bornu Training College made this appear plausible and it is not untrue.) Consequently, there might have been a predisposition to discuss education. While the existence of such a predisposition is not certain, the point remains that there were many references to education. Since the families were aware only of my educational interests, there is no reason to believe that this type of bias was fostered in other aspects of the family's life.

one month other than that I could afford it in time and money. Three months would have been preferable and, better yet, two or more month-long observations over several years.) From the month's data I had to select the most useful socialization sequences and to organize them so that even a student of Kanuri culture would recognize the synthetic day as bearing the stamp of authenticity. Accordingly, this investigation intended to provide information and insights regarding socialization rather than simply to present a real day, a glamorized fictional day, or the basis for generalization about changing Kanuri society.

To summarize, each case study presents one Kanuri schoolchild in a compositely organized day based on observation notes recorded daily for one month. Each day opens with an introductory description of the child's parents, who also came under observation, and leads on to the child himself; it concentrates on his activities from the time he awakens in the morning until he goes to sleep. Parents appear as they would normally during preschool and postschool episodes with their children, but they are not intended to be shown throughout a total day.

## THE KANURI

The general details of Kanuri society are ably presented in Ronald Cohen's *The Kanuri of Bornu* (1967). As background for this study it is sufficient to state that the Kanuri are the largest tribe in Bornu Province; according to the 1952 census, they number more than 700,000 in a provincial population of 1.2 million. Approximately 600,000 Kanuri live in other provinces. Bornu's population in 1952 was 83 percent Muslim, 0.6 percent Christian, and 16 percent animist (Northern Nigeria 1965:16–17). Bornu is the greatest livestock center of West Africa and an outstanding producer of groundnuts, millet, and guinea corn. Hides, skins, and groundnuts are its most valuable export products.

There are a number of facts to consider in regard to the Kanuri and education. Cohen writes that a major characteristic of the Kanuri is a strong sense of pride (1967:12) generated by their historic importance in West Africa. The Kanuri kingdom, in existence for a thousand years, is one of the few great kingdoms to survive the tumultuous history of the Sudan. In consequence, the revivalistic efforts of other African peoples to establish links with their past would be redundant in Bornu. Furthermore, the Kanuri have contemporary significance as the primary ethnic group in northeastern Nigeria in that their language and culture dominate Bornu.

For centuries the Kanuri have had commercial, political, military, and religious associations with sub-Saharan, North African, and Middle Eastern countries. They have been an acknowledged Islamic society for more than 600 years. Although not a nomadic tribe, the Kanuri have settled in most of Northern Nigeria's provinces and as far away as North Africa. They are not as prone to travel as the Hausa trader, but they are, nonetheless, a mobile people. Each of the four fathers in this study traveled beyond his native environs: the tanner bought animal skins throughout Bornu Province and in Chad as well; the village head's client conducts business in neighboring villages on behalf of his patron; the mallam[7] has been an active traveler, first in pursuit of his religious interests and later as a political activist; and the retired policeman served as a soldier in Asia during World War II.

The Kanuri have only a weak literary tradition, and the preeminence of English and Hausa will probably prevent a strong one from developing. But a wide range of artistic achievement is evident in their songs, riddles, and storytelling, in their dancing and song-games, as well as in their genuine appreciation of the well-turned phrase in conversation and speechmaking.

Finally, growing up for the Kanuri child never has meant invariably assuming the role and status of his parents. Persons of religious or military talent could rise to positions of leadership and, most important, the old client-patron system[8] has always provided openings for the advancement of children from lower socio-economic groups. Added to these traditional means of mobility have been the limited opportunities made available for almost fifty years through Western education.

It is clear from the foregoing facts that after independence, when Western education became a major impetus for change in Kanuri society, it interacted not with a simple, insular tribal group, but with a culture characterized by a sophisticated language, a social order enriched by Islam and centuries of active cultural diffusion, and a keen awareness both of its past greatness and of its important role in modern Nigeria. Thus, it must be underscored that although this study focuses on "the mechanisms [school, home, community] by which the . . . child's attention is turned toward the outer world" (Mead 1953:vi), and the consequences of these mechanisms for socialization, the Kanuri have been turned toward "the outer world" for many centuries.

## NOLA: THE VILLAGE OF AISA AND BUBA

While Nola is located within a number of political jurisdictions, it is controlled basically by the Bornu Native Authority (hereafter referred to as N.A.), one of five such authorities in Bornu Province. The Bornu N.A. is in Maiduguri, a city of an estimated 100,000 people located almost forty miles from Nola. Maiduguri is the administrative headquarters for the entire province and also the home of the Shehu, the traditional ruler of the kingdom of Bornu. As both a district headquarters[9] and a village, Nola contains a district head, who is appointed by the N.A. and may be transferred to any one of many districts, and a village head, often a local man who inherits the position from his father. Since neither

---

[7] The word *mallam* was attributed first to those who were learned in Arabic, then extended to include those who became literate in English, and finally used in both these senses and as the English *Mr.* It will be written hereafter in its abbreviated form—*M.* The reference here is to a Koranic mallam whose work includes religious teaching, advising, making charms, and the like.

[8] See Cohen 1967:50–51, 93–94.

[9] See Cohen 1967:99.

*Village tailor working his foot-operated sewing machine.*

occupant of these positions is literate in English, they rely upon Western-educated scribes to handle correspondence and other business.

Nola was first settled over 100 years ago by persons seeking fertile land. In the past perhaps its greatest source of pride was its many learned Koranic teachers who attracted students from Chad, the Cameroons, and other parts of Nigeria. Old people say that when Koranic learning in Nola was in its prime, fires lit for nighttime study were visible five miles away. The village still has respected teachers, and Koranic students are very much in evidence.

In the nineteenth century, Nola was enclosed by a large mud wall, none of which still stands. Today its most distinctive physical feature is the sandy avenue called a *dandal* that begins at the main road as a narrow car-width lane and broadens to a vast expanse as it reaches the school area. Then it passes Nola's only brick buildings, housing the police and other N.A. employees, and comes to a dead end at the entrance of the district head's residence, the finest house in the village. The *dandal* always leads to the house of the major local leader. The district head's Land Rover is parked at the entrance of his zinc-roofed house, and nearby under a large shade tree the district head usually reclines on his "big man's" canvas folding chair, the type that is taken to the beach in America. His naturally gray beard edging his jaw from ear to ear is blue from constant contact with the dye in his billowy tentlike gown.

N.A. employees in Nola, such as the health inspector, the agricultural assistant, the leprosy inspector, and the medical dispenser, conduct certain modern administrative functions. The dispensary is noteworthy in that it provides modern alternatives to and complements traditional medical practices, and because it employs Amina as an assistant.

Amina is one of the few women in Nola who are not housewives, farmers, prostitutes, or petty traders. Possessing no special qualifications to recommend her for dispensary work, she became an assistant because she was willing to work, had received her husband's permission, and was the village head's daughter-in-law. Supervising Amina's work is a dispenser with no more than secondary-level education who is trained in a special short course to diagnose and treat such "ordinary" diseases as malaria, bilharzia, and dysentery. He distributes pills, gives injections, and makes judgments which can send a patient to the hospital. With physicians and nurses in desperately short supply, a village dispenser's contribution is of great importance.

Although more representatives of both traditional and modern political offices reside in Nola than in the average Bornu village, it would be inaccurate to picture Nola as a busy administrative center, bustling with government officials at work. In fact, the pervasive feeling is one of somnolence, particularly during the end of the dry season when temperatures often exceed 100 degrees and there is neither tilling, planting, nor harvesting to do. People try to avoid unshaded sections of the dirt streets crisscrossing this settlement of 2300 persons, especially after midday when the heat is so intense that physical activity is kept to a minimum. Many tall neem trees provide relief, and such life as is visible goes on in their shade: women selling beancakes, groundnuts, and onions; children playing; tailors working their treadle-operated Singer sewing machines; and clusters of men talking and playing cards and other games.

Nola's big market that operates each Wednesday[10] throughout the year offers a striking contrast to the general somnolence of the dry season. Market day is too important for school to meet, so the village's almost 200 students join hundreds of sellers and shoppers from Maiduguri and all over the district for a day distinguished by commerce, sociability, and entertainment. A new market is under construction nearer the main road and the small depot where lorries stop to collect loads of passengers and freight. The N.A. decided that a roadside market would attract more people than the present one hidden in a grove of tall trees beyond the view of both pedestrian and motor traffic.

One busy place almost any day or time of the year is Nola Primary School, built by order of the education authority in Maiduguri about twenty years ago. It opened with a single room and grew until in 1967 it became a complete seven-class institution. Because education in the colonial period was so closely associated with Christian initiative, even locally sponsored, nonmission schools were suspect as Christian places. Western education was, and often still is, perceived as a threat to Islamic beliefs. Consequently, Nola, primarily a Muslim village, did not welcome its new school. Many parents hid their children in the bush or fled the village, fearing not only the school's "godlessness" but also that their young ones would be shipped abroad and eaten by Europeans.[11] Even today such fears have not been totally dispelled.

Between Nola and Maiduguri there is considerable movement of men, goods, and, presumably, ideas. As yet, however, Nola has no electricity, no running water, no industry, and no promise that these harbingers of modernization are about to arrive. Cemented wells, a school, a large and thriving market, shade trees, a dispensary, and its location on a good motor road—these are the most prominent signs of change marking the material progress of the village since its inception.

## MAIDUGURI: THE CITY OF MALIKI AND BINTU

A visitor from Nola to Maiduguri is not necessarily overwhelmed by its modernity: the city shares much with the village. The majority of the city's houses are built of mud which must be repatched after each rainy season, and zana grass and cornstalk structures are seen in many family compounds. Domestic animals often wander untended on its streets, perhaps no sight so cogently conveying the village-ness of the city as pregnant goats waddling across its main motor roads. Other common features differ merely in scale. Its daily market, resembling all village markets in appearance and organization, is substantially larger than any other in Bornu; its population, largely Kanuri as in Nola, surpasses most in Northern Nigeria; and the indicators of wealth, similar to those in the village, are just

---

[10] See Cohen 1967:86–88.

[11] Iwanska 1965:141 found Mexican villagers reluctant to send their children to school because they feared that the Russians would come and eat them.

*Koranic students in Maiduguri.*

more common in Maiduguri. They are discernible in the material and ornamentation of clothing, in the relative grandeur of many houses, and in the displays of a wedding ceremony. In addition, the city and the village share affection for Islam, but the main mosque in Maiduguri is massive by comparison with any other in the Province. And Koranic students, tea-kettles and blankets at their sides, abound along the city's streets. They sit swaying before wooden slates containing handwritten Koranic verses, reciting them over and over again. Finally, there is a *dandal,* as there is in every Muslim village in the Province, but here it is essentially a paved motor road that begins at a large brick gate located at a crossroads and leads to the Shehu's palace. The gate is distinguished by Bornu's only traffic policeman. He stands under an umbrella-shaped concrete shelter and signals vehicles to go north down the racecourse road, south past the N.A. police barracks to the big government hospital, west toward the three European banks, (a fourth Nigerian-owned bank is located elsewhere), or east down the *dandal* passing the Premier Cinema and many N.A. offices.

For decades political power has resided with the Shehu [12] and the titled persons of the kingdom.[13] Despite the opening of new N.A. departments to serve the development needs of the province, traditional political norms prevail. Thus, individuals aspiring to positions of trust and responsibility must prove acceptable

---

[12] The Shehu in power at the time of the study died in December 1967; he was approximately 100 years old.

[13] See Cohen 1967:104–110.

to the Shehu and his advisers. The possession of talent or money is insufficient for success in Bornu; one must still be legitimated by favorable response from the traditional oligarchy.

Described above are some of the more familiar aspects of traditional Kanuri society. Factors contributing to social mobilization are also abundant.

Trains, trucks, airplanes, and cars converge on Maiduguri, the transportation center of Bornu. While these mechanical wonders can still attract a crowd of boys, their dramatic effect pales beside two recent developments. The first is an extensive scheme to provide broad, deep, open concrete drainage ditches alóng the main streets of Maiduguri. One is struck not only by the transformation of the city's streets but also by the powerful machinery, directed by Italian foremen, used to produce this change. The second, perhaps even more startling than the drainage scheme, is a local road improvement program. Virtually overnight the French company that won the contract shipped in its equipment, set up a small satellite community for its workers where formerly millet and groundnuts grew, and stunned Maiduguri by the instant destruction of its old road and fine shade trees. Within a swath miles long and 20–30 yards wide, giant tractors tore through everything in sight, creating a treeless plateau ready for tarring.

Darkness and laborious water-fetching are landmarks of village life. In the city they are mitigated by occasional street lights and the availability of electricity to some homes some of the time, and by running water from public taps. Great numbers of kerosene cans converted to water containers are often lined up before a tap, saving the place of the absent owner. The comforts of electricity are involuntarily and periodically forgone during groundnut harvest when the Maiduguri Oil Mill requires a substantially enhanced share of the available current. Maiduguri's old generators struggle under the load of the mill, other factories, and the Europeans' air conditioners and fans.

Compared to any village market, the markets and shops of the city offer a veritable cornucopia of goods: synthetic fabrics from Europe and Japan for the trousers and jackets of young men favoring Western styles; imported canned and frozen foods; fresh fruits from the Nigerian highlands area; an abundance of phonographs, air conditioners, refrigerators, tape recorders, and the always popular transistor radios; and new Peugeot sedans and pick-up trucks sold at a French trading company, one of several firms that import a wide variety of goods.

The Koranic student is a common sight in the city[14] and religious learning

---

[14] Precise data on the number and size of Koranic schools were unavailable, but the following figures for Northern Nigeria may be helpful:

| Year | Number of Koranic Schools | Enrollments | Population of No. Nigeria |
|------|--------------------------|-------------|---------------------------|
| 1932[a] | 37,431 | 207,000 | 11,400,000 |
| 1965 | 27,500 | 550,000[b] | 29,800,000 |

[a] Figures for 1932 taken from Bittinger 1941:229–230.
[b] This is an estimate made by assuming twenty students per school. The more than doubling of the population between 1931 and 1965 is the basis for this assumption.

retains its adherents, but the rapidly expanding system of Western education is capturing the interest of many urban families. The demand for admission to primary schools outpaces the supply of classrooms and teachers. At present there are twelve primary schools (two are mission establishments that primarily serve the Nigerian families of southern origin), two secondary schools, two primary school teacher training colleges, a craft school, and an Arabic teacher training institution. Published material is available from two bookstores and the N.A. lending library, and many small enterprises sell daily newspapers and both domestic and foreign magazines. Radio programs are received in several Nigerian and foreign languages and a local radio station broadcasts news in English and Kanuri.

Projecting an image of the good life in Western terms is an expatriate community, consisting essentially of Englishmen in business and in Northern Nigerian government service, and of Americans serving with the State Department's Agency for International Development or the Peace Corps. In addition, there are many Frenchmen and Italians under short-term contract for supervising construction work and some Lebanese businessmen, perhaps the most permanent foreigners in resi-

*Advertisement for one of Maiduguri's four banks.*

dence. The expatriates, though not a particularly cohesive group, do share one salient trait: a style of living which contrasts notably with that of the traditional Kanuri. They all drive cars and dress well; they buy expensive canned goods and frozen bacon, butter, and fish sticks from the Indian and Lebanese shops; their social life centers around a club, a colonial relic offering swimming, tennis, dancing, a library, and a bar; they vacation abroad; their houses are large and made of brick; and they invariably enjoy the luxury of a number of paid, full-time servants. At least with regard to material attainments here indeed is an elite to be emulated.

For the time being, the core of Kanuri society—the family, the polity, the marketplace, and Islam—appears to be vital, respected, and vigorous. Yet the forces of social mobilization are widespread, and merely to be alive in Maiduguri is to be experiencing them. Channels to change are provided by the cinema and various news media, by the presence of a sizable foreign community and an expanding Western-educated local elite, and by the numerous administrative services and comforts—all of these derived from achievements and skills that originated beyond Bornu.

## EDUCATION IN BORNU

The Kanuri no longer compose an empire that reaches the city of Kano and stretches past the current boundaries of Nigeria into Chad and Niger. Their kingdom, confined now to a corner of Nigeria, does not extend its hegemony by military means. Its continuing influence in Nigeria partly depends on the quality of manpower it contributes to its own and to national development, and the quality of its manpower depends on educational progress. Before moving to the first case study, a brief overview of education is presented.

Control of primary education in Nigeria is centralized in four regional ministries of education which delegate some responsibility to local education authorities in each province. For the North, organizational details are specified in its Education Law (Northern Nigeria, 1964). The present syllabi for primary schools were prepared and approved in 1956 by the North's Ministry of Education, they were modified for some subjects in 1959, and they were later qualified by the introduction of new and superior textbooks. The Common Entrance Examination, given to all the region's students in their seventh or final year of primary education, determines whether or not a student can advance to a secondary-level institution. Marking and grading this examination is done under the auspices of the Ministry of Education.

Provincial education authorities influence the schools by employing teachers, providing the physical plant, and spending their own and regional funds for textbooks and other instructional materials. The Ministry's inspectors evaluate the work of the local education authorities and assist them to improve instruction.

Based on tables in the Appendix, it is clear that the ratio of schoolchildren from any primary school age cohort is small, despite recent increases in enrollments. The preindependence literacy base is about 3 percent in Bornu and about 7 percent in the Northern Region, and the shortage of funds and teachers, as well as the rejection of Western education, has kept literacy in English low. Nonetheless, between 1959 and 1966 Northern enrollments doubled from approximately 250,000 to 538,000, and the qualifications and number of teachers improved impressively. Bornu's expansion compares somewhat unfavorably with that of its region. The latter's enrollment is inflated by the relatively greater demands for schooling from its three southern provinces where Muslims are a minority and Christian missionary activity has been extensive.

Although there may be minor variations from province to province, the curricula for lower primary classes and for higher primary classes are basically as shown in Tables 1–1 and 1–2.

TABLE 1–1
CURRICULA FOR LOWER PRIMARY CLASSES

| Subject | Periods Per Week |
| --- | --- |
| English | 10 |
| Arithmetic | 9 |
| Religion | 6 |
| Physical Education | 5 |
| Vernacular (Kanuri) | 4 |
| Rural Science/Hygiene | 3 |
| Arts and Crafts | 3 |
| General Knowledge | 2 |
| TOTAL | 42 |

TABLE 1–2
CURRICULA FOR HIGHER PRIMARY CLASSES

| Subject | Periods Per Week |
| --- | --- |
| English | 13 |
| Arithmetic | 10 |
| Religion | 6 |
| Nature Study/Hygiene | 5 |
| Geography/History | 4 |
| Physical Education | 3 |
| Arts and Crafts | 3 |
| TOTAL | 44 |

The Education Law of the region requires religious instruction in every school "according to the pupil's faith and custom." Mission primary schools[15] teach

---

[15] Mission primary schools formerly constituted a separate system of education, parallel to that of the government. In the past few years the provincial governments increasingly assumed control of them. They were allowed to continue their Christian bias, and the mission boards which governed them could remain instrumental in the selection of teachers, but in all other respects they were to become integral parts of the provincial system of education.

Christianity and government primary schools teach Islam. Of the region's estimated 27,500 Koranic schools, 300 have introduced the secular subjects that entitle them to receive government grants-in-aid. Most remain outside the official stream of education where students sit for examinations, pass from one level of education to the next, and hold aspirations for salaried jobs.

This investigation did not proceed from a theory about the contribution of education to the socialization of Kanuri schoolchildren. However, one major impression had been formed about primary education based on more than a year's contact with schools in Bornu: the curriculum, as implemented by the classroom teacher, was not designed to effect social change. To be sure, the language and number skills learned in primary school created an eligibility for certain modest occupations. The connection, through an external examination, of primary education with the next higher level of education meant some students were sorted out for advanced schooling that led to high-paying jobs. Moreover, here, as in other developing nations, students who completed primary education were inclined to prefer urban living and nonagrarian occupations.[16] Beyond these important changes it appeared that *daily classroom experiences* were not calculated to have much immediate impact on a child's life either in his public or private roles. That is, he was not intentionally instructed to consider either new goals or new ways of thinking, improving his society, or ordering his life.

The subject matter of textbooks and teacher lectures lacked evidence of concern for nation building. This becomes comprehensible when certain facts about post-independent Northern Nigeria are understood.[17] For example, the then Minister of Education, Isa Kaita, represented his Ministry's attitude toward social change in these terms:

> Over 800 years ago, our contacts with North Africa and the Middle East brought Islam to Northern Nigeria and with it came the traditions of learning of that great religion and also the art of writing. Thus another factor was added to our educational system which ceased to be exclusively social and utilitarian. The age of scholarship was born and many of our ancestors achieved fame as philosophers, poets, and writers. But it was a leisurely form of scholarship. It established new religious and moral values, but *it did not disrupt the basic organization of the community.*
>
> The real revolution occurred with the British occupation of Nigeria and the consequent introduction of Western educational ideas into the country. Those ideas had come from countries which, because of recent and massive industrialisation, possessed power and wealth hitherto undreamed of. Combined with these were social differences and political notions quite alien to our customs and thought. Many of our people, and particularly the young, have been dazzled by the materialistic delights of the modern world. But there are many also who look on these things with some reserve. They see the possible destruction of the traditional social system. They see a drift away from religion and they are entitled to ask

---

[16] Data from another study I conducted in Bornu show that of 510 students questioned, 85 percent preferred to work in a town, a city, or another country rather than in a village, and only 6 percent included farming among their top five work preferences.

[17] See my "Education and National Integration in Nigeria," *The Journal of African Studies,* 5 (November, 1967): 323–334.

*Young primary school students doing craft work.*

whether there are altogether unmixed blessings. They wish to know whether the freedom to put a paper in a ballot-box is worth enslavement to the factory whistle, the airline schedule—to the monstrous domination of time which in Western terms means money (italics mine) (NNTEP, 1965:2).

And there is no doubt that Northern leadership in the period before the coup of January 1966 revered the traditional social order. Note the observations of the precoup governor of Northern Nigeria, Sir Kashim Ibrahim, spoken to the region's citizens on National Day in 1965:

... as we progress and strive after great achievements, we should not throw away indiscriminately age-old virtues and values which have given us our identity as a people. ... Our social solid foundation [sic] and fertile soil are in the good traditions established by the wisdom of generations of our forebears under the conditions of our country. We must not cast away our noble heritage in favor of ideas which have not been tried against the background of our needs and conditions. New ideas we must accept, if we have to keep pace with time, but like the cloth which we sometimes import from abroad, they must be tailored to African needs. Our stability which is the envy of many materially wealthier nations has its foundation in our traditional respect for authority, love of order and respect for the forces which enhance order (Sir Kashim Ibrahim, 1965:1).

Preindependence traditional leadership, controlling all levels of government in Northern Nigeria until the 1966 upheavals, protected both its political power and its social order. It welcomed economic development and Northern Nigeria made important gains in the post-1960 period. Desire for economic growth, however, must not be construed as desire for general social change. If education was intended to have any innovative effect, it was to be only in the area of providing skills— technical skills to staff railroads and factories, and administrative skills to manage the bureaucratic services demanded of an increasingly complex welfare-oriented state. But special and higher schools were responsible for developing such skills. Primary schools were held responsible for teaching reading and writing. If schools of any level were intended to have an impact on attitudes or values, it would be to reinforce those mentioned by Sir Kashim Ibrahim in his speech or those commonly-approved values such as honesty and loyalty.

A final explanation of the relative dearth of nation-building rhetoric is found in the North's concern for catching up to the other regions. The very substantial quantitative lag between Northern Nigeria and the southern regions in almost every category of educational achievement created tensions among the regions and provided an impetus for Northern educational expansion. That quantitative goals predominated is clear from the Northern Nigeria White Paper declaration that "the development of the educational system in Northern Nigeria has proceeded firmly in some areas, haltingly in others, toward *a vague and unspecific goal*. The task has seemed so great, the horizon so limitless, *that forward movement has been an end in itself*" (italics mine) (Northern Nigeria 1961:1). In subsequent years the horizon was no less limitless. The gap between North and South was not closed; the late premier of the North, Sir Ahmadu Bello, continually advocated "northernisation" in an effort to get northerners into jobs currently filled by better-educated southerners; and if "northernisation" constituted something more than "a vague and unspecific goal," the rhetoric of social change through education was notable largely by its absence.

# 2/School is the same as home: Aisa and her family

## CASE STUDY CHARACTERS

| | |
|---|---|
| Aisa | Seven-year-old schoolgirl |
| Ya Falta | Aisa's mother |
| M. Musa | Aisa's father |
| Lawan Abba | M. Musa's employer |
| M. Ibrahim | Aisa's teacher in Class 2 |
| Falmata, Magaram, Agujja | Aisa's girlfriends and classmates |
| Ya Abduram | Ya Falta's friend |
| Nana | Ya Abduram's daughter |
| Kyellu | Ya Falta's friend |
| Karu | Kyellu's daughter |
| Baba Mala, Zara, Buba, Baba Sheriff, Mallam Dallah, Isa, Harun, Amina, Modu Gaji, Moda Musa | Schoolchildren |
| Baba Madu | M. Musa's friend |

## MALLAM MUSA

AISA'S FATHER is an undistinguished man living the life of a basically traditional Kanuri, encountering the problems and joys of work, marriage, and manhood like tens of thousands of fellow tribesmen before him. If he differs in any noteworthy respect, it is in his permissive attitude toward Western education and his acceptance of modern medical practices. He was born in the small village of Kachallari and lived there for twenty-eight years, leaving when political pressures forced him to give up his land and his family claim to village leadership. The relative affluence of his childhood now no more than a memory, he still recalls with pleasure that his grandmother never had to farm because she had so many slaves and maids to toil for her.

M. Musa and Ya Falta, his wife, have been childless in their thirteen-year marriage. Aisa, actually the daughter of Ya Falta's sister, has been raised by them since she was two and they are her parents in all but a biological sense. The practice of

21

adults raising children other than their own is common in Bornu due to the exceptionally high divorce rate and the custom of fostering, whereby children, for political and other reasons, are raised by grandparents, relatives, or friends.[1]

At sixty-five, M. Musa tires easily but not so much that he does not farm when he is well or labor regularly on behalf of Lawan Abba, his employer and village head[2] of Nola. For Lawan Abba he delivers and receives messages, represents him at meetings, and does whatever he is ordered to do, expecting in return financial support but not regular wages. M. Musa's relationship to Lawan Abba is the common one in Kanuri society of client-patron, involving an exchange of security and services between a clearly designated subordinate and superior. M. Musa's original patron died years ago, leaving his son Abba to "'inherit" M. Musa, although the new association was a matter of mutual consent in recognition of mutual advantages.

It is now the dry season in Northern Nigeria and during this time of the year the tall, blue-gowned figure of M. Musa is usually seen sitting in the shade by Lawan Abba's entrance hut. Lawan Abba reclines on a canvas folding chair in a corner demarcated by a row of empty, green, quart size beer bottles stuck in the ground so that only an inch or so of their fat bottom ends are showing. From his location, Lawan Abba talks to friends, listens to stories, or settles the numerous issues which daily come before a man of his responsibility. M. Musa changes his behavior to suit the situation. When the occasion merely calls for talk to pass the time of day, he joins in with stories and incidents from his own life. When there is a controversial issue before the village head, he offers advice or reinforces the opinions and feelings of his master. When there is business involving other villages, he may go to them as Lawan Abba's agent.

With his old age and poor health M. Musa finds all work a strain, and though he can still tell a good story to amuse his friends, his pessimistic moments come readily. When Laina came into his compound last Wednesday on her way from market, he asked her how business was. She said she had made some pots, but a few were broken on the way to Nola and that was the end of her profit. To this M. Musa replied, "Yes, because the world is coming to an end. Everything's getting worse and worse. The time is coming when there'll be no rain unless everyone gives alms to the poor every year." Another time, when a visitor informed him that he was not sitting completely on his mat and he was getting his robe dirty, he responded that as a poor man it didn't make any difference where he sat and added, "Poverty is the worst enemy of man. If not for poverty who would stay in the bush?" *Bush* is a derogatory term given to anything that is considered sub-standard, unsophisticated, rural, or uncivilized. He suggests here that if he was not so poor he would go to live in the city.

From his work with Lawan Abba, his occasional farming, and his very small-scale trading in grain, M. Musa manages to earn a modest but adequate living. Neither rich nor poor, he can provide for the everyday needs of his small family

[1] See Cohen 1967:62.
[2] See Cohen 1967:94-8.

and for the maintenance of his home. Recently issues arising from a shortage of cash have created conflict with his wife, and from all appearances their divorce seems imminent.[3]

## YA FALTA

Ya Falta, a tall, smiling, pleasant-looking woman, has lived in the vicinity of Nola all of her forty-six years. Her father was an ordinary farmer who moved several times during her childhood to seek better economic opportunities, but never very far from Nola District.

Hard work is a natural part of her day. Her home tasks include the usual cleaning, cooking, child tending, and constant fetching of water. Throughout the year she sits at one of the village's small markets or at the main market if it is market day and sells grain. During the rainy season she farms both her own plot of land and the one she shares with her husband.

At the age of fourteen she was married to the first of six husbands, remaining in his house for nine years and bearing two sons, both of whom are alive today. The fact that she bore no children in her later marriages and that she has a keen sense of responsibility to her own kin are two major reasons for her many divorces. Her third husband, the one she remembers most fondly, was a successful trader who owned a truck and twenty cows. Finding her life intolerable after he took two more wives, she packed her belongings and ran away. Even though she has lived with M. Musa for many years, she still feels she has come down in life since the days of her trader. In fact, she does not think she will stay married to him much longer. Having always farmed and continuing to be in good health (the only noticeable sign of disease is a spreading discoloration of the skin on her hands and lips), she feels that if necessary she can make her own way in life.

Tension has mounted between her and M. Musa during the past few weeks in proportion to her anxiety to purchase gifts for two marriage ceremonies. The obligation to buy these gifts is more demanding than that she feels for M. Musa and her debts promise to increase as she prepares for the second marriage.

A few weeks ago she and M. Musa quarreled about their farming plans for the coming rainy season. M. Musa wishes to raise millet, whereas Ya Falta hopes to plant groundnuts on a plot of her own. Doubting that she will get her own piece of land, he fears that she will want some of his.[4] Their conflict climaxed recently when they fought over a bottle of groundnut oil she was selling him.[5] M. Musa, perturbed by her refusal to set what he thought was a fair price, was ready to divorce her, but the village head intervened and made him reconsider.

Her ultimate insult, M. Musa explained, came when "she stood so proudly and defiantly before the village head," instead of being submissive and knowing her

---

[3] See Cohen 1967:41–45.

[4] See Cohen 1967:77–80, for discussion of farming and land tenure.

[5] When M. Musa wishes to obtain something that belongs to his wife in her economic role, then the relationship is that of buyer-seller and not husband-wife.

place. He says boastfully that he could get a new wife, no older than Ya Falta, the very day he decides he wants one and, after all, that at his age the only need for a wife is to cook food.

Ya Falta is not quite ready to break up her marriage, although she is aware of being young enough to attract another mate. When a friend visited her recently, Ya Falta said, only half-jokingly, that she could still look attractive if she tried. First, she would clean herself very carefully; then, she would polish her teeth white —they usually are stained red from constant dabbing with tobacco flowers; and,

*Vendors in one of Nola's small daily markets.*

finally, she would arrange for a new hairdo and clothes to complete her youthful appearance. Such changes, she felt, would win her "a husband young enough to be the son of Musa."

AISA

Aisa is six or seven years old, somewhat darker in complexion than her schoolmates, with her hair divided in three parts and shaved in between like most other young schoolgirls in Nola. On an old string tied diagonally around her chest and neck is attached a charm that she wore for years without knowing its purpose. Just recently she asked her mother about it, learning that it contains a Koranic verse that keeps her safe from "devils and evil doings."

Her home consists of three huts, one of mud and two of zana grass, clustered within a compound wall made of woven zana grass mats. She shares one hut with her mother, the other two serving as her father's bedroom and the kitchen. The latrine, a deep hole in the ground, is located in back of her mother's sleeping hut completely out of view. Some large clay water pots stand near the kitchen. To the right of the entrance is an open-sided shelter area made of cornstalks where guests are received and the family eats or sits during the day. It is here that Aisa and Ya Falta rest throughout the afternoon that is described later. Beyond this area is a space for quartering a horse. M. Musa travels so frequently that he is thinking of acquiring one. Kanuri men on horseback are a common sight along the paths that parallel the motor road to Nola.

Aisa's home is near the cement well located outside the village head's compound. It is an easy walk to her school, to the grinding machine where she goes frequently with her mother's grain, or to the small market where her mother sits to sell groundnuts or millet.

Throughout any ordinary day Aisa is at school from 6:30 A.M. to 12:30 P.M., the coolest daylight hours. After coming home she alternately helps her mother with chores or drives her to distraction with questions and interruptions, plays with her toy "daughter," or entertains Nana, the little girl from the next compound. Late in the afternoon, when the day begins to turn cooler, she may run errands or play with her friends, the young daughters of one of the four wives of the village head.

At home she is a cheerful, playful child, sometimes impudent to her surprisingly permissive parents, but at school she is quiet and respectful, seldom involved in the fights that break out when students are left alone. She listens intently to her teacher and tries to understand and to do the work.

Aisa's parents are not in complete agreement about the value of education. M. Musa already has raised a young man who completed three years of postprimary training to earn a Grade III teacher's certificate. Much to M. Musa's pleasure and pride he is now headmaster of a nearby primary school. Ya Falta, however, is of two minds about Aisa's education. On the one hand, she is impressed with her daughter's accomplishments, few though they are; on the other hand, the traditional importance of marriage in the life of a Kanuri girl makes her feel uneasy about Aisa's possible presence in school beyond puberty—the right time for marriage. Furthermore, although she is proud that of all the members of her family only Aisa and her cousin have attended primary school, she fears that an educated daughter, rather than remaining faithful in her husband's house, will be adulterous. And if this happens, "God will punish the mother whose job it is to keep her daughters well-behaved." Neither M. Musa nor his wife have great ambitions for their adopted daughter; they pay no attention to her wish to be a nurse. They say that if she succeeds in primary school, somehow they will find money to support her in a postprimary school in Maiduguri, and, if not, she will get married just like any other girl.

At 5:00 A.M. M. Musa is just beginning to stir on the two ragged mats which separate his body from his mud bed. The bed is built up about three feet from the floor of his hut. He pulls up his old blanket around his shoulders and scratches his thigh. His small, wood-frame zana mat room is crowded with his wife's possessions. Across the room, opposite the mud bed, Ya Falta has built an embankment of sand on which her property is placed: a mirror, some baskets, an empty sweet tin, small bottles of scent and oil, and calabashes, pans, and bowls. An old blanket and a new mat hang from a rope strung high across the center of the room. Two more mats are on the floor, one by his bed and another that is covered with a ram skin and used only for guests.

He shakes his head as if to clear it and rises deliberately and somewhat unsteadily from his mud bed. After returning from the latrine he performs his ablutions in preparation for the first prayers of the day. When the formal prayers are complete, he continues to sit on his mat reciting verses from the Koran, only his lips moving, his well-practiced fingers counting the verses on his prayer beads.

It is now 5:30 A.M. Bush dogs and roosters have been making noise for at least an hour. Ya Falta comes out of the kitchen after saying her prayers and steps into a heavy but brief downpour. It is unusual for rain to fall like this in April. She enters her room and comes out again followed by little Aisa, who is completely naked. Aisa looks around and then goes to the latrine at the rear of the hut. She returns, twisting her body and clapping.

"Fetch some water and wash yourself," orders her mother.

"What kind of washing?"

"Your whole body."

"Just yesterday I washed my body."

"O.K. Then wash only your hands and face and feet before you come back here."

When she is finished cleaning herself, her mother sends her to buy breakfast.

"Get that small pan and go to Ya Gana who sells cakes. Buy some for us. Do you know her, Aisa?"

"Yes, I know her very well. That's the big old woman who sells cakes near our school."

"O.K. Run and come back right away while I wait here for you."

"Are you going to Kallari on market day?" Ya Falta asks M. Musa.

"No, but I'll be gone all of today."

"I have no transport money, otherwise I'd go to Kallari."

"What for?"

"Because I want to meet my brother."

Ya Falta goes out of the hut, leaving her husband sitting in front of his mud bed at the middle of the room. He continues reciting Koranic verses.

He stops praying to call to his wife, "I've not taken food for the past three days because of the pain in my chest. I've only eaten a little gruel."

He rises to sit on his bed, steps into his trousers, and takes off the black gown he is wearing in order to put on a blue shirt. Then he lifts the large black gown over his head, takes his cap and beads, and prepares to leave the compound.

"I'm going to greet the village head," he says to Ya Falta. He turns left out of his compound and in a minute is at the entrance hut of the village head, who is sitting in the shade on his canvas chair.

Mother and daughter share the cakes and afterwards Aisa changes into her school uniform, an unadorned, royal blue dress worn with a matching headkerchief.

"Yesterday," Aisa recalls, "those who came late to school were punished. Last year when you were away I was late once and my teacher hit me."

Without waiting for a response she grabs her broom and dashes off to school. On her way she stops by the village head's compound to greet her father, who is meeting with Lawan Abba before departing on an all-day errand. They are standing in front of a blue and white Volkswagen that belongs to the Englishman who works with Ali, a truck driver. The Volkswagen is jacked up and the owner is sitting on an overturned wooden mortar removing the bolts from the punctured rear wheel. As the two men talk they unconsciously brush away the mass of flies swarming persistently around their heads and backs. When the men sit quietly the flies will simply settle on them.

"What's wrong with the car?" asks M. Musa. "He never brought this one before. I think it's the first time."

The village head is as interested in the car and its problems as his friend.

"Yes, this is the first time I've seen him in such a car. I think the engine is at the back."

"Yes, right there, where the holes are."

The village head points his chin toward the European. "Look at him. When he learned his tire was punctured, he just got out of the car, brought his tools, and started repairing."

"Oh, you don't know these poeple. They've no thought of their importance. Any time work comes, they do it."

"What's he going to do with the tire he took off?"

"Now that he's finished, he'll take it back to Maiduguri."

With his spare tire bolted in place, the driver picks his tools out of the sand, reverses his car, and drives off toward the main road. The village head looks in dismay at the departing car. "Wonderful. He didn't even say goodbye. What's wrong? Did he forget or was he too busy?"

"Well," says M. Musa, sounding worldly-wise, "that's the way the white men are. Sometimes they greet you. Sometimes they don't."

Aisa leaves and when she reaches the school compound she goes straight to her designated work area where she meets a number of girls sweeping.

Falmata, Aisa's classmate and friend, stops her. "Aisa, you've come late, you know, and your place isn't swept yet."

"I'll sweep as soon as I finish my cakes." She goes to a vendor near the school, buys a penny's worth of beancakes, and returns to eat them at her sweeping area.

"Aisa, try and finish quickly," demands Falmata. "You know there may be an inspection today."

"I'm almost finished eating. I'll start to sweep right away."

The girls work together sweeping and carrying their rubbish to the garbage can in order to be ready for inspection. Their daily morning chores are carried out under the supervision of the head girl, an upper class student appointed by the headmaster. The children work industriously knowing they will be beaten by older students if they do poor work or none at all. As they approach the garbage can they are joined by three other girls, all classmates. One of them remarks to Falmata, "You didn't wash your clothes yesterday and today the headmaster will inspect us. What'll you do?"

"Can't you see that I have washed them? They're so old. Father says he'll buy me a new uniform after the holidays."

"Zara, what about mine?"

"Aisa, yours is new."

They reach the garbage can, throw away the neem tree leaves and other sweepings, and return to their area to begin all over again a procedure which lasts for approximately thirty minutes each morning.

The headmaster signals for the morning assembly to begin, and all the children and teachers gather outside the junior primary classrooms. They form a semicircle in the center of which the headmaster stands and greets the children. They bow slightly in response and sing out in chorus, "Good morning, sir," their voices rising on "morning" and prolonging its first syllable.

The headmaster addresses the children in Kanuri. "Good morning. Boys, I've heard what went on the last two days and I know it was due to one stupid boy who deceived you to take the stuff. Where is he? Come out here to the center."

Baba Mala comes out and stands before the assembly. Yesterday he encouraged some students to eat seeds from the aljang (datura) plant, some varieties of which are poisonous and one is narcotic. If enough seeds of the Bornu variety are eaten, serious degrees of mental confusion result, the victims beating their heads, running about, and becoming generally uninhibited.

"Now, please look at him. If he thought this aljang stuff was good and wouldn't cause trouble, why didn't he take it himself?" The headmaster turns to the boy. "Why did you deceive others to take it? Look at his clothes, please. All in rags. Now, I'm telling you that those boys who were taken to Maiduguri General Hospital may be in serious condition or they may get better. But if they aren't brought back safely to school, think of the worst thing in the world. That's what'll happen to you. I won't decide your punishment now because I must first have an idea about the children's condition. Mind you, I say this with regret, if it happens that one or both those children die (I hope not), their parents will have to deal with you any way they like. You good for nothing. Do you remember I warned you that many of my staff were complaining about you? And still you behaved badly.

"Boys," he continues, facing the assembly, "now that we've burned most aljang plants in the village, it doesn't mean that we've removed all the aljang in the world. I'm telling you that anyone caught eating or even holding the stuff in his hand will be dealt with severely." He turns toward Class 7. "Prefects."

"Yes, sir. Yes, sir."

"I want you to watch every boy. If you see one eating or even holding aljang, write down his name and bring it to me. During school hours don't bother to write his name. Bring the boy straight to me. Do you hear me, Buba, Baba Sheriff, and the rest of you? Tell Mallam Dalah what I said. Clear?"

"Yes, sir."

He turns to all the children. "One more point. Today, as you must've heard, your terminal examinations begin. If anybody is brought to me for misbehaving in any way, he'll be punished. I won't tolerate any nonsense. Is everybody clear about that?"

"Yes, sir."

"All right. Say your prayers and go to class."

After reciting *fatiha,* the first verse in the Koran, all students rush off to their classes with the headmaster shouting after them, "Don't lose hope. Have your pens and pencils and your rulers and ink ready before your teachers come to class."

Aisa's class no sooner enters its room when the teacher orders them out to sit under the neem trees while he writes their exams on the blackboard.

M. Ibrahim, the class teacher, is twenty-nine years old and has lived and taught in Nola for the past nine years. His own education was obtained in Nola Primary School at a time when all instruction was in Hausa, the lingua franca for most of Northern Nigeria. English was introduced as the medium of instruction before he completed his primary education, so that he had some experience with it before receiving the one year of postprimary teacher training which qualified him as a Grade IV teacher. He tries to be an effective teacher as evidenced by his effort to help children rather than letting them struggle unaided for answers to problems he assigns. He threatens but does not beat his students as readily as some teachers do.

Moreover, he is thoughtful of the needs of the students and often delights in their accomplishments. During a recent vernacular lesson, for example, he asked if anyone would tell a story. Isa volunteered.

"This time I'm going to tell a riddle not a story."

"Yes, we like riddles very much," said M. Ibrahim.

"Now, give me the answer after I say one. When I stood in the center of the forest I heard something saying, 'kok, kok, kok.' What was it?"

A boy raised his hand. "An axe."

"Is that correct, Isa?" asked M. Ibrahim.

"Yes, that's what I mean. Listen to this one. I have a gown. If I wear it, it'll be new, but if I stop wearing it, it'll be old." Everyone sat thinking and when no one could guess, Isa was asked to answer. "The answer is 'a road.' If you follow it, it'll remain good, but if you don't, it'll grow bushy. Here's another. My herd of cattle can't raise any dust or noise."

At once a boy raised his hand to answer. "A parade of ants." He was correct. With each riddle M. Ibrahim became more impressed and when Isa had exhausted his store of them M. Ibrahim said, "I'd be so pleased if everyone would try like Isa. Now let's all clap three times for him."

Class 2 is taking their terminal examinations, thus ending term one which began four months ago in January. Two more terms remain in the school year, with holidays separating each term. M. Ibrahim has been working on the four basic arithmetic processes for the past month. Few children in Aisa's class are able to understand division, but since the Ministry of Education-approved arithmetic syllabus includes division, it must be taught. Recognizing that many children have not developed even a rudimentary knowledge of arithmetic, M. Ibrahim has divided the class into two groups: one works on the regular assignments while the other merely practices writing numbers from one to ten. Unlike M. Ibrahim, most teachers do not attempt to adapt instruction, even in a gross way, to student differences; once a child lags behind, in learning to read, for example, he may complete the seven classes of primary school without ever mastering the simplest reading skills.

Aisa and her classmates do not show much anxiety over today's examinations. M. Ibrahim would like the children to do well, but promotion from grade to grade is automatic and in contrast to Bintu, Aisa's urban counterpart discussed later, there is no pressure from home for Aisa to succeed.

When the class is admitted to their room, they see the following problems on the board:

### 1st Term Arithmetic Examination, 26th April 1966

1. (a) $21 \div 3 =$   (b) $18 \div 6 =$   (c) $24 \div 8 =$   (d) $15 \div 3 =$

2. (a) $4 \times 9 =$   (b) $6 \times 8 =$   (c) $7 \times 8 =$   (d) $7 \times 6 =$

3. (a)  H T U[6]   (b)  H T U   (c)  H T U   (d)  H T U
    8 4 7       2 4 5        6 7       8 7 0
  +1 2 5     +5 0 6      +3 3      +3 0 4

4. (a)  T U   (b)  T U   (c)  T U   (d)  T U
    6 7      5 2      2 4      8 3
  &minus;3 3     &minus;3 6     &minus;1 4    &minus;1 5

"First of all," says M. Ibrahim, "write the heading. I don't want you to talk or turn and look at your friend's work. Do everything by yourself. Try and write the heading quickly." For a moment the children quietly stare at the blackboard before

---

[6] These letters stand for hundreds, tens, and units.

beginning to write. "Remember, this is your first exam in this class so I want you to do your best. I've already written your names on the exam sheets because some of you don't write clearly. Anybody caught talking or turning around will lose points. Do you want to lose points?"

"No, no."

"O.K. Then mind your own business."

"Yes, sir."

"Look, all of you. I'm going to explain each type of problem, but you must look at the blackboard and listen so that you don't keep asking me questions later on." Each word of his explanation is repeated by the children and he concludes by advising them to write clearly.

The children work silently. Some of them work the problems using ordinary pieces of gravel as counting stones, while others count on their fingers. Aisa looks puzzled. She turns to peek at her neighbor's paper.

"Do not look at others' work. Just do your own. Don't turn around, Amina. Try hard, try hard, and you'll do well." He gets up from his table and walks between the rows of desks.

Two boys raise their hands. M. Ibrahim ignores them, noticing instead that one girl is writing numbers one to ten over and over and not doing the problems. He cautions her about her error and then comes over to Aisa who has done nothing more than write the problems on her exam sheet.

"Write the answers underneath the problems," he gently encourages her. "Don't just copy the sums and leave them like that without answers. You'll get nothing if you do."

Though Aisa bends over her paper as if to continue her work, she looks as confused and uncertain as ever.

One boy raises his hand.

"What's the matter?"

"I'm finished."

"O.K. Bring your paper and go out."

Aisa peers desperately at the board. Looking intent, she covers her paper with one hand, grips her pencil tightly with the other, but does nothing. When M. Ibrahim announces that it is time for breakfast, she places a ruler on the edge of her paper and happily joins two of her friends for the walk home. In their playfulness they ignore the morning's ordeal.

Ya Falta has cooked gruel for breakfast. She pours some into a calabash and Aisa drinks from it while the gruel is still hot. Afterwards Aisa covers the calabash with a small grass mat, goes outside to wash herself, and returns with a small can of vaseline. She rubs vaseline on her own head and tries to dab some on Nana, the little girl from the next compound who has stopped by with her mother for a visit. At first Nana resists Aisa's attempts to play with her, but then she acquiesces and the girls begin to shout and scream in fun.

"Aisa, please stop yelling. If she doesn't want to play with you, leave her alone." Aisa ignores her mother and continues to be noisy. "You don't respect my words? Starting right now you will," Ya Falta threatens.

Ya Abduram, Nana's mother, comments, "The trouble is with her education."

"What do you mean? What's the trouble with her education?"

"Well, from going to school she's come to believe she knows more than her parents and regards them as fools."

"So that's what they think of uneducated people!" Ya Falta pauses, pensive for a moment. "Yes, what you say is right, because she started behaving like this only recently. If she weren't in school I'd surely get her married when she's twelve."[7]

"A child who's been to school is no more your child. The authorities won't let you take her out so you just have to stand by and wait until she finishes."

"Ya Abduram, will you send Nana to school when she grows up?"

"That's up to her father. If he feels like sending her, he'll do so."

"Do you think he will?"

"Yes, because he's the district head's bodyguard, you know, and the children of such men are the first to be sent. When more children are needed to enroll, the authorities notify the district head and immediately he sends the children of his servants and other workers."

Ya Abduram lifts up Nana and goes home through an opening in the zana mat fence. When Aisa sees her friend Magaram pass by, she runs out of the compound to escort her to school. They meet Agujja, another friend, and join hands with her to run to class.

"Aisa, let's peek in the window," suggests Agujja. "Maybe M. Ibrahim has written the next test on the blackboard."

"No. Better not. He'll beat us if he sees us."[8]

"But he hasn't left his house yet."

The girls climb upon the window ledge and peer at the blackboard. "Nothing new," says Aisa. "It's arithmetic from this morning."

"Yes. Nothing new."

"Let's run. Come on. Don't let the teacher see us." Hand in hand they move toward the southern part of the school.

Just as Aisa leaves to join some other girls, the bell rings and all the students enter the class only to be dismissed while Ibrahim writes the English examination. Outside the monitor keeps order among the children. Aisa sits with the eight other girls in her class of thirty-five; the boys sit apart from them. This division, so natural among young children all over the world, may receive extra incentive in this Islamic culture where segregation by sex often is considered a virtue. Each morning the girls work together sweeping the school grounds and fetching water

---

[7] In Kanuri tradition girls are expected to marry at puberty. Boys marry several years later. See Cohen 1967:63–64.

[8] Corporal punishment is common in Nigeria's schools, so Aisa's comment is to be taken seriously. However, she does not usually get beaten by her teacher because, unlike at home, she is very quiet in class. Beatings with the branch of a neem tree are given to children who are tardy, disturb a lesson, or do poorly in recitation. Many teachers seem to assume that children willfully refuse to learn, and a beating, a slap, or a kick will help improve their academic performance. Notwithstanding the fact that corporal punishment results from all sorts of teacher idiosyncracies, it is supported by the belief that it is an effective and appropriate mode of reforming misbehavior in Nigerian children.

for the teachers. They are excused from the afternoon games and work period required of the boys. However, with the exception of informal activities, only physical education is taught to the children in separate groups.

The girls sit in a row leaning against their classroom wall. Most of them draw pictures in their notebooks. One girl begins to cry.

"Who made you cry?" the monitor asks.

The girl refuses to answer.

*Boys and girls are separated for physical education.*

"Zara was slapped by Amina," volunteers another girl.

"Why did you slap her, Amina?"

"I didn't slap her! Yesterday she took my beads and when I asked about them she said they were lost. She started crying because I told her to find them."

"Don't cry, Zara. Look for the beads at home," says the monitor as he returns to sit among the boys.

At 10:50 M. Ibrahim invites the children inside. They rush to their desks and wait for the English test papers to be distributed. With her ruler, pencil, and paper neatly arranged on her desk, Aisa looks at the test written on the board.

1st Term English Examination, 26th April 1966

*Fill in the blanks*

1. We can eat . . . . . . . . . . . . . . . . . .
2. We can . . . . . . . . . . . . . . . . . bananas.
3. Can you . . . . . . . . . . . . . . . . . . . . rice?
4. Can you . . . . . . . . . . . . . . . . . meat?

*Answer these questions*

5. What is your name?
6. What is your father's name?
7. What is your mother's name?

*For those who cannot write or do the work*
*properly, to copy [sic]*

1. Mary sits in the desk.
2. John sits in the desk.
3. The desk is in the room.

After explaining the work, M. Ibrahim orders them to begin. All the children are now very busy. Aisa looks steadily at the board. Then she hunches over her paper, and, after studying the work of the boy sitting next to her, she searchingly scans the room, gradually becoming gloomier and gloomier. In the first ten minutes she has completed no more than part of the top line—"Ist Term English Examination." Sometimes she moves her pencil, pretending to write. Ten minutes later she has added only her name and the date.

Children in Bornu's primary schools begin to learn English in Class 1. Although teachers are trained to teach English as a foreign language, it is, perhaps because

*Learning English through alphabet games.*

of its difficulty, among the least effectively taught subjects. In spite of this, some children become competent in English as it gradually takes over from their vernacular, Kanuri, as the medium of instruction in all subjects except religion and the vernacular.[9]

Ideally, after Class 4 or 5, children should be reading, hearing, and speaking English throughout the school day. In fact, teachers frequently lapse into Kanuri for teaching all subjects, particularly when their own mastery of English is weak. Since most village parents do not speak English, it is seldom heard outside of school. That some children learn English more slowly than others is appreciated by M. Ibrahim as he willingly gives credit on today's examination to those who can do no more than copy the last three sentences he has written on the board.

Aisa's class studies English daily for two thirty-five minute periods. M. Ibrahim gamely, intermittently, and impatiently guides Class 2 through a variety of experiences. The examination on the blackboard is based on Lesson 23 in the children's textbook, which he began teaching two weeks ago. First he wrote the letter "w" on the board, asked what it was, and made certain it was pronounced correctly; then he proceeded similarly with the letter "e." Drilling followed, each letter being recited repeatedly in sets of three, and finally as a word—"we." Exactly the same tedious procedure was used with "can," the next word, eventually the "we" and the "can" being joined with the other words in the sentence.

Last week he let the children practice doing the type of test he gave them today. On the board he wrote such sentences as, "He is looking at the_____." and "Can you bring the_____?" taken directly from the English reader. The children were expected to fill the blanks with words of their own choice.

As Aisa prepares to do the first sentence, the teacher announces, "Marks will be given for neat work and clear handwriting. You'll lose marks if your answers are correct but your handwriting is bad."

Within minutes Harun raises his hand saying that he is done. "Go through it again," M. Ibrahim advises. "Don't miss apostrophes and periods. They'll count much against you if you do. Remember that neatness and clear handwriting are very important. Harun, bring yours now if you're finished."

Aisa is still on number one. She writes very slowly. There is murmuring among the children as they surreptitiously discuss the test.

"Look at Modu Musa's paper," says M. Ibrahim. "He did all ten. What a clever boy! If all children did so well they'd have bright futures."

Aisa appears to be progressing from question to question. About one-quarter of the class have handed in their papers and gone out to play. "Amina, don't look at your neighbor's paper. Do your own work. And Modu Gaji, what's wrong? Why aren't you finished yet?" A girl falls off her bench. "Always playing. That's why

---

[9] The Western-educated Northern Nigerian has a tradition of high-level English competency. In recent years, with the rapid expansion of enrollments, this tradition has been difficult to uphold. However, English is the official language in Nigeria and it is used extensively in business. I should expect, therefore, that in the future the standards will return to their traditionally high levels.

you fall down. I say pay attention, but you always fool around." All the children laugh at her.

Now there are only eight students in class. M. Ibrahim is busy correcting the exam papers. When the girl who fell off her bench turns in her paper, he says out loud but to no particular student, "Most of you can't answer in writing 'What is your name?'" At 11:55 M. Ibrahim reminds them that they have five minutes more to complete their work. He rises from his desk to pray and afterwards collects some finished examinations. Ten minutes later he picks up the last papers, Aisa's among them (she merely copied the sentences as they were written on the blackboard), and sends the students out to the school compound. Aisa eagerly joins some girls who are pretending to be dogs, but their play is soon interrupted when the bell rings and the headmaster orders everyone to go home.

Since her mother is away, Aisa finds the calabash of gruel left over from breakfast and drinks it. Having also heard the school bell Ya Falta soon returns from the small market where she sells grain.

"Mother."

"Yes. What's the matter?"

"I'm going to take that fish," referring to a smoked fish her mother has just bought. As Ya Falta shows signs of disagreement, Aisa insists, "Mother can I take it? Mother, can I take it?"

"But you have to leave my room before you eat it."

"Mother, here's a worm." She shows it to her mother, who shouts, "Take it away and throw it in the garbage pit."

"Which place?"

"There, at the back of the hut, near the firewood."

When Aisa returns and moves toward the water pot to wash her hands, Ya Falta immediately stops her, saying that she must not touch the pot until she has scrubbed her hands with ashes. Ya Falta is trying to prevent Aisa's fishy hands from contaminating the water supply that she alone laboriously fetches each day from the nearby well. Aisa is too young to carry much water, and M. Musa will never carry any. Boys do it as one of their daily chores; no grown man does. With no water tap in all of Nola, water for personal washing, bathing, and drinking, for cleaning kitchen equipment and watering animals, and for performing ablutions for the five times daily prayers must be drawn and carried by hand from one of the many wells, some of them no more than openings in the earth, scattered throughout the village.

Ya Falta is concerned about cleanliness. Before Aisa goes out to play, Ya Falta inquires whether she has washed her hands and mouth. Weekly school-directed baths, inspections, and washing of school uniforms help to reinforce her teachings. When Aisa needs her nails trimmed in order to pass inspection, she cuts the nails on her own left hand with a razor blade and her mother cuts the nails on her right hand. Afterwards they are careful to bury the pieces so that they cannot be used against her in witchcraft.

Aisa lies in front of her mother on a mat.

"Are you putting sand in your mouth?"

"No, I'm playing with my saliva."

*Village woman drawing water from a simple well.*

"What a sloppy thing to do."

Aisa scratches her toes.

"What's wrong with your toes? Didn't you wear your shoes today?"

"No, but I didn't feel hot on the sand."

"In this season do you think people have shoes just for the heat?"

"What else are shoes for?"

"To protect their feet from worms."

"Mother, give me a mirror."

"What for?"

"To look at my face." After lying still for a moment she remarks, "Tomorrow is market day in Nola. When is market day in Maiduguri?"

"Monday, but every day seems to be market day there."

"If that's so, Maiduguri must be a nice place to live. We can buy special things only one day a week."[10]

"Mother, please cut my fingernails."

"Some other time, Aisa. I'm too tired now."

"Something's fallen into my nose. Will you blow it for me?"

"No. Bring that rag and I'll clean your ears instead." She brings the rag and Ya Falta cleans her ears.

"Mother, please give me a needle to sew my doll's dress. May I get some cloth for my doll from the tailor?"

Ya Falta is dozing and does not answer Aisa.

"Won't you tell me?" Again no answer. Aisa goes into the room and searches for a needle. To herself she says, "I don't know where she put the needle and now she's sleeping."

"Mother, where's my needle?"

"Did you forget where you put it?" she asks drowsily.

"I remember. It's with the dress I started sewing yesterday. I'll also make a bed for her, a mud bed that will lean against the kitchen wall. Let me draw it." In the sand she draws a picture of her doll's bed. "Let me draw an airplane now." And she does, her enthusiasm mounting with each drawing she makes. "I'll draw another picture, Mother. This one is a latrine. Let me draw a sedan car for you. Mother, look at the picture of a sedan car."

"Who taught you how to draw?" she asks, surprised by Aisa's skill.

"Our teacher, M. Ibrahim. I'll draw a N.A. truck."

"That you cannot do," says Ya Falta and she is right. Aisa does not even attempt to draw one.

Ya Falta is impressed by the accomplishments of her young daughter. While Aisa, to a very limited extent, is able to read, write, and speak English, it is most

---

[10] Aisa's comment refers to the fact that on market day goods are available which cannot be purchased any other day of the week. Items such as soap, cigarettes and matches, hard candies, and grain are always sold at Nola's small markets, where women vend their wares from the ground or from small stalls made of zana matting. On market day, however, trucks and traders bring in an extensive array of products from all over the district. Therefore, she reasons, if Maiduguri has a daily market, a rich supply of goods must always be on hand.

doubtful that her mother will learn these skills. Despite Aisa's continued depend-
ence on her mother—"blow my nose" and "cut my nails,"—Ya Falta is never
certain what amazing and unforeseen thing will come next from her "educated"
child.

Aisa stops drawing altogether and lies down beside her mother. Suddenly she
jumps up and begins to climb the wooden pole which supports a zana mat roof.
"Get down. You'll fall on the mat and break it."
"It's father's mat, not yours," she replies provocatively, but climbs down all the
same and again lies beside her mother.
It has been a long afternoon for Aisa and Ya Falta and at 2:45 it is far from
over. Nola is hardly awake at this time of the day in April because the heat is
unbearably intense, especially as it is reflected in the sandy soil covering the village.
After jumping on her father's mat Aisa again lies down with her mother and
as quickly sits up.
"Mother, when I have something with me, my friends always take it away."
"Well, if they take your cakes and other things I won't let you eat outside the
house."
"But I always eat my cakes inside the school."
"Isn't school outside the house?"
"No. We call it home."
"Is it enclosed like this house you live in?"
"Even if it isn't, it's the same as home to us."
Following no response from her mother, Aisa turns to another subject. "If it
rains again today, we'll play in it. When we're in class and its raining, we feel
happy."
She begins to sing a song, stopping when Kyellu, her mother's friend, enters
the compound with her daughter Karu.
Kyellu joins Ya Falta to chat and Karu goes to play with Aisa. The two girls
run around, hide, and play first with water and then with the dye Kanuri women
use to stain their hands and feet a reddish-brown color. Stained hands, feet, and
teeth are thought to be quite beautiful.
With the girls occupied, Kyellu talks about her elder daughter. "Ya Falta,
I hate the thought of sending her to Maiduguri for marriage."
"I wouldn't like it either," sympathizes Ya Falta. "Because once she's taken to
Maiduguri as a married woman, she might never be here when you need her. I
mean when you have a marriage or a naming ceremony in the family, maybe her
husband won't let her come. And if one of the family dies and the report reaches
her, sometimes she won't be allowed to make the condolence call. Remember the
Nola girl who married that big Mallam—Maliki Audu? Well, for three years he
didn't let her return. Even last year when her sister who finished primary school
was given in marriage, that Mallam refused to let her attend her sister's marriage.
Last week for the first time he let her come to say goodbye to her family because
he's moving to Kaduna for business."
"That is bad. I wouldn't tolerate such conditions," says Kyellu.
"To us villagers, that's very bad. We always want to see our daughters with us
when there's any happiness or sorrow. Look, during the recent marriage ceremony

when my whole family was together, we were so pleased to see our daughters fetching water, bringing firewood from the bush, cooking food, and doing all the work for the ceremony, while we elders remained resting in the shade advising them to do this and that. Well, if those daughters of ours weren't here, who would do all the work? We would!"

"Ya Falta, at the marriage you just attended, did you have drums and flutes?"

"We usually do, but this time there were none because both sides of the family were in mourning. It would've been shameful to have music during the ceremony."

When Kyellu and Karu leave, Aisa lies down to be deloused by her mother. (Killing lice is an endless task in this and most other rural households. Some days ago, as Ya Falta was searching for lice, she teased Aisa that she could not be married until all the lice in her hair were killed, a rather serious threat to the Kanuri girl who hears about her own marriage from infancy until puberty. But when Aisa took the tease seriously, Ya Falta cheered her by saying that she would become a doctor when she grew up.) At the same time that Ya Falta works on Aisa's head, Aisa searches for lice on the string of charms hanging around Ya Falta's neck. Suddenly she reaches up to suck her mother's breast.

"Hey, what's this? You're how old? You don't need a breast anymore or are you trying to be funny?"

The delousing temporarily halted, Ya Falta leaves for the kitchen and Aisa goes into the sleeping hut for a mirror and face powder. She liberally pats powder all over her face; then dyes her lips and uses the same stuff to make small red circles on her cheeks. After coloring her eyebrows with a pencil, she spits on her jumper and rubs her brows with it. As she goes to join her mother, a neighbor's chicken comes in to search for grain. She drives it away and returns with an onion in her hand. In addition to liking onions, she has been told by her mother that onions are good during the hot season because they prevent sudden attacks of measles.

"I'm going to eat this onion, Mother," she announces.

"It's not mine. It's your father's."

"I'll eat it and tell him when he comes."

"Eat it if you like, but it belongs to your father."

"When is Baba coming home?" (He is still away on an errand for the village head.)

"I don't know. He didn't tell me what time he'd return."

Aisa taunts Ya Falta. "When he comes I won't tell him I took the onion. I'll tell him you used it in the soup."

"But I don't eat the soup alone. You know we share it."

"If that's so, I'll put in half of it," and she enters the kitchen, returning with half the onion in her hand.

"I hope Baba comes back tonight, Mother."

"I don't know," she responds peevishly. "Don't ask me. Besides, he didn't tell me what time he'd come."

Aisa, quiet for a moment, sits and swings her legs while eating her onion. "Mother, we did a test in school this morning."

This is her only reference all day to examinations. Her mother ignores the remark. Aisa, herself, does not seem to care that she received no reaction to her statement and the matter is dropped. Ya Falta expresses little interest in Aisa's daily school affairs. She shows concern over Aisa's presence in school possibly interfering with her marriage which, if reaching puberty is the indicator, is five to seven years away. But beyond getting her daughter to school on time and keeping her body and uniform clean, she ignores the details of Aisa's academic life. There is obviously no anxiety about the results of today's test. Later in the day when someone asked Aisa if the tests seemed difficult, she only laughed and turned away.

At 5:00 P.M. it is time for Ya Falta to prepare the evening meal. She gathers up her cooking pots, washes some old black ones, breaks up torn zana matting for tinder, and generally busies herself around the cooking hut. Aisa chases another chicken, digs near the water pots, and, as usual, interrupts her mother's work.

"What are you doing in that room, Aisa?"

"Nothing."

"Are you climbing on the roof?"

"No, I'm looking for something."

Aisa comes out with a piece of paper and a pencil and begins to write, stopping when she hears a beggar approach their compound door. She stares at him while Ya Falta offers some guinea corn from a very small calabash. The beggar thanks her and goes away.

M. Musa's old, torn shoes are put on by Aisa and she drags and stamps her feet. Tiring of this, she collects some dried neem tree seeds, using them to count in Kanuri and English. She makes frequent mistakes whenever she counts beyond twenty in English. Her counting play is stopped when Ya Falta sends her on an errand to borrow a sieve.

At the same time her mother is cooking, Aisa prepares dinner for her doll. She goes into the kitchen for some beans, grinds them on the grinding stone, and squats down like her mother, pretending to cook. After dressing her doll and putting her on a bed made of old sugar packets, she gets water from the big pot. Soil, used for make-believe grain, is ground and smoothed, mixed with water, and finally stirred with a zana stalk.

Ya Falta goes out to her nearby neighbor's house and shouts at Aisa when she tries to follow through the fence opening. "Didn't I say don't follow me? Can't you ever stay without me?" Aisa returns through the opening and lies down on the mat. She sings to herself in English, "In that little farm, moo, moo. In that little farm, moo, moo. Audu Jim Birru," stopping when her friend Agujja enters.

"Aisa, did you see my little brother go by here? I don't know where he is. Please help me find him because he's lost somewhere."

"My mother won't let me go."

"Let's go ask her."

She shouts to her mother, who is few yards away in the next compound, "Mother, Agujja wants me to help find her brother."

"Night is near," she calls back. "Let Agujja go to her mother and father."

"We'll come back right away," pleads Agujja.

"I can't go, Agujja. You better go alone."

Ya Falta returns and pours water for her ablutions which she completes before doing her prayers. Ablutions and prayers together take only five minutes and by then dinner is ready. She pours food into one pan and water into another for Aïsa to wash her hands. Aisa comes into the kitchen and they both sit and eat in silence.

From outside their compound wall they hear, "For the sake of Allah. For the sake of Allah." One of Nola's many Koranic students has come begging food as alms. (These students seek food for themselves and their teachers, who do not receive fees but, instead, are compensated by the services their students perform for them, such as begging for food, washing clothes, tending animals, and farming.) Aisa mocks the student, trying to imitate his voice and for this Ya Falta slaps her, saying that had she been outside the student also would have slapped her. In M. Musa's house there is no mocking with impunity anything relating to Islam. Its sanctions and injunctions are probably more important in guiding the life of the family than those which come from any other source.

Unnoticed by Ya Falta, a boy enters the compound carrying two leather bags. When Aisa sees the bags and recognizes them as her father's she shouts, "Mother, Baba has returned."

Ya Falta comes out of the kitchen to receive her husband's belongings and without a word returns to the kitchen. Aisa, however, is quite excited by her father's arrival. She opens one of the leather bags.

"Mother, Baba has brought some fish again."

"Who told you to open those bags, you naughty child?"

Just then M. Musa enters carrying another bag. *"Assalam Alaikum"* (Peace be on you), he greets them. He deposits his sword and stick on the mat and says, before he goes out again, "I'm taking this bag somewhere. I'll be back soon." Ya Falta comes out of the kitchen too late to greet him, so she continues to eat.

Within ten minutes M. Musa returns home looking tired and dirty after a long hot day on horseback. He removes his gown, takes a piece of soap from his pocket, and, without actually facing his wife, orders her to pour water for his bath and to go buy some items for him. Their uneasy relationship has been evident in Ya Falta's and Aisa's previous conversation about the mat and the onion and is indicated now in their restrained meeting. Ya Falta carries in his shirt and gown, makes another trip with his string of nine charms (every precaution is taken on long trips away from home), and then goes outside to purchase Key brand soap for three pence, candy for a penny, and one razor blade for another penny.

It is almost 6:30 P.M. and the voice of the muezzin is heard calling Muslims to prayer for the fourth and next to last time of the day. He stands at the door of Nola's mosque, a modest mud building without a minaret, and raises his voice for all of the village to hear.

"Ya Falta, bring some water so I can say my prayers," M. Musa calls out.

Since she is busy, Aisa brings the water for ablutions. As soon as he completes his prayers, Ya Falta brings him his dinner. She and her daughter never eat with him because to do so would be shameful; in fact, they are embarrassed if any male adult sees them eating. After M. Musa eats, he calls to his wife to bring his gown with the prayer beads in it. She kneels in respect as she hands the gown to him and returns it to his room when he has found his beads. He leaves to join his friends by the village head's entrance hut.

Aisa goes into her room to get some pillows. At seven o'clock it is almost too dark to find anything inside. The uncomfortable heat of the day is gone, but it will be awhile before the thick-walled sleeping huts cool off. In the meantime, pillows are placed by the mats under the shelter where mother and daughter have been sitting or lying all afternoon, and a tired Aisa lies down beside her mother and sings several Kanuri songs. "Shehu Sanda's handkerchief. How can I get it? It is beyond me."

She repeats these lines several times before singing a song made popular by the personal musicians of the Waziri, the prime minister to the Shehu. "He is called Galadima,"[11] she sings. "Even his grandfather was called Galadima. There's your school at your gate. There's your court at your gate. There's your treasury at your gate." Aisa frequently sings one song after another just to amuse herself. Many of them she has learned at school, while others, like those above, are more traditional and sung by Kanuri youngsters all over the Province. Then she sings a song which seems to be derived from "Ba Ba Black Sheep." "One, two, three abishala. La, la, la. One for the master. One for the lady. And one for the little girl. La, la, la." And finally she sings, "A bo bo bonsue.[12] A bo bo bonsue. A bo bo bonsue. Virgins two pence each. Prostitutes two for three pence."

A girl's voice is heard from outside. "Aisa."

"Who's calling me?"

"Come out. Let's go to school."

"No, I'm afraid of scorpions."

Her mother responds to this. "Even if you weren't afraid of scorpions, who'd let you go?"

Aisa says disparagingly, "Your kind of school isn't good because you go all the time but our school closes at 12:00."

"Aisa, this school is quite different from yours," explains Ya Falta. "It's a Koranic school, while yours is a European school."

"Even in our school we learn about religion and the Koran," Aisa replies. She is amused at this conversation. The "European school" is the only one she really knows and she likes it. She laughs as she lies down to sleep beside her mother. Nola is dark and quiet except for the sound of drumming coming from near the district head's gate.

Outside, M. Musa sits comfortably with his friends relaxing for the first time after an exhausting day. As tired as he is, he actively joins the discussion with a comment or an opinion on almost every topic. These are old men in conversation and it is not surprising that they talk about their ailments.

"Baba Madu won't recover using medicine from this small dispensary. His knee is swollen like a kettle so he can't even stand up. He must go to the General Hospital."

---

[11] Contrary to other honors, "Galadima" is a very high title granted by the Shehu to only one man at a time. Formerly the Galadima was placed in charge of the western part of Bornu's kingdom, now located within other states. The present position of Waziri is filled by a man who has been awarded the title of Galadima.

[12] These are alliterative sounds without any meaning.

"You're right," agrees M. Musa, "but some people are still afraid of going there."

"Well, death is with God, not the doctor. If you're meant to die, you can die anywhere."

"You're a good example of that."

"Yes, remember last year when I was sick all the time. I had no idea that Alhaji would come with a car and take me to the hospital. What could I do? I just went along with him and thirty days later I was out."

"When I stay home I can never cool off," complains one of the men. "If I go out to the shade, I can sleep easily, but I really don't like to sleep in public."

"Actually, I don't like it myself."

"I'm not very well these days."

"You'd better get an injection," remarks M. Musa knowingly. "Go to Feni or Maiduguri. I prefer Feni. If you want to be admitted, tell the doctor you don't know anybody at Feni. That time I was there, when I couldn't urinate, I told the doctor I was a stranger in town so I wouldn't have to be an out-patient. Even when he asked me if I knew anybody in Feni by sight, I told him I didn't. So he had to admit me."

"Well, I'll try to see a doctor when I have time. I'm not sick enough to stop working."

A boy with a fan in his hand approaches them.

"Come here, boy," calls M. Musa. "What are you holding?"

The boy gives him the fan without saying anything. He opens the fan and spreads it.

"What is it?"

"A toy fan."

"The boys of today enjoy so much. In our childhood who would get such nice toys to play with? We'll die and leave many changes behind us."

"That's the world. It's always changing from one thing to another."

"Here's your fan. Go and play with it."

The boy leaves and M. Musa continues with a description of his recent stay in the hospital. "When I couldn't urinate again I stayed in the hospital for about two weeks. I did this to regain my proper health because there's nothing better than myself. If you know our local medicine is not as good as hospital medicine, you move with the times and go to a hospital whenever you're feeling sick.

"When I was there, some kind of machine was put into my penis and soon I could urinate again. This treatment lasted for about three days and finally I could go all right, but later on the trouble came back again. I asked the nurse to bring the machine, but he said he wouldn't do it without the doctor's consent. I said to him, 'Since the doctor's away and you can't ask him, what'll you do if I die before he returns?' But the nurse ignored me and went away.

"So, when the Senior Nurse came in, I told him the whole story and he said to the other man, 'Well, if he dies because you refuse to fix the machine for him, you'll be charged with his death.' Then the nurse saw that he had to bring the machine back and soon I was able to urinate again. From that day I never would say if I felt all right. I stayed with the machine for three extra days to be sure I'd have no more trouble."

"You were a wise fellow. Otherwise he'd have discharged you before you were perfectly cured."

After the first scorpion is spotted a flashlight is brought out and for several minutes the men explore their sitting area. M. Musa announces that he knows of a charm for safety from both scorpions and snakes. It must be read at the end of each Muslim month when the new moon appears.

"I'm surprised about educated people," M. Musa says, "because most of them don't believe in charms. There was a certain educated mallam I accompanied on tour around the district. He used to comment on the number of charms I put on before going out."

"Yes, that's true. Some of them don't even say their prayers."

"In Maiduguri we were ten in the same house but only two of us prayed. All the others called themselves Muslims and didn't pray."

When the scorpions become too bothersome, M. Musa excuses himself and goes home. He lies down on his mud bed, his old black sleeping gown wrapped around his body. His left hand is under his head and with the other he fans himself until he falls asleep.

Startled by a shout from nearby, M. Musa jumps up. "Ya Falta, what's the matter? Is that from our house?"

"No. It was our neighbor to the east. He was bit by a scorpion."

"Hmm." He is asleep before he can hear his wife sigh and say, "It's been so hot today. I feel very tired now."

# 3/"The world is for new people": Buba Nola and his family

## UMAR

UMAR'S PASSPORT to enter Fort Lamy, the capital city of Chad, describes him as five feet tall, brown in complexion, with brown eyes and black hair. He was born and raised in Nola, and except for business excursions has spent all of his fifty years there. His parents came from Dikwa Division of Bornu Province where both his father and grandfather were hunters.

The record of Umar's marriages and divorces substantiates what is well known —that marriage among the Kanuri is a fragile affair. It would be necessary to consult his former wives for a more complete and balanced picture of his marital experiences, but, for what it is worth, Umar recalls that he left Fanna because she had leprosy and Dija because she stole the corn that he had buried from a previous year's harvest, whereas Boram lost interest in him and ran away after first informing a neighbor that she was merely going to market for sour milk. He recovered the nine shawls, six jumpers, and five blouses he had given her as wedding presents. Unable to account for his four other divorces, he states categorically that if a wife failed to bear children in three years of marriage, then he divorced her. He has been married to Zara, Buba Nola's mother, for nineteen years; with no other wife did he have any children. Perhaps with his former wives he never took the onion treatment that he once advised to a childless friend: eat seven white onions and do not let your wife chase other men.

Before World War II Umar traveled all over the province, to Marte, Gubio, Gashua, and Bama, buying hides and skins from the local people for resale at a profit to his European employer. After the war he heard of great opportunities in Fort Lamy, so he continued his hides and skins business there, earning for four month's work some thirty or forty pounds toward the family's yearly living expenses. When his health was good he farmed during the rainy season, harvesting thirty sacks of threshed millet and six to eight sacks of unshelled groundnuts. He sold the groundnuts and stored the millet for his family's consumption. Since the death of his older brother, Buba's namesake, he has tanned and sold ram, deer, goat, and reptile skins. Umar inherited the tanning business from his brother and also the huts he lives in.[1]

For many months Umar has been unable to work regularly because of stomach pains. Occasionally he goes to market with his skins so that people will not think he is very ill and come to inquire about his health. His faith in Western medicine, and Western education, as well, does not match that of M. Musa, his co-villager. "I've been to both Feni and Maiduguri hospitals," he relates, "but I still don't feel well. I think I'd better get some of our own [traditional] medicine. I was in each hospital for fifteen days without results from their pills and watery medicine. I think they don't care for villagers or else they'd have given me injections." Injections are the only modern treatment he says he respects. To substantiate his trust in the purveyors of traditional medicine, he tells the story of a wizard who informed him that somewhere in his ward a woman would die. "So I bought a red cock and sacrificed it. A month later my wife was sitting in her hut with Ibrahim and the walls cracked and fell toward them. Fortunately they weren't touched by even one piece of mud. Just a week later a woman died who lived right behind my house. If a wizard can protect my wife, I'm sure he can cure any kind of sickness. He can predict and his predictions come true. I don't think a small pill can cure a person as quickly as a wizard can. I'm going to find one to cure me. I won't depend on a dispensary."

Like many men of his generation, he could not avoid being drawn toward modern medical treatment. His suspicions of what is new are confirmed, however, when a cure does not follow hospital confinement or a dispenser's tablet. He can explain the failure of traditional modes of treatment—by shaitans,[2] by an enemy's stronger prayers, or by disregarded details of the wizard's instructions. These are familiar

---

[1] The matter of Umar's own legacy arose sooner than anyone anticipated because he died one month after this study was made.

[2] *Shaitan* has several meanings such as devil or "a power that opposes God in the hearts of men." Its meanings and appearance in Islamic tradition may be extended considerably, but for my purpose it is sufficient to present it as an evil spirit. (See Houtsma 1927:286.)

and comprehensible explanations. But how to account for the failure of the white man's medicine! Such understanding is beyond his grasp, as is acquiring the unthinking faith in science of other ordinary people who chanced to have grown up in a modern milieu.

If his son Buba's milieu is not strikingly modern, there are indications, nonetheless, that his school experience is a move away from traditional norms. For example, one night after dinner Buba sat in the family compound with his friend Bunu, a Class 4 student. As the older of the two, Buba was quizzing him.

"What would you do if you were very thirsty and could find only dirty water?"

"I'd boil it or filter it."

"Suppose you had neither fire nor filter?"

"I'd pour the water into a container and drink it through a handkerchief and if I didn't have a hankerchief, then through the edge of my clothing."

Zara, Buba's mother, is greatly amused by this sequence and she asks, "What if you're thirsty and have only dirty water and you drink it with the mud and everything? Anyhow, you'll certainly die some day." Everyone laughs and the boys return to their question-answer play.

Umar is ambivalent about education. He never went to school and, moreover, he still remembers with emotion the time "city people" came to Nola recruiting children for Class 1. After they beat him, trying to force him to enroll, he ran away for a few days and they never returned again. At first he was completely opposed to Buba's enrollment and at times he still refers to school as though it were a sickness like smallpox or cerebrospinal meningitis, two diseases which occasionally assume epidemic proportions in Bornu. Since Buba's success in school holds the promise of higher education and well-paying jobs, Umar is more or less reconciled to Buba being in school. As regards the education of his younger sons, his feelings range from never sending them at all—"one son is enough to lose to school"—to leaving the problem to Buba—"if Buba finishes his education and becomes a big man he can send all his brothers to school if he wants to." He is not the least ambivalent about sending girls to school. Girls, he claims, are ruined by education, becoming too proud and wanting only to marry an educated man. If they work for a salary—and obtaining a salaried job is the goal of an educated person—they are not at home to prepare a man's meals. When they come home they complain of tiredness. "How can you get tired from writing on paper?" Umar asks. "We bend down farming all day and never complain, while all they do is write and write and take so many pounds of our tax money. Schools are terrible. I don't like them." Consequently, he is completely opposed to Buba marrying an educated girl and he states, in his humorously bombastic fashion, that if Buba wishes to wed such a girl he can arrange his own marriage.

Umar is a kind man. Without the means to make any grand displays, he still manages to be generous. When Buba requires new clothing Umar tries to accommodate him. In the market he urges his companians not to overcharge their customers. Among his finest deeds is the provision of a home for Karibe, a divorcee, and her daughter. Karibe's home is in a nearby village. When she came to Nola in search of a place to live, Umar took her in as a rent-free boarder. Although not a relation, she is fully accepted by all members of the family, eating with them, joking with Zara's old father, and being a companion to Zara.

Karibe's position as a *zower*, or prostitute,[3] does not involve the promiscuity or low status of her Western sisters. Her behavior as a divorced woman is within an accepted, stigma-free role in Kanuri society. She plans to remarry soon; in the meantime, she does the expected, taking as lovers a few men who will reward her with money and clothing. If her second, third, or fourth marriage will not be the marriage of a young virgin, her husband will have no illusions about her. Men marry *zowers* for the same reasons men marry women in any culture, with the advantage in Bornu that marriage to a *zower* is cheaper to arrange than to a virgin. Umar, for example, never could afford to wed any woman other than a *zower*.

## ZARA

Nola has been Zara's home throughout her thirty-five years. The village had no Western-type school when she was a girl and it is unlikely, considering the still prevailing prejudice against female education, that she would have attended had there been one. Her family was quite rich until her father unaccountably departed for the Cameroons, returning months later to find his cattle sold and his wealth squandered by relatives. Now almost ninety years old, he lives with Zara and his wife lives in Maiduguri with one of their other children.

At the age of seventeen, one year after her marriage to Umar, her second husband, Zara gave birth to Buba. Since then she has had eight more children, six of whom are still alive. Her two daughters live with their aunts in different towns; she seldom mentions them. Living with her in Nola are her sons, Buba—seventeen, Kaka—eight, Ibrahim—four, and Yahaya—one.

Zara is the mainstay of her family and probably has been ever since Umar regularly spent so many months each year away from home. These days, with Umar sick and idle much of the time, she is constantly busy; cooking millet cakes for sale; collecting loads of firewood; farming in season; caring for her children; and preparing meals for her family and Musa the miller, a young man she befriended when he came to Nola as a stranger. Her endless physical labor keeps her short figure lean and wiry and, with one notable exception, she appears to be in good health. A positive diagnosis is uncertain because she has never been examined by a doctor, yet judging from a recent experience she appears to have epilepsy.

Zara, together with Umar, Musa, and her sons Ibrahim and Yahaya, sat in front of her sleeping hut.

"Ibrahim, come stand on my feet," Zara requested. He did, stepping on and off her feet a number of times. Yahaya, the baby in the family, took a piece of kolanut and handed it to her. "Thank you, Yahaya. Grow up to be tall like this."

She lifted her hands high above her head to show him how tall he would become. Yahaya laughed, lifted both his hands above his head, and nearly fell down. Zara caught him and then lowered her face in the crook of her arm. When Yahaya began to climb on her she told him to get down. He laughed again and crawled off as Zara turned away from him.

---

[3] See Cohen 1967:40.

"Have you sold all your cakes yet?" asked Umar.

She did not reply.

"I'm talking to her. Is she gone?"

"No, she's here," answered Musa.

"Well, why doesn't she answer?"

Ibrahim touched his mother but she signaled to be left alone.

"If there are any cakes, bring some for threepence," her husband persisted.

She still did not speak. Instead, she began to roll on her mat, groaning and striking the ground with her hand. She accidentally touched Ibrahim.

"Mother's sick. With her eyes closed she's hitting me."

"Is that so? Well, something's wrong with her," said Umar with concern, finally aware that Zara was troubled. He hurried to his hut, returning with a bottle of scent.

"Musa, come and hold her hands for me."

As Musa held her, Umar dropped scent into her nose and tapped her head with a piece of millet stalk that he had blessed first with Koranic verses.

Zara continued to lie with her eyes closed. Musa suggested taking her to the dispensary.

"Don't worry, Musa. Leave her alone. She'll be all right. No need to take her away because she'll get better at home."

Umar explained that dispensaries do not have medicine for someone in her condition. "This happens to her when she talks to a person who has been with a cannibal. She doesn't know this until her head feels like it's spinning and the hair on her body stands straight up. She's been like this since she was a small girl. Her mother has the same sickness and so does our little Ibrahim. You can't touch his head or he'll fall down. Something he inherited from his grandmother. Too bad."

"So, did she see someone today who's been with a cannibal?" asked Musa.

"Very likely. Otherwise the shaitan wouldn't have touched her."[4]

Later in the evening Zara spoke about her morning's experience.

"I don't know why I feel tired today. Even though I didn't work so hard, all my muscles hurt. They feel as if someone is cutting them with a knife. I hate seeing cannibals. Thank God none of the children is affected like me. [She does not acknowledge that Ibrahim is similarly afflicted.] I'd rather die with the trouble than turn it on to my family and I could do that by asking a juju man [a wizard] to transfer it. It's easily done but very expensive."

Buba's mother is an unsophisticated woman. She has traveled no farther than the villages immediately surrounding Nola, and she takes little interest in affairs outside of her family. In this respect she is no different from most village women. Last market day she returned home with a story about a European she saw there selling books written in Arabic. Having been there himself, Buba corrected her, saying that the man was an Ibo, not a European. "What's an Ibo?" she asked. "A tribe in Eastern Nigeria." "Who knows what Eastern Nigeria is!" she said with a

---

[4] It is believed that some people are man-eaters. Without actually killing and eating humans they can draw all the blood from a body until it becomes lean and sick, perhaps to die. They are thought to have other powers as well. For example, if one should say, "You'll break your leg," then, your leg gets broken.

laugh. To Zara, anyone wearing Western-style clothing is a European and the Ibo males who worked in Northern Nigeria primarily wore Western dress.

Nonetheless, for all her supposed parochialism she is keenly interested in Buba's education. "The world," she says, "is for the new people and the new people are mostly educated. If you're not educated, you won't feel good because you can never understand the world as they do. Even if my time has passed, I'm happy the school has taught my child how to live with the people around him." She acknowledges that children get beaten in school, become too lazy to farm, and forget their religion, especially if they advance beyond primary school. However, if necessary, she is ready to sell her farm products to pay Buba's school fees, believing that "Buba is a good boy. We know he'll take care of us when he starts earning a salary."

## BUBA NOLA

One would never guess that Buba Nola is seventeen years old because he is just a few inches over five feet tall and has the type of face that will look young when he is fifty. The thick scars lining his yellow-complexioned cheeks and running down the bridge of his nose mark him as a Kanuri. His younger brothers have not been scarified with tribal markings because nowadays people believe that such identification is old-fashioned.

An irregular row of squat, gray, smooth-trunked baobob trees, their green, melon-shaped fruits dangling from long stems, separate the village from its open fields. Just east of the trees, and partially in their shade, is Buba's house. The almost continually unpleasant odors emanating from his father's tannery, situated a few yards from the house, necessitate this location at the edge of the village. Unlike most houses in the village, Buba's has an "other side of the tracks" appearance. Eight buildings originally covered the grounds when Buba's uncle and namesake lived on this property. At present the zana grass compound wall is in disrepair, broken calabashes and other discarded items litter the grounds, and the three remaining huts are shabby. In addition to dirt and disorder, the only other change attributable to Umar's occupancy was the building of a hut for his old father-in-law.

To assist his parents, Buba runs errands, helps his father on market day, and fetches water from a well on the other side of the tannery. He is home for short periods during mealtime, in the afternoon for the few hours between the end of school and the beginning of the games period, and after dinner for an hour or so. Most of his time is spent at school. Buba is pleased to have arranged to sleep at the house of Musa the miller, not only because there is insufficient space in his own compound, but also because he can better control the cleanliness of this sleeping quarter. In every respect he is the cleanest member of his family. Perhaps more than anything else he studies at home. Eating takes no more than a few minutes, and if given no chores he gets a textbook and works in a quiet corner. He says that he reads so much in his spare time because he wants to do well on his terminal examinations; otherwise, he can think of no reason to read.

Buba entered Nola Primary School when he was six years old because of the insistence of his namesake uncle. Umar, as the junior brother, always acquiesced to his older brother's plans. After completing Class 4, then considered the top class in junior primary school, Buba left school for four years, only to return again at the request of the education authorities. He is in Class 7, the final year of primary school, hoping to be admitted next January to the teacher training college at Maiduguri. Whether or not he is eligible to continue his education will depend on the results of the Common Entrance Examination he sat for last month. He believes that if his uncle had remained alive, he would now be finished with the teacher training college or the secondary school instead of just expecting to begin.

Zara's and Umar's recollection of this early period of their son's education differs from Buba's.

"Buba suffered very much at school."

*Village houses and wall of zana grass mats.*

"Oh, yes, he certainly did," Zara agrees.

"He was taken to school and beaten and then thrown out after four years. Later, when the village head said he'd recruit him again, I was about to say no."

"I even cried. I said they'd kill my child just like that teacher Abba Idris killed Amina." (Amina, a schoolgirl, was hit by Abba Idris on the head with a blackboard ruler. Bleeding from the nose and mouth, she was taken to the hospital where she died three days later.)

"Even now if you mention Abba Idris' name while Amina's namesake is listening, she'll burst into tears."

"Everybody hated him and feared for their child's life."

"One of us would die the very day he struck my child."

"Did you forget already? Don't you remember he hit Buba so hard with a stick the poor boy couldn't walk for forty days?"

"You know I was in the hospital then."

"Not the district head, the village head, or any teachers came to ask about the boy's health."

"How could any of the teachers come? They knew one of them hit him."

"If I ever have a child, I won't send him to school," says a neighbor.

"Nowadays it's safe," Umar reassures her, "because the Europeans don't allow teachers to beat children."

"What if the Europeans go home?"

"We'll be dead before then and won't care what's going on in the world."

"Who knows whether we'll be dead or not. Only God knows. Let's hope the Europeans don't go away."

It is not surprising that Umar and Zara are unclear about the role of Europeans. For most of their lives Nigeria was a colony and there are as many, possibly more, Europeans present in their part of the country as before independence. In fact, Europeans do not control education either in Bornu or elsewhere in Northern Nigeria, and those administrative positions in the Ministry of Education that are held by Englishmen are filled by Nigerians as the former retire. Bornu's post-primary institutions are especially dependent upon expatriate teachers; in contrast, primary school teachers and local education authorities are entirely Nigerian. Therefore, if teacher behavior is more moderate now than when Buba began primary school, it is not due to European leadership. While brutality on the scale of Abba Idris never has been common, the evidence from Bornu Primary School, attended by Buba's urban counterpart, indicates that moderation in corporal punishment does not prevail everywhere.

Among the educational legacies of the British in Nigeria is the system of prefects, monitors, and games which they believed both at home and in their colonies was instrumental in developing character. Buba's duties as monitor are confined to his own classroom where he dispenses school supplies, runs errands for his teacher, and arranges for the cleaning of the blackboard. As prefect, he shares a variety of school-wide responsibilities with the two other prefects and the head boy. They conduct the games period which all boys must attend from approximately 3:30 to 6:00 each afternoon, excluding Wednesday, market day, and Friday, mosque day. During games period they take roll, supervise student work, such as filling the personal water pots of all the teachers, and organize the boys for a soccer game. When other students misbehave in school, the prefects often are held responsible. This part of the job is unpleasant to Buba, but he is happy with the prefect's power to beat other students and not get beaten in return.

According to his teacher, Buba is a good worker, regularly ranking among the top five students based on terminal examination results. During class his hand is always raised and he listens attentively. His ambition, as yet not strongly formed, is to be a doctor, and if not a doctor then an officer in the Department of Agriculture, or a teacher—anything that helps his country. He wants to live in Nola after completing his education because he thinks the city leads young people to smoke and to drink.

All members of Umar's family arise early. Zara prays, then begins to prepare her cakes for sale. Umar, feeling fit for the first time in weeks, arranges his materials for tanning.

Zara calls out to Karibe, the *zower* who lives in the family compound, "Let's go to the marriage place."

"Are you ready?"

"Yes, I'm getting ready just now."

Zara finishes pounding okra and goes to wash her face and hands before putting on a clean dress. From her husband's hut she gets a blue shawl for tying baby Yahaya to her back. Umar follows her into the compound wearing a sleeveless shirt and long baggy trousers, both garments smelling from close contact with the tannery. He unrolls skins which have been soaking in water, then finds some potash to grind in his mortar.

"I'm going now."

Umar murmurs a protest.

"No, no, I'll be back soon," Zara reassures him, "because I have much to do at home."

"All right, Zara, let's go," says Karibe.

Karibe walks out through the private entrance Umar built to prevent her customers from passing directly through his compound. Otherwise, he explains, strange men might see his wife and forget who it was they meant to visit.

"Let's go this way, Karibe." Zara points toward the tannery.

"No, we better stay on the main paths."

"This way is nearer, you know."

"Yes, but it's better to follow an odorless long way than an odorous short way."

Zara laughs and trails Karibe who stops after a few paces when up ahead she sees a group of men sitting near a well. "Oh, my goodness! Look at them. How can we ever pass by?"

"I told you before, didn't I, but you insisted we follow this way. Let's go. It doesn't matter. This is a good chance for you to exchange glances with your man friend."

Karibe laughs. "How do you know he'll be there?"

"I'm just saying so in case he is. If not, one of the others might be your choice."

"How about you?"

"People won't look at me in your company. Besides, with this child on my back they'll think I'm old."

Just before reaching the well they lower their heads and begin a coquettish walk. In a moment they are past the men and in the compound where the marriage reception is being held. Women have crowded everywhere in the entrance hut and in the open compound, talking in loud fragmented conversations. There is considerable movement and chatter, everyone wishing to talk but no one appearing to listen. Zara and Karibe squeeze into the noisy mass, receiving greetings from all directions. They congratulate the newly wedded woman and accept her offer of kolanut for chewing and tobacco leaves for staining teeth. In five minutes, their obligations met, they pay their respects and this time follow the shorter, aromatic road.

After changing clothes Zara gets some guinea corn and her grinding stones. She arranges two plates on either side of the stones, one for the unground and the other for the ground corn. As she rubs a small stone back and forth over the grain, Yahaya clings to her breast, trying to nurse.

Then Zara mashes groundnuts in a mortar and pestle for Umar's work as he spreads powdered potash on ram skins stretched on the ground and fastened tight with wooden pegs. She is pleased to see him working again. Most of the time his stomach pains confine him to his mat, so despite her gentle nagging (she believes he is healthier than he claims) he passes most days lying in front of his sleeping hut, moving only to relieve himself and to avoid the sun.

Buba, meanwhile, has come home for breakfast. He eats some cakes and strolls to school.

When the bell boy clangs his bell at 7:20 A.M. the children assemble in a semicircle in front of the school. Buba stands near Isa and Kalli, his best friends. As the headmaster and the staff appear from around the corner of a classroom block, Kalli, head boy of Nola Primary School, calls out, "Attention . . . greet." And all the children sing out, "Good morning, sir."

"Good morning. Stand easy," answers M. Zannah, the headmaster.

He calls forward some children wearing dirty uniforms and orders their group leaders, who are held responsible for such matters, to wash the dirty clothes. Another child, who left school yesterday without permission, is asked to stand before his father to receive six lashes on the buttocks. The father is advised that his son will continue to be beaten as long as he ignores school rules. Finally, the headmaster holds up three stolen mangoes before calling out the thief, a small boy of six. M. Zannah steps down from the verandah, catches hold of the boy, and lifts his little gown to expose his buttocks for lashing. After the children are reminded that a similar fate awaits anyone who steals anything, they say their prayers and leave for class.

M. Zannah stops near his office to watch a boy and girl squabbling.

"Our teacher went to Maiduguri," argues the boy.

"No. I saw him this morning," answers the girl.

"He went to the lorry station just this morning."

"No. He can't go anywhere today. It's not our day off."

"His wife had a baby and the naming ceremony is tomorrow. So he must go."

"No. You're wrong."

"Don't be stupid."

"You too don't be stupid."

"I'll take you to Zannah."

"Who is Zannah?"

The boy turns to run to the headmaster and almost bumps into him. "Alima says she doesn't know you and she abused your mother saying she has a big vagina." The children's class monitor who has been waiting nearby lifts the crying girl and stands her in front of the headmaster.

She shouts, "I didn't say that. I didn't say that."

"What didn't you say?" the headmaster asks. The girl is quiet. Lifting his whip threateningly, M. Zannah warns her not to fight with boys or to abuse teachers, and then he continues toward his office.

In this school, as in many others with recent additions, the headmaster's small office is located between two classrooms. The three rooms, sharing a common zinc roof and concrete foundation, constitute a classroom block. Sometimes each new block contains a headmaster's office even though there is never more than

*A Nola tanner.*

one headmaster in a school. M. Zannah's office desk is cluttered with textbooks and old exercise books. On the wall are announcements from the Education Authority and the complete timetable for the school.

He hangs up his big white gown and barefooted sets off to meet his twenty-nine children in Class 7. His desk at the front of the classroom is in disarray with chalk boxes, a blackboard ruler, and piles of marked and unmarked exercise books (each student has a different school-issued exercise book for each subject). A locked wooden cupboard containing school supplies stands near the rear door. Leaning against the cupboard are the children's brooms. Bulletin boards line the walls displaying a world map, a map of Africa, and a scene from Italy; a picture of a pineapple and its uses; and a student-drawn sketch of the life cycle of an insect. These materials have been shown since at least the beginning of the school term and they may continue to be shown until they fall off the walls. Of more ancient vintage by bulletin board standards are pictures of the Queen of England and also of the Duchess of Kent's visit to Nigeria that were posted for the 1960 independence celebrations.

"Have you finished the last three days' assignments?" asks M. Zannah. (He speaks in English because this is an advanced class.)

"Yes, sir. All of it."

"Mallam Abdalla, Kalli, Ashigar, Kaltum, and Buba. Bring your arithmetic exercise books here. And Isa, too." The six children place their books on his desk. "Have you taken all the decimals to three places?"

"Yes, sir."

"Good. Sit down."

After marking the work of his six brightest students, he can ascertain whether he made any miscalculations in his own solutions. Now the remaining students are invited to bring him their exercise books. The room is mostly quiet except when M. Zannah calls out "Next." A student returns to his desk once his problems are corrected. No other assignment has been given, so many pass the time looking out the window. Buba takes his English reader, tips his chair back, and reviews several old lessons, as he does whenever he gets a chance.

M. Zannah ignores the bell when it rings and continues marking into the next period, which also is for arithmetic. When he asks, "Did I mark everyone's book?" and hears no reply, he walks to the blackboard to write "Corrections" and, underneath this heading, "Find to the nearest penny the value of £5.718."

"What are we going to do first?"

"Multiply by twenty to take it back to shillings," the class replies in unison.

"All right, let's do it. Zero times eight equals . . ." He pauses to hear an answer before recording the zero on the blackboard. He continues in the same manner with the remaining numbers, finally announcing the answer as "£5:14.360."

"All right, class, what are we going to do next?"

"Multiply by twelve."

"Two times zero."

"Equals zero."

"Two times six."

"Twelve."

"So we put down two and carry one. Two times three?"

"Six. Plus one equals seven."

"Making £5:15.4320. Three is not up to five. So our answer should be £5:14.4d. How many made mistakes in carrying it to the nearest penny?" Twelve children raise their hands. "How many got all correct?" Only eight children raise their hands, Buba among them.

And thus the teaching-learning cycle passes through one stage: first, the technique for doing a new type of problem is demonstrated (this step and the next one were done on previous days); second, the problems are assigned and worked in class as the teacher walks up and down the aisles supervising the work; third, the problems are marked at home or in class; and, finally, the problems are solved on the blackboard, frequently in choral response as was done today. The second, and possibly even the third and fourth, stage is a repetition of the same arithmetic principle using different examples. This long, slow, deliberate process should ensure understanding by all students, but it does not because each type of problem assumes, too often without justification, previously mastered knowledge and skill. Buba and his friends are among the fortunate ones who understand, while the ignorance of so many others is masked by the choral response to the teacher's questions.

Ten minutes remain in the period. A villager comes by and stands outside the door until he gets the headmaster's attention. They talk and meanwhile the children sit restlessly in their seats until M. Zannah returns.

"O.K. As I've told you, don't mutiply the whole number part of the pounds or shillings by twenty or twelve, only the decimal part. Those numbers on the right-hand side. Clear?"

"Yes, sir."

A girl raises her hand, but then the bell rings and M. Zannah does not recognize her. Instead, he stands silent for a moment rubbing his hands. "All right, during this English period I want you to take out your grammar book. Open to Lesson 1, Exercise 1." He reads from the book. "Useful words and phrases. 'Much to see, much to do, little to see, little to do.' Let's discuss the words I've just read out. 'Much to do.' Who can tell me their meaning in Kanuri?"

Various children try the phrase in Kanuri before the headmaster is satisfied.

"Now, 'lost to sight.' Nobody can tell how far it is from here to Maiduguri just by looking. Another example. An airplane goes far up and we see it, but we can't tell how far it travels and finally we can't see it at all. So we say it's 'lost to sight.' Now, 'much to see.' During the day there is much to see. During the night there is little to see. Idle people have little to do. What is 'idle'?"

"One who is lazy."

"Give a sentence with 'much to do.'"

"If you go to Maiduguri there is much to do."

"O.K. If you go to Maiduguri you'll lose your way at night. There's little to see at night."

The class laughs.

"Village people have little to see," comments M. Zannah. "Why?" And before anyone can respond he continues, "In some places there is little to see. This is in reference to our last sentence. For example, in Nola there are the same round huts everywhere so there's little to see and little to do. In towns, though, some people are walking, some are in cars, some are selling in shops, and some are rushing about. There is much to do." (M. Zannah is a man of the city and his comparison of Nola and Maiduguri reflects more than an attempt to provide interesting examples for his English lesson. His mother is a well-known seller of *burukutu*, a local type of wine, and he spends his holidays with her in Maiduguri.)

Jiddah raises his hand to speak. "If you go to Man O'War Bay you'll have much to do.[5]

"Yes, you will have much to do there. From early morning to late at night you'll be very busy. I attended Man O'War in 1957. They give little time for prayers whether you're Muslim or Christian. Only one and a half hours free time all day. So whatever you're asked to do you must do fast."

Buba stands up to recite. "Lazy people have little to do."

"What? Say it in a different way."

"Women have less to do than men."

"No. Women have much to do because they prepare food and take care of the house. What do you say?"

Buba leans back on his chair and scratches his nose; he looks embarrassed for having made a mistake. Somewhere in the room a mirror falls and breaks into pieces. The headmaster, ignoring the sound, studies his book.

"What's behind that classroom?" M. Zannah asks. When the children look, he says, "The garden is there hidden from our view."

"Also the dispensary is hidden from view by the teacher's house."

"Yes, unless we destroy the teachers' houses we can't see the dispensary. Therefore, it's lost from sight."

Buba looks at the door and once again at his English book. The bell rings.

"The farther the lorry goes the smaller it looks," M. Zannah continues, "until it goes far into the horizon and disappears. We can say it is lost from sight." He rushes to complete the lesson. "We say on foot, by lorry, by car, by train, etc. You can cross the Sahara by camel. You can cross the ocean by ship, by canoe, and by ferry. By the way, what is a ferry?"

"A canoe that carries cars across the sea," somebody answers.

"Yes, that's right. And people can go to Lagos by ferry."

The headmaster signals that the class is dismissed and they rush out of the room with a great burst of noise.

Buba quickly walks home. He goes directly to his father's hut, pouring a bowl of water before heading toward the latrine. Zara enters the compound, removing her shawl as she approaches her own hut. Finally, Musa the miller comes in. Buba asks him how he feels but Zara interrupts before he can answer.

---

[5] Man O'War Bay was originally a training center located in the Cameroons. Its citizenship-building activities were considered so valuable that independent Nigeria established its own facilities at Kurra Falls in the highlands area of Northern Nigeria. The emphasis of the training programs is on reducing tribal hostilities and promoting a feeling of social responsibility, both particularly important aims in contemporary Nigeria.

"Musa, for what you did to me yesterday, I shouldn't speak to you today."

"Ya Zara, what could I do? I wasn't there when Usman refused to grind your millet. If I'd been there it wouldn't have happened."

"We were grinding and eating long before you brought that machine to this village. Only our vanity makes us take our grain to it."

"But mother, what is this? I tell you I wasn't there yesterday."

"All right, we'll see what happens next time."

Zara sets one bowl down and goes back to the kitchen for another. "Here, take this and eat," she says to her son as she passes him. "There's no other food for breakfast." The bowl contains five cakes. Buba and Musa begin to eat.

"Musa, how's your backache?" teases Buba. Musa was the only nonschoolboy who ate aljang seeds in the incident discussed previously in Aisa's day. He claims he took them to relieve his back pains.

"Don't mention it, please. I'm having another one right now."

"Backache? Well, why don't you take that stuff again? You know it gives relief."

"Yes, it does, but I won't take any more."

"Why? Is it bitter or painful? Anyway, why did you take it at all?"

"You see, when I took the stuff it had a fruity taste. I saw the schoolboys taking it and I thought, 'I've tasted so many intoxicating drinks from so many places, why not try the seeds and see what happens? If it comes to death, well, everyone has to die sometime and so I'll die with two children.' That's why I took aljang in the first place."

"Well?"

"After I swallowed some seeds I waited about ten or fifteen minutes before they took effect. When they did I began singing in different languages. A few minutes later I found I didn't want to sing anymore and I started thinking of strange things. I even talked to people outside our gate about things that I myself don't understand. When I stood up and walked around the village I felt like I was dragging something very heavy. At last I got to my compound, but before I could enter I collided with a zana mat. I drew back because everything looked terribly fuzzy and I collided with the same mat. Next time I got around it and headed toward my hut. After searching a while for the door I gave up and slept on the ground for the night. Next morning I felt so bad I couldn't recognize who was who or what was mine. I even mistook my own gown and flashlight and said they were my neighbor's. This craziness lasted until noon. Finally, my stomach felt like it was being pumped. I started making bad air so I drank potash in water with lime juice. This helped a lot and I fell asleep until evening."

Buba reaches school at 9:45 A.M. Children are concentrated in the shaded areas because the sandy soil of the school's playground already is burning hot. The bell rings at 10:00 and Buba and his friends reluctantly move from under the neem trees to their stuffy room where they wait for M. Alhaji to come and teach religion.

M. Alhaji walks in three minutes late and, speaking in Arabic, calls on Abdullah to read the lesson about the sky. Abdullah reads in Arabic and the teacher translates into Kanuri.

"Ashigar, in what tense is the verse Abdullah has just read?"

"The first two lines, where it says, 'The fox drove the sheep,' are in the past tense and the last one is in the future tense."

M. Alhaji reads another sentence, translating it himself. "This means, 'You see a handsome boy and a very beautiful girl.' Do you know that a female of twenty is beautiful but still a girl? At thirty she's a woman and at sixty an old woman. Over ninety she's too old to fast because there's no blood in her so for her sake people must give alms of one cup of millet to the poor."

Many children laugh at the mallam's joke.

M. Alhaji, often very punitive, is also lively and entertaining, thus making religion a popular subject. Much time is devoted to translation from Arabic to Kanuri. The children generally are indifferent to this work, yet they are ready with full attention when the mallam departs from the lesson to launch into a story or to offer advice based presumably on Islamic lore.

A few days ago he was reading a verse in Arabic when a student interrupted.

"Sir, I've heard people say that *dudjail*[6] is the European we see now. How can that be? Europeans have two eyes while *dudjail* is supposed to have just the one on his forehead."

"Oh, yes. People sometimes think the *dudjail* will come before the *Mahdi* [the Messiah], but this isn't true. People also say the *dudjail* will appear from among white men because the *dudjail*'s time is supposed to be one of easy transport and no famine. Everyone knows the white man invented airplanes and cars so that a distance which once took forty days now takes only a few hours. And food can be moved so fast that people don't suffer from hunger as before."

No other teacher moralizes as much as M. Alhaji. He makes his point in a manner that disarms an offender and amuses the momentarily innocent. After the last examination he called forward each student and publicly announced his score. Sulum expressed dissatisfaction with his results and asked to see his paper.

"Do you think you deserve more than I gave you?" M. Alhaji asked.

"Even Bukar got 35. What can he do that I can't?"

"Oh, I see. So you want to be compared with Bukar! Do you want me to compare you in other subjects, too?"

"Yes."

The teacher, annoyed, asked Sulum to come to the front of the room. "How many questions did I ask on the exam?"

"There were 20."

"And you got only 15 out of 100 percent? Good. You did all 20 questions as well as you could? Now, can you correctly answer 10 of the 20 questions? Any 10 and I'll give you 99 percent."

The other students were greatly amused at this offer.

---

6 The *dudjail*, Bornu Muslims believe, is a man who will come to earth and convert people of different religions to paganism. According to one source, he was a particular person who made "a great public display of his wealth and was swallowed up by the earth with his palace. He is thus an example of those who prefer the fleeting wealth of this world to gaining by alms and humility and righteousness the abiding riches given by Allah in the world to come" (Houtsma 1927: 780–781).

"Believe me sincerely to God I'll give you 99 percent. You think those who got higher marks are my favorites? No. They aren't. They're the same as you. Have you ever heard the story of Prophet Musa's [Moses] time when nobody was poorer or richer than anybody else and people were the same in all ways? But then came the complaints. People begged the Prophet to change things, at least to make them rich and poor, good and bad, etc. Their wish was granted and that's why in our community today certain people are cleverer than others. In God's case there's no appeal. Once he makes a change, that's the way it is.

"Sulum, if you're going to make such a fuss you won't get anywhere. Unless a student has good character and respect for his teachers even scores of 100 percent on every examination won't make him eligible for school in England. Maybe when you go to higher school in Yerwa [this is another name for Maiduguri] you'll learn that cleverness is not enough. You must respect your elders or it'll be too bad for you. I'm telling this to all of you and not only to Sulum."

Sulum goes to his seat and covers his face with his hands.

On another occasion M. Alhaji tried without success to get Class 7 to answer questions. Buba paid no attention. He stared vacantly at the blackboard, his fingers in his mouth, while the teacher taunted the class.

"I'm going to bring a Class 4 child to teach Arabic."

"He couldn't teach us," some students replied.

"He will if you won't pay attention."

"We will. We will."

"Class 7 boys are now being rejected as laborers," M. Alhaji says provocatively.

"We're better than laborers."

"You'll see. You'll cry one day." This comment evokes many no's from the class. Buba hits his desk with his fist as he joins the others in protest.

"I'm only advising you."

"Yes, your highness," says a boy.

He is corrected at once by a classmate. " 'Your highness' is only said by slaves and servants. 'Yes sir' is what we should say."

"No one is going to enter paradise," concludes M. Alhaji, "just because he's a Koranic mallam, a son of an Emir, or a European. Paradise is only for those who obey God's rules."

"I'll go to Arabic school to study," Kalli calls out, and he is joined by others shouting, "I will too, I will too."

At the end of a period of translation back and forth from Kanuri to Arabic, the class is asked to stand up and stretch their hands high in the air. As they do this the bell rings and M. Alhaji leaves immediately. Two students clean the blackboard in preparation for the next subject.

Buba and his classmates relax during the few minutes in between classes. When the headmaster arrives, he walks briskly to the board and begins unceremoniously by writing on the blackboard, "General Study of South America."

"South America consists of how many countries?" M. Zannah asks the class.

"Brazil, Uruguay, Argentina, Colombia, Paraguay," they answer one by one.

"Which is the largest country?"

"Brazil."

"How large is Brazil?"

"More than three million square miles."

"Buba, what is the capital of Brazil?" Neither Buba nor any other student knows the correct answer.

M. Zannah goes to the blackboard, writes "Washington,"[7] and asks, "Have you heard this name?"

There are many yes's and no's shouted at him and he angrily reminds them to answer one at a time.

"Why do we hear the name Washington most of the time?"

No answer.

"Because Washingon is the center of radio and television communications," he answers himself.

"Which town in Bornu do you hear of most?"

"Nguru."

"No, Yerwa is the town."

"Yes, Yerwa, Yerwa."

"Why do you think it is? Because Yerwa is the capital and the Shehu and Waziri stay there. O.K. Is South America mountainous or just plains?"

"Mountainous and plains."

"Who can guess the heights?"

"Fifteen to twenty thousand feet above sea level."

"How was this found? Did they start at the sea? If so, why?"

No answer.

"Because rivers and seas are the lowest places. If you've noticed, rivers start from the highest places and settle in the lowest places. Which are the lowest places in Nigeria?"

"Chad."

"Where else?"

"Rivers Niger and Benue."

"Yes, and also the coasts of the country. So rivers and seas are the lowest places and only rise when they're heated."[8]

Geography and history appear as a single subject on the timetable, although they are taught separately. The content of these courses is presented by M. Zannah in lectures drawn from his own notes taken as a student or from different books provided by the local education authority in Maiduguri; each student in the class has an atlas and his dictated notes. It is not uncommon to find students possessing only English and arithmetic textbooks.

The range and type of topics Class 7 studied in geography and history this term is evident in their final examination questions.

---

[7] M. Zannah may be unaware of the distinction between North America and South America. This section on Washington and Nguru is not meaningfully related to the rest of the lesson, but it is the way the lesson proceeded.

[8] Neither geography nor science are strong points in M. Zannah's education. In this reference he may be thinking that if water turns to vapor, the vapor rises and that this also happens to rivers and seas.

1. What do you know about the duties of the following: (a) the District Head; (b) the local council; (c) the Forestry Officer.
2. Why is the market necessary? (Give reasons.)
3. What do you know about South and North America in general?
4. Why were slaves taken to America many years ago? (Give full reasons.)
5. Who are the following? (a) Head of the Federal Military Government; (b) the Military Governor of the Northern Provinces; (c) the Chief Justice of the Federation; (d) the Chief Education Officer, Bornu Education Authority.

The profoundly limited ability of the students to write English prose reduces even the most discussable of these questions to several ungrammatical sentences.

At 11:10 the bell is rung and the entire school begins a fifteen-minute break. Buba remains writing at his desk until he is reminded that it is time to record the temperature and the amount of rainfall.

The rain gauge and the thermometer constitute the school's sole science equipment in use. Kits of science materials have been given to Nigeria by UNESCO; Bornu's share is locked securely in a special storeroom in Maiduguri. Even if they were distributed they would not be used properly because teachers have had minimal or no science education. Buba's weather recording activities constitute his science experience in school. Rural science, a mandatory subject, is offered, if only on the timetable pinned to the headmaster's office wall. At worst, students work the headmaster's farm during the rural science period. At best, they are divided into groups to tend the school garden.

Yesterday, for example, the headmaster sent the girls to fetch water as their gardening activity. From the storeroom they collected leather buckets to draw water from the well and kerosene tins to transport it to the garden. Buba's group of five boys was responsible for four paw-paw trees. They broke up the soil at the base of each tree and placed thornbushes and cornstalks around the trunk for protection from goats. Other groups worked on lemon, mango, and guava trees.

While Buba records the rainfall and temperature, most other children play or rest. A group of girls under the leadership of the head girl, a classmate of Buba's, fill and carry water pots back and forth from the headmaster's house. One girl announces that even if the bell of heaven were to ring she would finish her work rather than stay after school.

Arithmetic, Class 7's next subject, is taught for the third time today in continuation of the lesson from before breakfast. For those who have completed their corrections M. Zannah writes more of the same type of problem on the board and again demonstrates the correct procedure for its solution. Students soon flock around his desk while he patiently corrects and advises each one. The great attention to detail in working percentages of Nigerian currency may be useful not only for passing school examinations but also for satisfying job requirements in government departments or locally based foreign commercial firms.

It is nearly midday and the students are wilting. When their problems are corrected, they sit quietly fanning themselves with their exercise books. The onion-like smell of the neem tree's seeds penetrates the classroom. During a quiet moment the soft rumble of a truck is heard passing by on the paved road to the west.

English is the last lesson of the day and at the headmaster's command the arithmetic exercise books are immediately replaced by grammar books.

Within ten minutes M. Zannah and the students change from talking about English expressions to considering different languages and customs, and finally they drift into a discussion of the old and new names of various objects. They now speak only Kanuri, a more comfortable language than English for both teacher and students.

"What did we call matches in the olden days?"

Many children speak together. Some say "*tashar*" and others say "*mosuwa*."

"'*Tashar*' is correct. '*Mosuwa*' is the name of our old lamps."

"Long ago they used a tin filled with groundnut oil and a cotton wick," explains Ashigar.

"Yes. Do they exist now?"

"Yes."

A girl shouts at the top of her voice, "I've seen that type of lamp recently."

"Changing times often make us forget our old things. Who knows the name of the earrings worn by our older women?"

Many children guess. None, however, are correct.

"That's why Europeans are better than we are," admonishes M. Zannah. "They record everything while we can't even remember the names of our four grandparents. And we learn the history of other people in the world before mastering the history of ourselves and our area. Some of you know about modern things and ancient history better than your fathers, but European children know better than you because whenever they ask a question they get an answer. Your grandfather will drive you away if you ask more than two or three questions, won't he?"

Kalli says, "When I asked my father when I was born, he said, 'Go away, I don't even know my own birthday. My parents didn't tell me!'"

Everyone laughs at this response. M. Zannah reminds the class that it is time for prep and leaves the room. A moment after he departs Ashigar diverts the prep period, ordinarily a twenty-minute homework session, to the telling of riddles.

Ashigar begins. "What moves but can't be seen?"

"Air."

"What sleeps without closing its eyes?"

"A buck."

"What has life but never moves or talks?"

"An egg."

"What goes downhill, never uphill?"

"Water."

"No, but it involves water."

"A river."

"Yes."

Falmata takes her turn. "What contains milk only after birth?"

"You and your breast."

The class laughs.

"Not me but your mother's breast," jokes Falmata.

"What walks on land, flies in the sky, and swims in water?" asks Buba.

Many children call out, "There is no such thing." Others guess unsuccessfully. Buba laughs and says, "If you can't get it, I'll tell you."

"All right, tell us."

"A goose or a duck."

Buba's classmates clap in appreciation and he returns to his seat looking proud. As the final bell rings, Kalli announces he has one more riddle to ask. "After nine months and seven days the Koranic mallam comes. What does he say?" Everyone is silent. "Should I tell you?"

"Yes."

"I mean your name. You stay for nine months in your mother's stomach and seven days after birth the mallam comes to give you a name."

When all the children are gone, Buba selects some books from his desk, goes to the headmaster's office for a set of keys, and proceeds to shut the windows and lock the doors of all classrooms. After depositing the keys at his teacher's house, he walks home.

There he finds his mother and father shelling groundnuts in front of her sleeping hut. Yahaya, the youngest child, sits playing with a pile of shells. Karibe, the family boarder, is winnowing millet outside her own hut. She asks Umar if she can borrow some groundnut oil and as she reaches for the oil Umar asks her, "When are you going to Maiduguri for Mangu's marriage?"

"Tomorrow."

"I won't be able to go. I'm too sick. That's the bad part of putting a girl into school."

"I don't understand. What's the bad part?"

"That girl Mangu lived with us for almost ten years. She went to her first school from my house. When she joined her aunt in Maiduguri to go to a big school she never came back, not even to greet me. Now that she's going to be married and it's time for a gift she suddenly remembers me."

"Boys also forget their fathers, you know," Karibe reminds him.

"Yes and no. They'll forget you if you treat them too well when they're young. But if you don't pamper them and you give serious warnings and correct each mistake, they'll never be rude. And they'll never forget their parents."

For the next hour Umar alternately rests, complains of stomach pain, chats with friends, and watches Yahaya while Zara visits a sick neighbor. Buba, meanwhile, has gone to the headmaster's house to meet two other students who also have agreed to prepare and cook a chicken for their religion teacher.

Buba joins Ashigar, the riddle teller from his class, and Zarami, a boy from Class 5, under a neem tree behind the headmaster's house. The headmaster and his wife have gone to Maiduguri for the afternoon. The boys pluck chicken feathers.

Zarami picks up a piece of paper lying nearby and reads from the half-torn sheet, "Common Entrance . . ."

Ashigar finishes the line. "Examination. Oh, it makes me remember the examination we took last month."

"Me too," says Buba.

"Buba, if you had a choice, where would you go?" asks Zarami.

"I'd go to TTC [Teachers Training College] if I could. I really like it best.

But marks make the difference for going to any school and I'm worried that I didn't pass at all."

When the feathers are all plucked, they cut open the chickens and wash them with water before placing them over the open hearth for roasting. Around the hearth the intense heat from the fire compels them to take turns wearing their two available pairs of shoes, two boys working while one rests.

"Ashigar, go buy onions for threepence," orders Buba, "and by then I'll be done praying." He takes a dirty kettle, fills it with water, and sits down to perform his ablutions.

"But you didn't give me any money."

"Oh, take threepence from my gown on the headmaster's verandah." Ashigar is back in a few minutes and since Buba has finished praying, they pick up the chickens and onions and set off for their teacher's house. On the way Buba turns again to the subject of their recent school-leaving examination.

"When are the results coming out?" he asks.

"Maybe in June, because they usually come out then."

"I really think it's better to go to TTC and become a teacher," says Buba.

"No. Secondary school is better because if you finish five years 'and stay a few more, you can sit for your HSC [Higher School Certificate]."

"But to go on you must get a high pass. If you get division one, you have a chance for a [university] degree. If you get lower, what have you got?"

"Anyway, it'll be a long time before you reach that point."

"The world will come to an end first."

"And we'll have nothing, not even one salary before we die. If you go to a Grade I course [advanced teacher training] it's the same as getting a salary because you're paid eight pounds a month pocket money."

"That's why I say it's better to go to TTC and get your Grade II. After that you can go for Grade I."

"Teaching is terribly hard work but office work is nice. You get good pay and a comfortable place to sit."

"Aha. You're comfortable only until the auditors check your office and discover you've taken bribes or lost government property. Then you end up in prison. If you're a teacher there's no trouble like that because when the auditor asks where are such and such books, you say your pupils used them and then you're free. Besides, if you finish Grade II, you'll get twenty pounds a month teaching; if you finish secondary school and don't pass, you'll get less than a Grade II teacher."

Their assessment of the outcomes from attending a training college or a secondary school are highly realistic (a third postprimary alternative, the craft school, is too low in prestige for these able boys to consider in their discussion). Training college students are paid to go to school and, furthermore, they are assured of employment as primary school teachers or headmasters when they complete their course. A training college education, however, delays by one year reaching the university and is not as direct a route to it. While the financial costs of attending a secondary school are relatively high, the rewards—reaching the university or a government post—however uncertain, are also high. If students do well on their final examinations, the General Certificate of Education, they can enter the sixth form and possibly go on to the university. At present only a limited number of relatively high-paying, high-status jobs are available for the student with only a secondary school education. Some able students prefer the certainties of teacher education to the uncertainties of the higher potential, higher risk secondary school.

The boys are laughing as they enter M. Alhaji's compound. Seeing the chickens have been roasted properly, M. Alhaji gives the students sixpence to share and sends them away.

It has been a busy afternoon and they are surprised to learn that it is almost time for games. Instead of going home they head toward the school grounds where Buba walks to his usual sitting place near the well and begins the roll call. The boys of Nola Primary School sit silently, waiting to announce their presence. Once the roll call is over, some form groups for watering the garden and filling the teachers' water pots while others kick a tennis ball, eat groundnuts, or just sit around until summoned for the regular afternoon soccer match. Isa and Kalli join Buba at the well. They read for a while before deciding to work exercises in their English grammar book.

After some minutes of taking turns on the English exercises, Buba excuses himself to prepare for prayers. He walks to a quiet part of the school compound to urinate and wash his penis. Then he washes his hands three times, rinses his mouth three times, and flushes water through his nostrils. Next he washes his face three times, returns to his arms and cleans them up to the elbow, and then passes his still wet hands back and forth over his head. Finally he washes his legs and ears. When his prayers are complete he returns to Kalli and Isa.

It is almost five o'clock and time for the soccer match to begin. Buba puts his book aside and goes to inspect the watering and cleaning that have been under way since the games period began. He walks over to a group of six boys who are about to share a large onion. The owner, after failing to break the onion into smaller pieces, thinks for a moment, then lays the onion on his gown and invites all the boys to smack it with their hands. By the fourth blow the onion splits and the owner distributes the pieces, saving the largest for himself.

An older boy wearing a white shirt and yellow trousers cycles up to the group. Everyone admires him as he gets off his bike and allows Kaka, a schoolboy, to park it for him. As Kaka proudly walks the bike to a shady area, other children crowd around to ring the bell and stare into the rear view mirror. Kaka fumbles with the lock on the bike's rear tire, unable to work it, and a voice calls out from behind him, "Kaka bushman. Doesn't know how to lock a bicycle."

Kaka yells back, "Thank you, city boy, who knows how to drive a car."

Just then a whistle is blown from the playing field to urge the stragglers to hurry. Buba, Kaka, and the onion eaters join the other players and for the next hour they are happily absorbed playing soccer. At last a bell is rung to announce the final roll call. When it is finished Buba walks home with his friends.

"Come on, children. Come and eat your food." The three younger children gather around their mother. Buba gets the plate of food that he shares with his father. As usual, both groups eat in silence, but after a few mouthfuls Buba complains to his father that there is not much oil in the food.

"You have money. You're the son of a European.[9] Why don't you buy oil?" Umar smiles at his own humor. "Did your great-grandfather eat food with oil?"

"Did I know my great-grandfather?"

"Do you think he ate food with oil?"

"No, I don't think so."

"So, why should you?"

"Oh, I just said so. I'm not serious. By the way, Baba, did my great-grandfather go to European school?"

"No. In those days who thought of going to school?"

"Well, then, why am I in school if my great-grandfather didn't go?"

Zara and Umar both laugh at their son. They are amused and impressed by his reply. Zara says, "I told you, Umar, these schoolboys have been given too much brain by the white man."

Dinner is over and Zara collects and washes the bowls and utensils before making preparations for tomorrow's cakes. Umar resumes a prone position on his mat, but when he sees his wife doing work usually done first thing in the morning, he asks if she will ever stop working. Since she will be busy in the morning, she explains, she plans to cook the cakes and leave them overnight near the fire to keep warm. She continues her work and for a time the pleasant smell of cakes baking competes with the tannery aromas. While cooking, she sees three hunters pass by carrying guns over their shoulders.

"I think those guns can shoot far," she says to Umar.

"These days they go farther than in the olden days."

"Your father's knees . . . "

Umar interrupts her. "Aha. My father really suffered during the war with Rabeh.[10] He was shot just because he refused to hand over his property to the soldiers. Twelve bullets were taken out of his knees." He continues without pause to tell one story about a man who transformed vultures into chickens and sold the birds in the market and another about the powers of a former Nola leader. "During the reign of Kachalla Duloma as district head in Nola, a certain terrible thief was arrested who couldn't be touched by a bullet however close to him the gun was fired. Nothing could penetrate his skin, not even knives or arrows or spears. This was because he drank many powerful juju medicines. When the district head finally caught the thief, he locked his hands with handcuffs, but the thief commanded the handcuffs to drop off. They did. Each time Kachalla Duloma was defeated until he became so disappointed and angry that finally he roared to the handcuffs not to drop off at anyone's command. He did this to show the thief his power. So saying, he took the handcuffs and with his own hands locked up the thief. Now it was the thief's turn to roar at the handcuffs. It was no use, though, and he was taken to jail in Maiduguri."

---

[9] I believe the father is referring to me and the fact that for some reason or other his son, of all the schoolboys in Nola, had been chosen for the European's study.

[10] See Cohen 1967:18.

*Village woman cooking in clay pots.*

Zara's father has joined the family for the story. He sits leaning against a hut, his prayer beads in his hand, and naked to the waist because Zara is killing the lice in his gown. After ten minutes of searching out what appears to be an inexhaustible supply of lice she asks him, "How do you ever sleep with this gown on? Don't you feel them getting into your blood?"

"No, there's not much blood in me to be sucked. Besides, I'm too old to care about such things. I expect death to come soon." He speaks dispassionately and Zara makes no overt response to his comments.

Suddenly there is a frightened shout from the next hut.

"What's wrong, Karibe?"

"Scorpion. A very big one."

"Did it sting you?"

"I'm lucky. Just as it was about to sting my foot I lit my flashlight and it disappeared under my kolanut basket."

"It's because this cool breeze is blowing. They come out of their holes for fresh air and they get you if you don't take care."

"I'm going in now. I'm afraid I'll be bit."

"What'll I do then? Scorpions go where they see light and here I am baking. I'm afraid for the children sleeping on the ground."

She wakes Kaka and Ibrahim to move them inside, lifts the baby onto her own bed, and returns to the fire.

"Now I'm happy," she tells Karibe. "I hope they're safe inside. For myself it doesn't matter."

"So am I. I took my little girl inside, but I can't stay with her. The room is so hot I could never sleep. I'll stay out for a while in the fresh air." She hears Umar snoring. "Umar, Umar," she calls out.

"He's sleeping."

"Isn't it too early to sleep?"

"You know Umar with his sleeping. He lays down any time he feels like it."

Buba has long since left for the miller's house to study his English book by the light of a kerosene lamp.

# 4/Son of a donkey:
# Maliki Nguru and his family

## CASE STUDY CHARACTERS

| | |
|---|---|
| Maliki Nguru | Thirteen-year-old schoolboy |
| Ya Jalo | Maliki's mother |
| M. Ahmed Kura | Maliki's father |
| Isa | Maliki's youngest brother |
| Ya Alima | Maliki's married sister |
| Kaka | Maliki's baby sister |
| Ali | Bicycle renter and M. Ahmed's fellow vendor |
| M. Abba | Maliki's teacher of religion |
| M. Aji | Maliki's teacher in Class 7 |
| Fanna | Ya Jalo's friend and neighbor |
| Madu Shettima | Maliki's classmate |
| Mustafa | M. Ahmed's friend and fellow retainer in the house of Tijjani Kachallah |
| Abba | Maliki's friend |

## AHMED KURA

AHMED KURA was born in Ngerbuwa, Bornu Province. He was raised by his uncle, a Koranic mallam attached as a client to Sanda Kyari (who later became the Shehu of Bornu). His uncle's job was to provide charms and medicine and to pray so that God would grant his master's wishes. In addition, he gave his nephew religious instruction, and before their separation Ahmed Kura had memorized ten chapters of the Koran, an achievement of which he still is proud. When his uncle prepared to leave for Mecca on a pilgrimage, the young Ahmed returned to his own family.

By the early 1920s the British economic investment in Nigeria had created new job opportunities which lured the mobile and enterprising Nigerian away from family and farm. In most instances southern Nigerians seized these opportunities, but there were venturesome northerners as well and Ahmed Kura was among them. He remained on the family farm for three years before beginning the odyssey which took him to Jos, where tin mining had become an important industry, and to Zaria, where he obtained work with the Nigerian Railway Corporation first as a coal boy and later as caretaker of electric bulbs on the Zaria-Minna run. After nine years with the railroad, he collected sixty pounds terminal pay and again returned home to farm, but the quiet life of a villager did not suit him and he left to join the police force. Soon afterward it was his misfortune to catch syphilis, which at that time was grounds for dismissal. In 1939, without other means of employment in sight, he enlisted in the army. M. Ahmed was placed in a regiment that was sent to India in 1943 and remained in Asia until the war ended. By this time he has told and retold so often the story of his war years that it is difficult for him to separate fact from fiction (as we see later when he recounts his experiences in Burma). He claims to have attained the rank of lance-corporal and received the respect of a sergeant. It is certain, however, that after leaving military service in 1946 he rejoined the police force in Bornu, remaining in their employ until his retirement seventeen years later. "When I was young," he reminisces, "I always thought of going places my parents never even dreamed about." His thoughts indeed became reality and as a result he has, for a man of his generation, an uncommonly extensive awareness of the world beyond Bornu and an unusually large store of tales to relate to his friends.

While M. Ahmed has enjoyed good health most of his life, Ya Jalo, his wife, can recall the incident which almost proved fatal to her husband. "There was a certain policeman," she relates, "with the same name as my husband and he envied Kura's success. So, one day when the men were resting in the shade that other Ahmed Kura brought out a white kolanut and gave each man a piece. They all chewed their kolanut right then and there. When Kura came home he lay down and Maliki began playing with him, climbing on his stomach and hitting him with his dirty hands. I came out of the kitchen and asked whether he was well because he was lying there on the floor, but he didn't say anything. A visitor came to take him somewhere, but Kura gestured 'no' with his hand. As soon as the man walked away Kura began to vomit and he vomited all night long bringing up big clots of blood about the size of my fist.

"Early the next morning I went for Sergeant Zarma and told him to follow me before he even said his prayers. When he saw Kura all bloody, he ran at once to report the matter to the district head who sent a Land Rover to carry us to the Molai Mission Hospital. By the time we reached Molai his body had grown fatter and fatter; in fact, his watchband wouldn't fit around his wrist even on the last hole. He got some relief at Molai and the doctor guaranteed he'd send medicine whenever it was needed. I wasn't sure about that so when we reached Maiduguri, where we were sent for fifteen days' leave, I went to a famous [Koranic] mallam. Even though the mallam had never seen me before, he knew just why I'd come and he said the illness was caused by the other Ahmed Kura. He got some medicine and advised me to have Kura bathe in it nine times."

She takes pleasure in stating that the man who tried to bewitch her husband was later caught gambling in his own house, dismissed from the police force, and reduced to wearing rags.

At present M. Ahmed claims to be about fifty-five years old. He is tall and strong in appearance, although his back is slightly bent and many of his teeth are decayed or missing. In order to eat a kolanut he first must cut it into small pieces. He wears a big ring, a wristwatch, and a knife fastened just above his elbow. He rides his own bike when he goes to collect rent from his tenants or elsewhere beyond his immediate neighborhood, but mostly he sits behind his small business stand situated on the main road near his house. When he is not actually engaged with a customer, he chats with other vendors and visitors who stop to pass the time of day or recites Koranic verses while counting prayer beads, a common practice among men of his age. Occasionally he reaches under his table for a wooden slate containing verses from the Koran and reads them to himself. These acts of religious devotion are unremarked by anyone who happens to be present.

On most days he is joined in his market area by the young girl with the big red pot who sells gruel and by Ali the bicycle renter, who keeps his bicycles lined up, air pump handy, and a half-dozen wrenches thrown about on a dirty mat. A more transient group consists of the vendors of *ardeb* (a locally prepared brew drunk especially in hot weather), kolanuts, and groundnuts. Ahmed Kura presides over the social and business affairs of those around him in this little market. Here he is treated as a man of importance and clearly acts the part, settling disputes and dispensing advice with the authority of his combined policeman's background and gray hair. This dominating role is in contrast to his actual current occupation as a "petty, petty trader," who sells small quantities of a variety of goods from his four-foot by two-foot stand. For example, at one time he may have bars of Sunlight soap, bottles of perfume of different brands, jars of hair oil, individually wrapped cubes of sugar sold "by the loaf," open packages of cigarettes sold one at a time, matches, and toffee mints. Under the stand is a jar of drinking water. At night all his wares are packed in a large box and stored in a neighbor's compound.

In addition to his military and police pension and the return from his trading efforts he receives rent from two houses. Thus his income is adequate to ensure a comfortable standard of living, and the impression of his house, his food, and his clothing, as well as the relative leisure of his wife, suggests that this is in fact the case.

His aspirations for his children are similar to those of Aisa's and Buba's parents. There is no expectation that his sons should become big men in government or business; he hopes, rather, that they will obtain employment such that they can maintain him and his wife in their old age. Nonetheless, he has come to doubt the utility of education, a view engendered by the plight of many primary school leavers who wander around selling kolanuts or remain unemployed yet unwilling to follow their fathers in farming. Many are "idlers who smoke and drink." Fearing that Maliki will join this group, he now thinks it would have been best to send him to Koranic school where the teachers are more capable of "making a man of him." M. Ahmed's views reflect a dilemma of education, though from a slightly different perspective than that of Maliki's schoolmate (see page 87). M. Ahmed feels that Western schooling promises good jobs and diminishes respect for tradition, whereas Koranic schooling promises little hope for vocational advancement and perpetuates valued traditions. The dilemma is that in a very real sense both educational alternatives have undesirable aspects.

## YA JALO

Maliki's mother is a tall, attractive woman who at thirty-two is considerably younger than her husband. Since her father was a servant of Shehu Sanda Kyari (the one who employed her husband's uncle as Koranic mallam), she was born in Maiduguri. She has two brothers and two sisters, each one born of a different mother; two older brothers died during a mumps epidemic. She does not remember too much about her childhood, but the fun of selling kolanuts with a group of girl friends stands out in her mind. She did not sell from financial need as much as from a desire to have something to do which was lucrative and enjoyable. Her own girls, however, will never be allowed to work on the streets because "nowadays girls do not properly fear boys and boys do not respect girls. There is nothing so valuable in a Kanuri marriage as for a girl to be a virgin, no matter how old she is, and for her virginity to be proved by her husband."

Also from her childhood she tells of an incident that nearly involved her in witchcraft. "There once was a neighbor of ours named Amma whose husband divorced her and took a new wife. One day on the way to a relative's house I met this woman. We exchanged greetings and she said she'd give me a penny if I'd do her a favor. I said I would so she asked me to collect some dirt from under the feet of her former husband's present wife. I didn't take the penny because I wasn't going by the new wife's house, but I promised to help her.

"When I came home and told my sister what happened she was very angry and warned me that she'd definitely beat me if I helped the neighbor.

"After not hearing from me for a while, Amma came to our quarter one day and by coincidence saw the new wife walking by. Without her knowing it, Amma scooped up some dirt from under her rival's feet. Amma wasn't clever enough because some gentleman standing across the road saw her. The man told the wife and the wife told her husband. He immediately ran to his former wife's house to accuse her of witchcraft and the case finally came to court. I never did learn how it ended."

Ya Jalo's first and only marriage was arranged by her family to M. Ahmed when she was thirteen years old. Although a tailor was her personal favorite among five suitors, her family preferred M. Ahmed and their choice prevailed. M. Ahmed was then a policeman and the young Ya Jalo joined her husband in the village where he was stationed, subsequently spending much of her life in rural areas before returning to the city at the time of her husband's retirement.

She did not enjoy village life because something always seemed to go wrong. In Nguru (more reasonably called a town than a village), for example, she became pregnant with Maliki and was troubled in the last days before delivery by his constant movement. He did this, she explains, because a child visits while still within the mother's stomach all the places the father has been to in his life.

Her trouble with Maliki was not over after his birth. She recalls the time during his infancy when he nearly died. "One day Maliki became terribly sick. He got worse and worse. Nobody knew the cause and I got no help until some woman came for a visit. She saw the baby's condition and knew at once it was due to a certain wizard. She advised me to take Maliki to a learned mallam who was living in Lamisula ward of Maiduguri and said the mallam would be expecting me so I wasn't supposed to worry about finding his house.

"By this time Kura had lost hope that Maliki would survive and he told me that it was all the same to him whether or not I went. Anyway, I followed the woman's suggestion and left for the mallam's house that evening with Maliki tied to my back. Before I even reached his house, to my surprise he called out my name and he also knew Maliki's. We exchanged greetings and he asked to examine the boy.

"In a minute the mallam said, 'There's a wizard living near your house bringing this trouble to your child. Since you've brought him to me, the wizard's spell will be broken. Let me have that slate, the ink, and the pen.' I handed these things to him.

"He gave Maliki back to me so he could write a verse on the slate for my baby to drink.[1] Right there I did as he said and slowly fed the medicine into Maliki's mouth.

"The last thing the mallam did was to promise that the wizard himself would come to my house and confess, and he surely did. He came three days after Maliki took the medicine. Everyone, even his father, was surprised at the boy's recovery."

Her most negative impression of life outside Maiduguri is reserved for Damaturu, a town located on the main motor road between Maiduguri and Kano.

"Kura's bean crop was so good in Damaturu that he owned two sewing machines and one bicycle and all of us wore fashionable new clothes. We lived in a long narrow police barracks containing thirteen rooms and thirteen families. If you stood at one end you could see the outdoor oven of the last room at the far end. The rooms were awful, the walls so thin there was no privacy for a husband to talk to his wife.

"Kura wouldn't come home before midnight whether he was on duty or not. He wore his most attractive gowns when he went out and used 'Goma,' an expensive scent, while he gave me only two or three shillings for my own scent. You can imagine what he was up to!

"All the wives of the policemen gathered at the space in front of my room each night; that was because my son Isa was very playful and the women admired him so much. The husbands of the other wives came home between ten and eleven. Not Kura. He continued his misconduct and I didn't say anything. I just ignored him. Instead of sleeping with him when he finally did come home, I'd have Isa lie right in front of me on the floor. I did this so many times that Kura finally asked for an explanation. I told him he'd get one in Maiduguri because we

---

[1] To drink a verse or slate means drinking a liquid containing both the ink used to write a Koranic verse on a wooden board and the water used to remove the ink from the board. The charm is always prepared by a Koranic mallam in order to be efficacious. There is virtually no limit to the number and kind of charms, drinks, and prayers available with Islamic endorsement which may be purchased to ward off evil and to guarantee success.

were sure to have a fight and a fight in the barracks would give away our secret to everyone.

"Next, he began to gamble. I was informed of this but I didn't really believe it until I found out for myself. I wondered why Kura always insisted on yams for lunch. They're difficult to cook and later I understood this was just his way to keep me busy. One day I sent a visitor to look for him where I thought he'd be— at the mosque or under a tree somewhere. The visitor returned without him and I didn't know what to think until a neighbor told me he was gambling at Hamad's house. I finished cooking and went to this house, walked right past their outside guard, and found him and four others gambling. I was very polite. I just wished Kura good luck and gave his food to some other policeman.

"From that moment I refused to cook for him until finally he got angry enough to divorce me. When he did, I packed up the children and paid my own seven shilling truck fare back to Maiduguri. I was left off at the charge office where by coincidence my friend Sergeant Abubukar saw me and asked what was wrong and how could Kura be so stupid, etc. He was very friendly to me because he wanted his son to marry my daughter when she was ready. He knew that any girl I raised would make a good wife. Abubukar brought me home and sent a telegram to Kura to come to Maiduguri. When Kura didn't answer, Abubukar sent a letter to be delivered and read out loud by a messenger. This was done before other people so there'd be many witnesses. Finally, Kura had to return with all my belongings and to agree to come before a friend and talk out the whole incident. Kura was ready to reconcile after this but I firmly refused. Even though Sergeant Abubukar got me to wait a *bari*,[2] I wasn't ready to assure anyone I'd remarry my husband.

"On the fortieth day, a suitor arrived at my house with gifts and an offer of marriage. We were going to meet that night at a neighbor's house, but a relative of his had died that afternoon so when I arrived he was busy cutting pieces of cloth to wrap the dead body. We arranged another meeting.

"Now Kura heard about this meeting and went at once to Abubukar to see about an immediate reconciliation. Abubukar urged him to see my *luwali*.[3] Kura and his friend Adamu went to my *luwali* who advised them he'd do nothing unless he heard from me first. Adamu was a very clever man. When he learned that my big daughter, Ya Alima, had begun to menstruate and was therefore ready for marriage, he warned her that her marriage would be disappointing if it wasn't conducted by both parents, etc., etc., and that he'd contribute much to her marriage if she would tell the *luwali* that her mother agrees to return to her father. She did this and the ceremony for reconciliation was performed in my absence.

"What could I do? At last I agreed to go back.[4] From selling one of his houses Kura got money to buy me new clothes. He went on ahead to Damaturu to divorce

---

[2] The *bari* is a postdivorce confinement of three months and ten days which a woman waits to be sure she is not pregnant before accepting another marriage.

[3] He is a guardian appointed by a wife's relatives to uphold her interests in a marriage. See Cohen 1967:36–45 for more details on Kanuri divorce and marriage.

[4] She and her husband were divorced again a few months after this study.

*Lebanese canteen that sells the much-admired Honda.*

the wife he'd married in my absence and I returned there to a wonderful reception from all my old neighbors."

Since Ahmed Kura has retired from the police force, Ya Jalo no longer must face "hardships" in the villages or towns of Bornu; she no doubt will spend the rest of her life in Maiduguri.

## MALIKI NGURU

Maliki Nguru is a city boy, having been born in Nguru in the northwestern corner of Bornu Province and lived most of his thirteen years in Maiduguri. His mother knows his birthday, but she will never reveal it to him or to anyone else.

Such information, it is believed, can be used to charm you and bring about your downfall.

Maliki lives with Isa Mohammed, his eight-year-old brother, and Kaka, his sixteen-month-old sister, as well as his mother and father. An older sister, Ya Alima, has been married about a year and lives with her husband in another ward of the city. Unlike Buba Nola's home, Maliki's is made entirely of mud that has been treated with some type of oil to make it last longer and painted with whitewash. While it is by no means a grand house, it is solid and comfortable, containing three sleeping rooms, a kitchen, and an entrance room. In the court-yard are two folding chairs: the one a simple, wooden, straight-back card chair and the other a "big man's" canvas chair; these chairs are used only when important guests come to visit. The house is surrounded by a high wall shared on three sides by neighbors.

It is convenient for Maliki to reach almost any place in the city from his home. Just a few blocks to the south are the N.A. offices and the *dandal*[5] which leads to the Shehu's palace. A short distance down the *dandal* is the Premier Cinema. Less than a mile to the southwest is the big daily market, although there are numerous smaller markets nearby, and a half mile to the northeast is his school.

Maliki's day begins about 6:00 A.M. when he says his prayers for the first and usually the last time of the day. He feels religious, he loves Islam, but somehow he has not developed the habit of regular praying. In winter he is especially reluctant to pray because the water used for ablutions is uncomfortably cold. After eating a beancake or two he rides his bike to school, fearful that he will be stopped by the police because he has never obtained a license. Since bicycles are quite common in the city, he gets no special attention from his schoolmates as did the bike owner in Nola. Were he to ride a Honda, he would be very popular indeed. The motorcycle is a symbol of success and Maliki envies their owners, some of them boys not much older than himself. Hondas are sold in the Lebanese canteen near the race track, and many boys can recite accurately the technical details of the different models as well as the purchase price.

At 1:30 Maliki comes home for lunch and occupies himself in various ways until returning to school for evening games. At home he runs errands, watches his little sister while his mother goes out, or tends his father's stand. He performs these duties willingly and is never beaten by his parents. If he has nothing he must do, he sits by his father and Ali, the bicycle renter, and models clay or listens to the conversation of his elders. After games time at school he returns home to deliver food to his grandmother and to eat dinner. With no definite bedtime hours he has spare time each evening to play hide-and-go-seek in the unfinished drains on the big street near his house, to tell stories, or to repair his perpetually punctured bicycle tires. His father unsuccessfully urges Ya Jalo to keep him home after dinner by forcing him to read his school books or by telling stories to him and his brother.

Beatings and the constant threat of beatings make Maliki unhappy with school. Unfortunately for him he is frequently at the receiving end of both the beatings and the threats. He is active and energetic and somehow cannot prevent himself

---

[5] See page 11, Chapter 1.

from shoving, teasing, hiding, or pushing whoever and whatever is within reach. Although he is in the "A" stream of Class 7, a decision based presumably on academic achievement, Maliki stands near the bottom of his class in his terminal examination results. On recent examinations he received, of a possible 100 percent in each subject: 21 in English; 2 in arithmetic; 5 in nature study; 18 in geography; 12 in history; and 41 in religion. No test is given in art, his best subject. He takes pride in the occasions when his drawings are selected to hang on the classroom wall, the children then applauding him as they applaud those who excel on their examinations. While instruction is in process, his attention is seldom directed toward the teacher: for the most part he fidgets, concentrating only in art and in religion, his best academic subject. Whereas Buba Nola has several responsibilities, Maliki is only a garden keeper, a duty which requires him to tend the school's fruit trees. He likes this work because it gives him a chance to eat fruit, to hide from the monitors, and to obtain fruit for sale.

The Common Entrance Examination is offered to all students in Class 7. Based on his classwork, it seems improbable that Maliki will pass this examination at a level acceptable to any of the three types of postprimary schools. He knows that students with doubtful results can become a "remain" in Class 7, thereby redoing both Class 7 and the Examination. The thought of subjecting himself to another year of beatings at the hands of his peers has dissuaded him from accepting this alternative, although he is aware that nowadays the boy possessing only primary school qualifications has great trouble finding a job.

Maliki at thirteen is still in the "fireman this week, train engineer next week" stage of thinking about his future. Within the same month he wanted to be a primary school teacher, a soldier, a regional or federal member of parliament, the Prophet Mohammed, and to live in England married to an English woman or in India married to an Indian woman. The job of teacher was appealing because of the respect and fear he would receive from his students, and, moreover, the chance to beat others as he himself has been beaten. As a former soldier during World War II, M. Ahmed relates his adventures to those who pass the time of day with him. Maliki confesses that when he hears his father's stories he feels like entering the army at once and shooting people with a machine gun. Wishing to become a member of parliament places him in the large company of Nigerian boys who have seen that such positions, available since shortly before independence, have provided great power and wealth to many persons of formerly ordinary means and manners. As a government officer, Maliki imagines himself triumphantly returning home from Lagos, the federal capital, or Kaduna, the former regional capital, driving a new car (frequently traded in for new models), and living like the Waziri with four wives in a two-story house. He explains that the four wives are necessary so that if one is menstruating he can invite another to sleep with him. Because his religion teacher has made him conscious of the "evils of adultery," he is anxious to avoid "unlawful women." As for being the Prophet Mohammed, he explains that as the Prophet he would be sure to enter paradise, the desire of every good Muslim. Finally, Maliki would "like to live in London where the climate is nice and most people are white. Nigerians live there like English people and after a while the climate changes their skin; they become shiny all over as if they were smeared in oil. Where there are so many white ladies it will be simpler to marry one, not like Maiduguri where just to look at one amounts to a civil war." Then he thinks of India and changes his opinion to favoring the Indian woman for marriage. "If I married one of those Indians I wouldn't let her do a lot of housework and she wouldn't have to cook my food. I'd always provide her a clean place to live like those I've seen in the movies."

Maliki's aspirations are those of a young city boy who, despite prohibitions from the N.A., attends the movies whenever he can; who is keenly conscious of new status symbols—the Honda, the car, and the two-story house; and who is made aware of non-African culture by the English woman who is a volunteer teacher in his school, by the locally shown Indian films, and by the well-dressed, well-seated Americans attending public celebrations, their expensive cameras clicking away.

M. Ahmed is sitting on a mat, a kettle of water before him, finishing his ablutions. After praying, he throws water on Maliki, who turns over and sits up rubbing his eyes. "Get up and pray," M. Ahmed orders. Maliki rises, taking his father's kettle to refill at the water pot, does his ablutions, and completes five minutes of prayer. On his way out to school he gets twopence from his father to buy breakfast and walks his baby sister to a neighbor's house.

The preclass scene at Bornu Primary School is much the same as at all other schools in the province—children sweeping, picking up, and disposing of all kinds of rubbish found on the school grounds and in the classrooms, with older students standing watch, the ever-menacing neem switch in hand. Some differences seen here, aside from the greater number of students, are that students jostle and fight around two water taps instead of a well and get their skinned knees and other ailments treated at the school's own dispensary. For more serious illnesses the General Hospital is available, with Western-trained doctors on its staff.

When an inspection is announced most children leave what they are doing to line up with their class. Some, Maliki among them, run and hide in the garden or the latrine until they are caught and dragged before the headmaster, much to the amusement of those already in line. Maliki joins his class after the inspection is complete, explaining to his teacher that he hid only because his uniform is dirty, as in fact it is. In response he receives his first threat of the day, delivered in English. "You fool. You're known for this offense. If you hide like this again, you'll be dealt with severely." To one side of the assembled students the teachers stand debating who should win the inspection. Finally, M. Abba, the religion teacher, shouts that 7B is the winner and everyone should clap for them. The winner's flag is placed outside 7B's room, where it will stand for a week until the next inspection is held.

The first bell rings and Class 7A clambers onto the small verandah outside their room, entering through one of two iron-framed, glass-windowed doors. The newer sections of the school are built of such materials, but the older parts, like at Nola Primary School, have heavy wooden doors and wooden shutters instead of windows. Pairs of shoes are lined up on the verandah along the classroom wall. Only teachers wear shoes inside, although even they walk barefoot much of the time. The student ink-mixers come out to prepare a day's supply of ink.

As the final bell rings, M. Abba enters to teach religion, the first lesson of the day. The children rise to greet him and he answers in Arabic, as he usually does. After announcing the assignment of a writing lesson, he alternately writes on the blackboard and explains what he has written. (In the following description, the first quotation is what M. Abba had written on the board and the second is his explanation of the expression.)

"God is alone and present everywhere, having no beginning."

"We humans are born of parents. Therefore, we have a definite beginning, but God hasn't."

"Everlasting."

"We hear of people dying and ultimately we ourselves die. When we die it is the end for us, but God goes on forever, even after all the people of the world are gone."

"He has no resemblance to anybody."

"If we saw X in Maiduguri, then traveled to Kaduna and saw Y, and X and Y looked alike, then we could say that X and Y resembled each other. But God bears no resemblance to anyone or anything."

"He is alone."

"God has no mother or father as we mortals have."

"Self-reliant."

"God is able to do alone anything He wishes. We cannot always do what we wish. We have to rely on others."

"All-knowing."

"Sometimes mortals find certain books which they cannot read or understand. But God has knowledge of everything in the world."

His writing and explanations complete, M. Abba then asks the students to copy his words, remarking on their importance as part of a group of attributes of God which must be learned before a person is admitted to paradise.

One boy stands up. "Sir, what happens to kids who die as babies?"

"In the hereafter those children are taken to Sayidina Ibrahim's school where all day and night they recite a certain chapter from the Koran."

"Don't they get tired, sir?"

"They don't eat or drink or ever get tired. Now stop asking questions and keep quiet. Get on with your writing."

Maliki raises his hand. "Sir, suppose I died when I was a baby and I had a friend who died a few months after me. Would we both meet in Sayidina Ibrahim's school?"

"Yes, of course you would, and you'd both read the same chapter."

After checking exercise books M. Abba announces a reading lesson from the Koran. He begins reading and is soon interrupted by a request to explain what he has just read. "This verse," he comments, "is about a revelation to Prophet Mohammed when he was in Medina. God spoke to Mohammed saying, 'Have you not heard of the many events before your time? We created man from clay and also from combined sperm and ovum.' This means that in the beginning God created Adam from clay; the rest of mankind were born to mothers and fathers.

Farther down the page is another story about paradise. You know that in paradise everyone has a beautiful house full of things to enjoy. Some people have as many as seventy mattresses."[6]

"Mallam, I have a question." This is Maliki again. He usually is most active during religion.

"I haven't got time."

"Only one question, sir."

"All right, what is it?"

"Who will be allowed to enter paradise, sir?"

"Whoever God wishes. Usually people who believe in God and do good deeds like giving to charity and praying and fasting."

"All right, sir."

He continues reading another section.

"I want to know the meaning of the last part, sir."

"That refers to people who continue to do evil things, thinking they'll never die. If any child here is like that he'd better change his way of life."

His remarks stimulate much shouting from the students as they accuse and deny accusations about being such a person. M. Abba brandishes his neem whip and calls out, "Sons of donkeys. If you know what these evil things are, tell me."

"Adultery."

"Alcoholism."

"Thieving."

"Lying."

They shout until he raises his whip again.

"Now this next part," he continues, "refers to men who while hoarding money neglect their families and sleep in poorly-built houses. They are completely lost when they appear before God because striving for great possessions has blinded them to the need for doing good in their lives."

Maliki again questions M. Abba on a point unrelated to the lesson. "What should a man do if he has two wives and one visits Kaduna and gets beautiful clothes from her relatives? Should the husband buy the second wife some beautiful clothes, too?"

"A good question. In such a case the husband must buy beautiful clothes for the second wife and less beautiful ones for the wife who went to Kaduna."

After writing the word *punishment* in Arabic on the board M. Abba says, "The sins people commit in this world will be punished by God in the hereafter. How are people punished when they commit a crime in this world?"

The bell rings before M. Abba can conclude his lesson. The headmaster, Maliki's regular teacher, enters to teach the next subject. He stations himself on the raised

---

[6] M. Abba is combining prophetic revelation with Kanuri culture. He embellishes paradise, always depicted by Islam as a place of infinite pleasure and comfort, with the addition of mattresses because the Kanuri value them. One occasionally sees in the homes of well-to-do urban families a bed piled so high with mattresses that it is unusable for sleeping. This is reasonable when it is understood that the bed and mattresses are meant for conspicuous consumption and not for sleep.

area at the center of the room and says, as M. Abba leaves, "Keep quiet. It's nature study time."

"Why do you make noise?" calls out the monitor.

"Chalk," orders the headmaster. He teaches nature study and history to Class 7, the remaining subjects being taught by another teacher, M. Aji.

With his new piece of chalk the headmaster writes some sentences on the blackboard saying, "This work is a continuation from where we stopped last time." He reads his sentences and briefly explains each one. Then he asks, "What is the opposite of carbon dioxide?"

"Oxygen is the opposite."

"What is the heart made of?"

"It's made of muscle."

"Yes, the heart is made of flesh. And what is its use?"

"It pumps blood around the body."

"O.K. Now, take out your exercise books and copy these notes I'm writing." He completes the blackboard notes, asks if there are any questions, and, hearing none, leaves the class with the monitor in charge.[7]

Maliki removes his little ink pot from its hole in the desk and copies sentences until it is time for art, the last lesson before breakfast.

M. Aji takes over for art. He arranges for the distribution of materials—half the class will paint and half will model with clay—and demonstrates how to draw a picture of the Shehu's palace. For the remainder of the period he supervises student work or sits at his desk completing his own drawing. The children enjoy the art lesson because they can be more playful than at most other times.

"Look, I'm making a car."

"What kind of car is that with three parts?"

"You don't know! In front is the engine, next is the driver's seat, and last is the trunk for carrying goods."

One boy stands up holding a model of a snake charmer hypnotizing a snake. He moves his snake around, saying, "Player is safe. Audience is safe. If I turn, the snake turns. If I twist, the snake twists." The other boys in his group laugh.

A piece of clay is thrown at a boy who turns to the thrower and says, "You threw at your father."

"Your father's asshole."

"Mallam, Ali is insulting my father."

"Stop talking and get on with your work. Ali, don't insult his father."

"He insulted me first."

"Ali, first you hit me with a ball of clay."

"All right, now, get back to work."

"Look, this is a donkey," a boy says to his neighbor.

---

[7] The headmaster's style of teaching in this lesson is common. He goes through the motions of raising questions, then tries to elicit questions from the students, and ends with his notes being transferred from blackboard to student notebook. At best such lessons provide students a chance to practice handwriting.

"Wonderful! Have you ever seen a donkey without a tail?"

"Maybe it's the kind they have in his village."

"Are you insulting me?"

"No, I'm not. I only said that maybe you have donkeys without tails in your village."

Across the room the other half of the class is painting. Maliki, predictably, has not settled down to work. "Can I use your water to mix my paint?" he asks a boy near him.

"No. There's not enough for me and two of us are using it already."

"I want just a little."

"Please, go ask that girl. She has a lot in her tin."

He pours some of the girl's water into the lid of his box and while sitting down he spills some water on a desk.

"What are you doing, Maliki?"

"I see it."

"Won't you get something to dry my desk?"

"What do you want me to do, use my shirt?"

Now he moves around to borrow paint from his neighbors. His obtrusive movements plus a trail of grumbled protests finally are noticed by M. Aji. "Hey you. Get out of class. Leave the room, I said. Put all your stuff right here. I don't like to drive boys out of class but if I'm forced to do so, I will. Do you understand?" he asks the class.

"Yes, sir," the class answers.

"All right. Anybody else making noise follows Maliki Nguru."

When Maliki leaves he walks along the verandahs of different classroom blocks looking into windows. Feeling hot he sits down under a tree, his back against the trunk, and hits his toes with a twig. Then he gets up, dusts the sand from the seat of his trousers, and follows a shady path back toward his own room. Whenever he comes to an open stretch he runs until he reaches shade again. He sneaks up to the open window near his desk and gestures to Madu Shettima to pass out his paints and drawing.

Maliki joins four other students working on the verandah. Almost at once he gets into an argument and as the bell rings he and another boy are fighting. The sounds of a struggle bring the monitor rushing through the doorway, ruler in hand, to break up the fight, but they run away at the sight of him. Waving his ruler the monitor shouts after them, "Sons of an asshole."

The breakfast hour is half gone by the time Maliki reaches home. Ya Jalo, Maliki's mother, has prepared breakfast and sits rocking baby Kaka, hoping to lull her to sleep. She looks anxious while talking to Fanna, her neighbor in the next house, because Kaka was sick and had to be taken to the General Hospital earlier this morning.

"I went to the hospital to get Kaka's wound dressed and they gave me some medicine to rub over her body. They said to bring her back again after three days. Fanna, I met Birima on my way home from the dispensary."

"You met a funny person. Why doesn't she come to our quarter any more?"

"I don't know. When she saw me she said I was becoming younger and younger every day. She asked, 'What does your husband give you?' I said, 'What should he give me except ordinary food and drink?'"

"She would say something like that. That's the way she talks."

"But how can I be young after getting old? I can only get older and older. What a strange woman."

Kaka cries in her sleep.

"This girl is seriously ill. Look how she stretches her body in her dreams. Maybe witchcraft has been used on her? Fanna, please, can you help me? Do you have any charms or medicine I can use?"

Ya Jalo locates a charm in her own room and tries to tie it around Kaka's neck. Kaka resists.

"All right, all right. I'll leave it if you don't want it, but I have to put it under your pillow." To herself she says aloud, "I better put a knife under her head, too. That'll help against witchcraft."

She goes to the kitchen for a knife and places it under the baby's pillow.

"Jalo, take care. I'm throwing the medicine over the wall now," Fanna calls out.

"Throw it. I'm ready," and she picks up something wrapped in a piece of paper. "Is this for drinking or for bathing?"

"Neither. It's a powder to put in your fire."

"Is there fire in your house?"

"Yes, there is."

With the help of Fanna's ember, Ya Jalo starts a fire in a small clay brazier, drops the powder in the fire, and places the brazier near Kaka so that the smoke can pass over her body.

Maliki eats very quickly and returns to school, stopping momentarily to buy candy for a penny. There is disorder at school. Many teachers and students are late and the headmaster is busy attempting to establish order. He collects a large group of children and demands an explanation for their tardiness. Those whose explanations displease him are whipped by a big boy. When the headmaster is done with the tardy students, he goes to different classrooms to quiet them. In one he checks the timetable and, learning that they are supposed to have religion, orders students to read from the Koran. He interrupts a group standing outside their room being entertained by a boy pretending to be a beggar. The boy has both hands extended forward, palms upward in a pose of supplication, saying he is fatherless and anyone giving him a piece of beancake will be rewarded by God with gold or paradise in the next world. Class 2A is sitting outside their room in the shade, the boys and girls separated under different trees. Their teacher has asked them to tell folktales to each other; he sits apart from both groups, his gown in his lap, eating chocolates and hard candies. Class 3B, supervised by two student teachers from the Arabic Teachers Training College, is in chaos, with children climbing in and out of the windows and dancing in the room. Some children have left an unsupervised classroom and taken refuge in the garden, where they smoke and eat stolen oranges. One boy is washing his teacher's robe; he returns to the teacher when he sees he has no bluing and receives threepence and a reminder to take the robe to be ironed when it is dry.

In Maliki's class it is time for English. M. Aji is present. The class has not been called to order, however, because mail has been delivered by a school messenger and Aji is reading his own letter. With Bornu's postal system not yet fully developed, students and teachers use the N.A. Education Authority in care of their school as a mailing address.

With the teacher's attention diverted, Maliki looks around for someone to annoy. He notices a boy reading a letter. "What's wrong?" Maliki asks him.

"Nothing."

"Then why do you look like you just heard about someone's death."

"It isn't news about a death. I'm upset because I made a job application and this letter says there's no vacancy."

Maliki tries to read the letter, but the gloomy boy has already returned it to its envelope. The boy sits quietly, his head supported by his hand.[8]

At last M. Aji begins the English lesson. He reads from an English text in a dramatic manner, changing his voice to fit each character. While he is absorbed in his performance, some students are throwing paper wads. Maliki is restless. He picks his nose and plays with the buttons on his trousers. He taps his fingers on the bottom of his desk and works a needle into his bench. Once, he raises his hand volunteering to read, but lowers it when the teacher shouts at him.

"If you have no questions, look at Exercise 18 in *Grammar and Composition.* Are there any words here you don't understand?"

Many hands are raised and M. Aji explains the words one by one. " 'As a matter of fact' means 'in reality.' 'Walk up to' means 'to go to a person or place mentioned.' 'Actually' means 'really.' 'Settle' means 'to end a quarrel or dispute.' If you plan to go to secondary school you must learn to use such words or you'll face great difficulties."

Exercise 18 requires the students to insert the clause "it is worthwhile" or "it is not worthwhile," whichever is most sensible, into the blank spaces to complete the sentences. When it is Maliki's turn he stands up and reads, "It is not worthwhile patching a hole before it grows too big."

M. Aji asks if this response is sensible or not. There are many *yes*'s and *no*'s. He asks those who claimed the answer was sensible to raise their hands and when they do he tells them they are dogs and then calls on another student.

The boy behind Maliki is unable to read his sentence and the monitor is sent to fetch a *bulala* (a whip made of rhinoceros hide) from the headmaster's office. After delivering two lashes, M. Aji admonishes the boy, "It isn't worthwhile you being in this class. You're primary seven and still you can't read." He adds two

---

[8] Maliki's classmate will soon have company to share his disappointment, Maliki most likely included. Each year's new Common Entrance Examination failures join the growing numbers of semieducated in the search for employment. The drama of the educated unemployed has reached Maiduguri and unless economic development can keep pace with educational expansion it promises to have a long and sad run. At one time a primary school education provided ample credentials for many jobs. In fact, the completion of only a secondary-level teacher training course placed one in a group which contained a substantial number of the postindependence political elite in Northern Nigeria, including the former prime minister of the country. Maliki's neighbor should not be optimistic about finding a job with only a primary school education.

final lashes and concludes the period with some advice. "I'm now talking to all of you. At this stage you must be able to write as well as read such simple sentences. If you think you can't read good enough, then I'll let you take your books home for help from your friends. Who wants to go home with his books?"

Everyone raises his hand. It is safer to appear interested in M. Aji's proposition than run the risk of lashes with a *bulala*. The bell is rung announcing the fifth period of the day.

"Oh, we have geography now," M. Aji announces, and without pause moves his students to their next subject. "Take out your atlases. How many common-wealth countries are there?"

"Twenty-six."

"Nonsense."

"Twenty-seven."

"Nonsense."

Without indicating the correct answer he calls for the names of the countries and their capitals, listing the correct responses on the board. He next takes a world globe and holds it up before the students to demonstrate the principle of rotation. He shows the direction of the earth's movement and relates it to the sun in order to explain night and day.

Maliki occasionally writes down the sentences spoken by the teacher. His attention wanders easily and he amuses himself by rocking back and forth on his bench, apparently enjoying its creaking sound. He covers and uncovers his ears with his hands. The points of the lesson are mostly lost to him as he diverts himself with playful activities, but as the period is ending he hears the teacher say that the world is round like a ball and to this he utters an emphatic *No*, although not loud enough for the teacher to hear.

A student asks M. Aji to explain how their room remains in one place if the world is always moving. M. Aji ignores the question, commenting instead on Sierra Leone before releasing the students for their fifteen-minute break.

The arithmetic lesson which follows during the last period of the day is the prototype for hundreds of other such unremarkable lessons children in Class 7 have endured. Following a short debate between teacher and pupils regarding whether Exercise 26 or 27 is the correct one to do, the students settle down to their work, the knowledgeable ones getting practice in doing what they have already understood, and most of the others getting reinforcement of their own inadequacies or, possibly, the asininity of education. Maliki Nguru belongs to an intermediate group who are on the verge of understanding without fully attaining it. The group is not notable except insofar as it contains outspoken members like Maliki.

He dips his pen in the inkwell, writes $2\ 2/3 \div 1\ 1/6$, and after a moment's puzzlement over the problem takes his book to the teacher. "I can't do this."

"Look here. What's the opposite of multiplication?" M. Aji talks loud enough for the entire class to hear.

"Division."

"To divide we multiply and invert the divisor." He writes $8/3 \div 6/7 = 2\ 2/7$ on the board. "Do you understand?" he asks Maliki.

"Yes, sir."

And thus ends the instructional activity in this class. Before the final dismissal bell rings there is one brief moment of interest when a well-dressed young man visits M. Aji. He is introduced as a successful candidate for the Higher School Certificate who will enter Ahmadu Bello University in October when the new term begins. No moral is drawn from the visitor's academic success; none is necessary. The students fully recognize his attainment of the acme of scholarly accomplishment in Northern Nigeria.

Schoolchildren flood the compound, spilling out of their classrooms in every direction. They feel especially good because they have been released an hour early today, as they are each Friday, the day of congregational prayers.

Isa, Maliki's brother, is waiting by the headmaster's office to walk home with him. When Maliki comes, he tells Isa to go without him because he is going to collect the deposit on beer bottles that he bought last night for Falmata, a policeman's wife.

Maliki departs for the foreigner's section of town, where the non-Kanuri reside, to find one of the five or six bars in Maiduguri. On the way home, unencumbered by the bottles, he decides to run, stopping once when the road before him is blocked by a huge yellow Caterpillar machine. He arrives breathlessly in his compound and is met by a request from his father to eat quickly and perform his ablutions in readiness for attending mosque.

Both Maliki and his father are well-dressed when they leave the house. Along the way M. Ahmed rubs perfume on his chest. Some people say that perfuming oneself is required by religion; required or not, the crush of bodies praying under a torrid May sun makes it the thoughtful thing to do.

Although it is not yet time for the mandatory prayers to begin, hundreds of townsmen have joined father and son in arriving early at the mosque. The mosque itself can hold probably no more than five hundred persons, and when the neem tree shade outside the mosque is exhausted, the others must pray in the sun. Thus, beginning shortly after midday there is a steady stream of prayergoers arriving from every direction by a variety of conveyances: cars, motorcycles, bicycles, horses, donkeys, the latter used exclusively by otherwise immobile lepers. The lepers come to beg and also to pray at the special place reserved for them on the southern side of the *dandal*.

Beggars move freely throughout the crowd seeking alms from the charitable Friday congregation. They are joined by young children who have come merely to enjoy themselves. Some beg or try to be hired to guard somebody's car or motorcycle. Others play on the mounds of sand used for making cement. Order is maintained among this mass of people by the tall N.A. messengers who come each Friday, whips in hand, to chase away the small boys when they bother the prayers, to break up fights, or to stop the begging when the Imam arrives, because his presence signals total silence and the beginning of group prayer.

By the time M. Ahmed and Maliki reach the *dandal*, the mosque is quite full. The supplicants have begun to form lines on the *dandal* itself, their pattern clear and invariable: since they must face east toward Mecca their lines are uniformly parallel running from north to south. Those sitting in the sun already are drenched in sweat and for protection they have extended the edges of their big gowns over their heads. Maliki locates a place in the shade outside while his father walks into the mosque hopeful that he can find an empty space. He scans the large room and, thinking he sees an opening, forces himself down between two gentlemen who would not have agreed that a space existed. He is not alone, however, in sitting squeezed against the thighs of his neighbors.

There is ample time for M. Ahmed to recite his optional prayers and once seated he begins them, counting on his beads. Maliki sits with other schoolboys waiting for the compulsory prayers to begin. Everyone looks up with interest when the muezzin's familiar call is broadcast over the loudspeakers:

> God is great.
> God is great.
> There is no God but Allah.
> There is no God but Allah.
> There is no prophet of God except Mohammed.
> There is no prophet of God except Mohammed.
> Hasten to prayer.
> Hasten to prayer.

A second muezzin ascends the minaret and his voice is heard repeating the call.

A momentary crescendo of sound rises in the crowd following each muezzin's announcement. Much to the pleasure of those praying, who reward him with money, groundnuts, and dates, a man carrying a small clay cup of sweet burning incense now circulates throughout the mosque.

A trumpet is heard, followed immediately by the sound of a car stopping outside the mosque. It is the Shehu's car. This afternoon's congregation will feel further enriched because the Shehu has come for public prayer. In his entourage are twenty colorfully dressed slaves,[9] ten walking in front and ten behind his car, each one carrying a sword. One senses the satisfaction of the crowd at the presence of this almost legendary character whose reign as Shehu covers most of the years most citizens of Bornu have been alive. He is thought to be pure in behavior, and therefore assured of a place in paradise, and to be able to say his prayers in Maiduguri with the same effect as though he said them in Mecca. The Shehu sits in the second row, which is reserved for him and other dignitaries; his followers sit in the row behind him. Only the Imam and his muezzins may sit in the first row.

And as "Peace be on you" is heard in the mosque, the crowd turns toward the speaker, for this is the Imam having arrived at last, greeting the congregation and signaling by his presence for the third muezzin to make the final call to prayer. The Imam has come in his own chauffeur-driven, yellow Opel Kapitan. He is a dignified man who clearly conveys the importance associated with his role. Even his clothing communicates his status. He wears three gowns, the first, an ordinary one, the second, a burnoose, which marks him as leader of the congregation and a learned mallam, and the third, a crown gown, a gift of the Shehu. His entry in

---

[9] Though slavery was legally abolished years ago, former slaves had the option to remain with their masters. Slaves of the Shehu are considered to hold an honorable position; they are not viewed with disdain or disrespect.

the mosque is made through the special eastern door reserved for dignitaries, where he is preceded by five men and followed by two more. As does any other prayer, he removes his shoes at the gate. Before he can begin his service, the silence of the congregation is jarred by the arrival of the Provincial Secretary. He is the highest officer in Northern Nigeria's civil service stationed in Bornu Province. His driver pushes heavily on his horn, trying to squeeze his car through the rows of massed worshipers so that he can deliver his master to the door of the mosque. As the Provincial Secretary enters the door for dignitaries, his driver reverses the car, parks it under a tree, and prepares his own mat for praying.

The Imam stands on a platform facing the congregation. From his pocket he removes the papers containing the long verse he will read. Since the verse is in Arabic it is understood by a minority of those present, but these few clearly register on their faces the import of the Imam's words, pleased when he elaborates on the pleasures of paradise and pained when he describes the suffering of those condemned to hell. He reads for thirty minutes and ends with *"Allahu Akhbar"* (God is great), which is repeated by the muezzins as a signal for further prayers to be said.

Everyone is hot and wet. They wipe their heads with the edge of their gowns and alternately rise and prostrate themselves, following the lead of the Imam, who recites certain verses from the Koran and at last leads the congregation in reciting *fatiha*. The Imam raises his voice to thank God for sparing their lives to attend the service, and then prayers are over. The uniform parallel lines are broken as people rise to greet their neighbors and to find friends with whom to walk home or the small boy who guarded their transport. Before much of the crowd has departed, drums are heard from inside the Shehu's gate announcing the beginning of dancing on the palace grounds. Many people go to watch the dancers, to greet the Shehu, or just to mingle with some of the important people of the town.

Maliki walks directly home to set up his father's stand. M. Ahmed enters the palace, going to the Council Hall where the Shehu sits on cushions surrounded by the Imam, his Waziri, and many of the N.A. councillors. Students from the local boys' secondary school cluster in front of the Waziri, who is advising them that in the "new" Nigeria[10] the regime will not tolerate undisciplined or lazy students. Thus, he urges them to study hard, to show respect to their elders and teachers, especially their principal, and to remember that "an education without character is like a building without a foundation." Finally, he reminds them that the making of a new Nigeria is up to them and calls upon the Shehu to give them his wishes for their good luck and successful studies. M. Ahmed greets some friends and then leaves the Hall, making his way through dense crowds of people in the palace compound and out past the mosque to his own home, where he changes back into his old clothes.

Maliki is joined at his father's stand by his brother Isa and two friends. They are grouped around Maliki who is breaking up a large piece of molded clay. He

---

[10] The Waziri is referring to the changes of government which occurred four months earlier.

sends Isa for a bottle of *ardeb*. One of the boys wonders how he can drink "such dirty rubbish."

"Where were you born?" Maliki asks him.

"I was born here but I'm not supposed to drink something that will kill me."

"Nonsense. So you don't believe in our own customs! What do you think old people drank when there was no Coca Cola or Fanta?"

"Well, tell me, what's the good of that drink?"

"I'll tell you. During the hot season it cools you off and it also helps to purify the blood. Isa, get some more water for me."

He is almost finished breaking up the clay, which was originally shaped as a man's head. His father had ordered him to destroy his work, explaining that it is bad to make models because they give the impression of man creating, when this is God's function. Maliki obviously is not obeying his father. He finishes shaping a new head, makes the eye sockets with a stick, and places a piece of chalk in each one. He jabs a stick up into the clay nose to make the nasal passages.

"Hey, you're putting a stick in someone's nose."

Maliki just smiles and hands a piece of clay to his brother, telling him to make a neck. He comments on a Honda passing by driven by Modu, an older acquaintance.

"Modu is enjoying his Honda."

*Homeward bound from Friday congregational prayers in Maiduguri.*

"Is it his own?"

"Yes. His father bought it for him last year when he left school."

While Maliki as a final step is working the neck onto the head, he asks one boy, "Have you seen the village head staying in that house across the street?"

"Yes."

"He's no older than me yet men his father's age insist on calling him 'sir.'"

"His father used to be the ruler, but he became blind so the son took over from him. Have you ever seen Duloma on his Honda?"

"Yes. He passed here a while ago."

"He'll soon be spoiled because Garba gets him and they go to some bar."

"Does Garba drink?" asks Maliki.

"Oh, yes. He drinks all kinds of liquor."

When Modu passes by again Maliki exclaims, "I'm sorry for a person who has to return so soon from a ride. If I had a Honda I'd go a long way and visit some far-off village."

"Well, your father has lots of money. Tell him to buy you one."

"If he did he'd have no money left at all."

When M. Ahmed reaches his market area he takes over from Maliki, who remains at the stand and listens to the conversation of his father and other adults. A heated discussion is soon under way. The old woman who sells groundnuts is comparing the Kanuri and Hausa ways of life. A man in a blue gown says that while it is impossible to recognize a Hausa with fifty pounds to his name, one knows if a Kanuri has only five pounds in his pocket. He supports this statement by saying, "A Hausa man with fifty pounds doesn't show off. He continues wearing the same old dirty clothes and buying porridge and eating it whenever he wants to. When he pisses he does it wherever he is, just hiding behind his open umbrella, not caring about anybody. He also buys what he wants without thinking about his family, but he isn't so ashamed of his woman as a Kanuri man. What about the Kanuri man! Give him five pounds and he tries to live beyond his means, contemplating a second marriage, buying expensive clothes, etc. He also keeps himself apart from other people."

"But not all Kanuri people are like that," protests one man.

"If you listened better you'd know I was only referring to some Kanuri, not all of them," explains the speaker.

Thereupon an argument develops between the two and soon everyone is shouting so that no one can be understood.

Apparently tiring of the clatter, M. Ahmed turns away from the group to reach for his radio. He slowly adjusts the station dial from end to end looking for an interesting program. He eventually locates the local Maiduguri station that broadcasts personal messages to friends and plays popular records. All the people sitting under the tree are now listening quietly to the program.

"This is one of the records I like best. Ahmed Kura, if you see the film that features this music you'll really enjoy it. Maybe you've seen it already?"

"Is there any film shown in this town that I don't see? Kai! I can tell you Indians are great dancers and musicians because I saw them—in person. Listen to this. Once during our stay in India our officer said we'd been invited to a dance.

So we got dressed in our best uniforms and were ready at four when the order was given to march to the theatre. After the secretary of the club greeted us, the conductor gave an order and the music began. Hey, those people really know drumming. They started: toom-toom-toom-toom. Then, at the command of the leader, two beautiful girls came out of the tent and bowed before us. We all jumped to our feet without being asked. In fact, we didn't even realize we'd stood up. We just suddenly found ourselves standing. Hah! What beauty they had! Long hair falling down below their waists. Their shoulders shaking as they danced. Bodies so smooth and white we could see right through the skin to those blue lines underneath."

"But Chinese beauty is greater than Indian beauty, I think," remarks a man.

"Kai! Don't believe it. I saw with my own eyes while you only see pictures. The Chinese have short faces. There are some beauties among them but not like the Indians."

They see a Shuwa Arab girl walking on the main road. She is identifiable through her distinctive hairdo and skin color. One man comments that she is the type who marries southerners. "All girls are after those people."

M. Ahmed agrees. "Ibos have married many Shuwa Arabs in this region, but no one talks about it. Our customs and religion are really different."

"All this has happened since the Americans came here.[11] They gave money too easily to women and all women are too fond of money. When the Americans disappeared these Ibos took their place."

"When I was in the army I had one good lady," says M. Ahmed. "She slept with me for fifteen days. This was when we'd just come back from the Burma war. She brought me food three times a day for only threepence. When we were about to break camp I called the woman and gave her thirty pounds dash [tip]. She laughed at me and said she could get thirty pounds for just one night. At that time money was easy to get from the American soldiers. That's why there were so many whores then."

It is now late afternoon and M. Ahmed is left sitting with his sons and a few male friends, one of whom was his mate in the army and another who was a retainer with him in the house of Tijjani Kachallah, a former district head of Maiduguri. The latter friend takes three toffee mints from the table and tells M. Ahmed to deduct a penny from the amount he owes him.

"Haven't I paid you back yet?" asks M. Ahmed. "You had threepence with me and you bought candy for twopence on Friday and took a penny candy yesterday. So if you touch any of those mints, you'll owe me!"

"Didn't I give you any money besides the threepence?"

"You better tell me. I've forgotten."

"If you've forgotten, I won't remind you, but I think you'll give it back to me in the hereafter."

"Don't talk about the hereafter. How many times was I kind to you when we were together in Tijjani Kachallah's house? Now listen people," Ahmed pompously

---

[11] The man responding to M. Ahmed is referring to the Americans present in Maiduguri during World War II when they operated an air base on the outskirts of the city.

addresses the small group. "We were both servants to Tijjani Kachallah. Everyone was afraid of him. He had three wives and five concubines but best of all he loved the youngest wife, a girl about eighteen years old with high breasts. Nobody was allowed to visit her after dusk. One night he had a dream that the young wife was taken to bed by Mustafa here. I was away at the time drinking wine. Tijjani could not believe it was a dream so he called all his servants and said everyone must take an oath whether or not he'd seen or heard Mustafa. They all were lined up before him sweating in fright. Each swore he knew nothing. He'd already put his wives and concubines under lock and key and by now everyone was anxious to see me come home.

"When I returned and learned about the trouble, I appealed to Tijjani to let them go by telling him that if people heard of this incident he'd regret it. Tijjani said he wouldn't allow the servants to swear on a Koran because they'd merely falsify an oath. Instead, he was going to whip them. I let him think I agreed by pretending to go to his room for a whip, but instead I surprised him by dismissing all the servants and breaking open the room where his ladies were locked up. They were very grateful and thanked me, saying, 'We've been waiting for you.' Now, I turned to Tijjani and told him I was ready to face any consequence. He only frowned and glared at me, calling me a bad man. He said that if he could he'd kick me out of his house."

"Why couldn't he?"

"Because I had come to Yerwa with him from our home town of Ngerbuwa."[12]

[12] What M. Ahmed implies here is that although he was only the retainer or client of Tijjani, their long-standing relationship of dependency going back to a common village birthplace could not easily be broken.

*Premier Cinema in Maiduguri shows mostly Indian and American films.*

M. Ahmed proceeds to discuss Ngerbuwa, its former size and grandeur, relating how his townsmen still come to purchase goods from him. The retired soldier leads him away from Ngerbuwa by asking, "What about our suffering in the army?"

"Oh, that was terrible, especially our attack on Rangoon."

"Hey, British people are very clever!"

"What was the attack like?" one man asks.

"Well, the city is built between mountains which lie to the north and south. The eastern and western parts are walled and there are only two gates into the city, one on the east and the other on the west." He draws a rough map of Rangoon on the ground to illustrate what he is saying. "Our troops were thirty miles away in the jungle. Messages from headquarters were sent saying we should attack and conquer the city before Christmas. It was four days till Christmas and we made up our minds to spend the holiday in the city. So the order was given. We started moving early in the morning and marched for hours until we came to the edge of a jungle. Seven miles of open land had to be crossed before reaching the city. We were ordered to wait for dark. At 10:00 P.M. we began to advance, but the Burmese were also ready, waiting to shoot us on the open land. Whenever we stirred they caught us in their search lights, so we stopped until our two planes approached the city. The Burmese would cut the lights when they heard the sound of the planes and we'd advance again. Rap, rap, rap. When the lights were put on, our planes again flew toward the city."

"All this was to deceive them," his army friend adds.

"So they turned off the lights, but before they could put them on we had crossed the open land and reached some jungle just in front of the city. Orders were given to settle there till morning when we could see everything clearly. We entrenched ourselves and waited and at about eight the next morning they started firing at the open land, thinking we were still there."

"They didn't know we were just under the city."

"No they didn't and they continued firing in the wrong place till midday. Suddenly we heard planes—our fighters and bombers. First they flew like this," and he makes a V with his hands. "Then in a straight line. All that time we waited in the bushes for a command. The planes dipped down and dropped the bombs, two at a time, and at every burst of the bombs we heard people crying, sounding seven times louder than the people at a Monday market. After they stopped, the order to attack was given so we marched into the city and captured the few survivors."

Whether this story represents an old soldier's faulty memory,[13] his vivid imagination, or both is difficult to say, but with his tale complete he checks his watch and sees that it is time for evening prayers.

He prepares himself for his ablutions and in the meantime Maliki brings his dinner in two covered bowls, leaving them on the table. After delivering his father's dinner, Maliki returns home to check if his grandmother's is ready. It is customary to provide such elder persons with daily food. Ya Jalo points to an

---

[13] Rangoon is a port city located on a river. The city was in fact bombarded in 1945.

enameled bowl, which he places on his head before setting off for his grand-mother's house.

Maliki's dinner is waiting for him when he returns; it is corn and soup covered over with melted butter. He holds his bowl in his left hand and eats slowly with the fingers of his right hand. His leftovers are offered to Koranic students who in turn give them to a man they see also begging for food.

Maliki "drinks his slate"[14] and then has one remaining obligation before seek-ing his own enjoyment for the evening. He must visit Ya Alima, his married sister. She rewards him with two dates, one kolanut, and a penny for coming to greet her. Now he returns to his father's stand, joining Isa and some other friends for storytelling.

Maliki begins. "There once were four men whose names were Bismillahi [an Arabic word meaning 'in the name of God'], Not You, Curse You All, and Too Many Parasites. They decided to visit a village where a man lived who was so stingy he wouldn't even give food to his children. They reached the village and asked the stingy man for lodging. To their request he said, 'Why stay with me? You won't get any food or drink.' The four men replied that they didn't need food or drink and so the man gave them a room. That night the man's wife pre-pared dinner and he sat down to eat after first saying the usual *'bismillahi.'* Hear-ing his name called, Bismillahi ran into the room and began to eat. The host said, 'Not you. I didn't call you,' and Not You entered and began to eat. The stingy man became angry and roared, 'Curse you all!' and now the third man ran in to eat. The man was really mad and he shouted, 'Too many parasites!' so the fourth man came in. That's how the four friends ate well and left the glutton in ruin."

Abba says he wants to be next. "Now, you have a hyena, a goat, and a bundle of hay and you come to a small stream that has to be crossed. If there's only one boat big enough to carry you and one of these three things, how will you get across?"

"I'll first carry the hay, then come back for the goat, and finally the hyena."

"O.K. But before you return for the goat, the hyena will have eaten it. And if you leave the goat with the hay, then she'll eat the hay."

"Then you must give up one of them."

"But what if you want all three?"

"It can't be done."

"Yes, there is a way. First carry the goat to the other side, leaving the hyena with the hay. Then go back for the hyena, take it over, and come back with the goat. Leave the goat, take the hay over to the hyena, and finally take the goat over. That's the only possible way."

They all laugh at Abba's explanation, appreciating the cleverness of the plan. "Such stories really puzzle the mind."

They move to a new location under the exposed gate light of a neighboring house. In the rainy season there will be countless numbers of insects here, but for now it is a comfortable place to sit. Maliki leaves for a moment to help his father

---

14 The verse he drank is one that promises general safety.

pack away his wares for the night. After replenishing his father's water supply at home, he returns outside. Abba is telling another story.

"One day a man went hunting and lay down beside a river waiting for a deer. None came so he searched until he spied one standing by a tree. He shot an arrow at the deer, but ran ahead anyway and killed the deer with his hands. While he was dragging the deer away the arrow was still flying in the air. He took the meat home to his wife who was waiting for him. Deciding it was a waste of time to enter the house, he threw the meat over the wall while he walked toward the door. His wife caught the meat, lit a fire, cooked the meat, and she and the rest of the family ate it. Just as they were about to throw away the bones, her husband entered. Now who was the most expert, the husband or the wife?"

"It was the woman."

"Why?"

"Because the man entered within seconds after throwing the meat over the wall. Well, in that time the woman had cleaned the meat, lit a fire, washed the pots, and cooked and eaten the meat. Therefore, she obviously is the expert."

For a while they argue about this explanation. Then Maliki begins another riddle.

"A Koranic mallam, a strong man with a stick, and a Fulani[15] with a bow and arrow went together on a journey. They came to a river and decided they would have to find different ways of crossing. The Fulani shot an arrow across the river and grabbed the tail of the arrow as it flew over. The mallam set a page from his Koran on the water, it turned into a boat, and he sailed over. The strong man struck his stick on the water, it parted, and he crossed before the waters could join together. Now, which one was most clever?"

"The mallam."

"Why?"

"Because the Fulani would be worried that the arrow couldn't reach its target and the strong person would be worried because the waters might meet before he reached the other side. But the mallam was in control of the boat, not being controlled by the boat."

Again there is no agreement and the boys walk home discussing the merits of this and other answers, leaving Maliki and Abba behind. A Honda drives down the narrow street leading to Maliki's house.

"Hello. That Honda is going after Lokocha," observes Abba.

"I don't know why everyone loves this Lokocha."

"The people who want her can't get her because a big government officer always comes and parks his car at her gate. When he goes in he stays until bedtime and then takes her to his house."

The Honda drives past with Lokocha, a *zower*, on the back seat.

"That man is lucky to get her."

"Maybe the officer sent him."

"Maybe. Let's go home and sleep."

As Maliki enters his compound, he calls out, "Baba, I'm in. Shall I lock the door?"

"Yes," his father calls out from inside his bedroom.

---

[15] The Fulani are a major Muslim tribe in Northern Nigeria who extend into other West African nations.

# 5/A child of European times:
# Bintu and her family

## CASE STUDY CHARACTERS

| | |
|---|---|
| Bintu | Seven-year-old schoolgirl |
| Ya Amina | Bintu's mother |
| M. Zarami Goni | Bintu's father |
| Ya Fati | Bintu's stepmother; her father's second wife |
| Bulama, Harun, Usman | Bintu's brothers |
| Alhaji | Mourner at funeral of M. Zarami's sister-in-law |
| M. Garba | Bintu's teacher in Class 2 |
| M. Yusufu | Bintu's teacher of religion |
| Mukhtar, Madu Bultu, Hadija, Audu, Jiddah Abubukar, Bukar, Suliman | Bintu's classmates |
| Magaram, Fatima, Kyellu | Ya Amina's friends |
| Mairama, Zara | Bintu's friends |
| Shettima, Kalli | Schoolboys |
| Amma | Bintu's cousin |
| Ya Karu | Ya Amina's older friend who recently returned from Mecca |

## ZARAMI GONI

IT IS DIFFICULT TO IMAGINE the young M. Zarami memorizing the Koran, locked nightly in his room, wearing only a loincloth, and spurred on by his father's lashes. For today, he is a man of the world, bright-eyed, alert, well-dressed, and handsome. He is knowledgeable of both world and African politics from listening to the news broadcast in Hausa by many foreign radio stations.[1] In addition, he regularly reads both Hausa and English newspapers, although his English skills are relatively undeveloped. Another source of information about his country and continent is government officials, whose association he has enjoyed through active involvement in party politics for the past ten years.

---

[1] Foreign powers attempt to reach the people of Northern Nigeria by beaming in radio programs in Hausa, the area's most widely spoken language.

Missing in his understanding of contemporary affairs is the dimension contributed by Western education. When M. Zarami was "captured" as a child and taken to primary school, his father's appeal that he continue in Islamic education was accepted by the authorities. M. Zarami still regrets not having attended school, particularly as he recalls that his party denied him a chance to run for parliament because of his lack of education. He is, however, a man of great learning, for his name *Goni* has been merited by successful memorization of the Koran, and his claim to be an Arabist rests upon years of study of Islamic religion, tradition, and law. In his religious accomplishments he follows a long family tradition: his father was a *goni* who descended from a line of *gonis* traceable to Njibi and Birni Ngazargamo, ancient cities of importance in Kanuri history.

After terminating his studies, M. Zarami left home to become an itinerant mallam.[2] He provided the services expected from men of his training, that is, writing prayers to be drunk as medicine and praying on behalf of people, such as for men whose wives had run away or for the return of errant sons. At the end of six years of wandering he returned home and had his marriage arranged to Ya Amina, a gift to him from her uncle.[3] M. Zarami responded to her uncle's charitableness with the gift of a handwritten Koran. He took a second wife a few years ago.[4]

His first occupation after his itinerant years was the production of handwritten Korans. People considered such a Koran a valuable possession and were willing, if able, to purchase them for high prices. He estimates that he wrote thirty Korans.

Attracted by the excitement of politics, he became active in a political party originating in southern Nigeria. The persistent hostility of the local supporters of the predominant Northern Nigeria party, the Northern Peoples Congress (NPC), led to the abolition of M. Zarami's party. By shifting his loyalty to the NPC after the demise of his own party, he continued working in politics. Nonetheless, when he speaks of the excitement of politics, it is the "old days" that come to mind. For example, he recalls the election that brought a famous southern politician to campaign in the North. As M. Zarami was arranging meetings for his party leader in different towns, his Land Rover broke down and the party rescued him with a helicopter. Where motorized vehicles of any kind are relatively uncommon, a helicopter ride is a unique event.

In addition to his activity on behalf of the NPC, M. Zarami has been elected to the Maiduguri Town Council, serving on its education committee. Since the military coup, not only were parliamentary and party politics suspended but also political activity at the local level. That he believes this state of affairs is temporary is evident from a recent conversation with a friend outside the chambers of the local Islamic judge.

"What are you waiting for, Zarami?"

"I'm waiting for Alhaji Yahaya [a politician]."

"Don't you know there are no politics in Nigeria now?"

"Who says so? Kai! Politics will never die."

---

[2] See Cohen 1967:55–57 and 62.

[3] Brides occasionally are given dowry-free to Koranic mallams for the prestige and religious advantages that will result. See Cohen 1967:38.

[4] For more details on polygymous marriage, see Cohen 1967:42–43.

"You'll come to know Ironsi[5] as your stomach hunger."

"You can be sure politics will begin again soon and you'll see us with a big post."

"You know what happens to people who take the party as their mother and father, always praying to God and going on pilgrimages [to Mecca] for the good of the party." He is laughing as he says this.

"Anyhow, you will see us in politics. again."

M. Zarami makes clear that his career preference, given proper educational credentials, is to be a member of parliament. Perhaps this unrealized aspiration explains in part his unequivocal support for the education of his children. Among Maiduguri's population he is virtually unique in knowing what place his children achieved on their latest examination and what comments were made by their headmaster. In his justification for sending Bintu and her brothers to school he sounds much like Maliki's or Baba's father, his eloquence, however, testifying to an unusual degree of faith in the outcomes of education. He delivered the discourse below (he has the politician's weakness for giving speeches even under informal circumstances) to friends sitting in the local ward head's entrance hut.

"When I admitted my son to school," he said, referring to Bulama, his eldest son, "I heard many stories. Some said I went against Islam by giving my child to an English rather than a Koranic school. Some said I'd be punished by God because the Koran states that a child must be educated in Koranic schools. I ignored all such talk because the speakers were uneducated and they didn't know the fruits of education. They abused my child, saying he left his culture and tradition by following the Christian faith, letting his hair grow long, wearing shorts and shirts, etc. But let's say that after overcoming hardships to win a high post in government, my son visits me. He won't come empty-handed. He'll bring a lot of gifts, as civil servants do. The boy's arrival will bring out all of our old friends and neighbors to greet him—and I'm sure he'll have gifts for them too. The good news will spread over the village or town or ward and for the moment he'll have changed society by helping people with new clothes, comfortable bedding, and money for business affairs. The curse of his education is converted now to a blessing. Well, what'll be the feeling of those critics, particularly the reluctant father whose son is jobless, possibly a wanderer, a gambler, a thief, or a messenger with a low salary? The father will be blamed for not giving his son an education, and the son, formerly praised for not attending school, will now be cursed."

He concluded by summarizing a recent discussion of the Maiduguri education committee that considered the underdeveloped condition of education in their area relative to other sections of the country. "Now our people are beginning to realize the importance of education. Most of them suffered from short-term education or none at all. In recent years, even members of the royal family [the Shehu's relatives] have begun to appreciate its importance because learned persons have replaced them in their jobs as district heads, clerks, and councillors. We're greatly worried by this army take-over. We have few educated northerners, some were killed, and now they're talking about 'One Nigeria.' The best thing they [the

5 "Ironsi" is Major General Johnson T. U. Aguiyi-Ironsi, the first head of Nigeria's Military Government and later assassinated, his regime giving way to the present government under Major General Yakubu Gowon.

Military Government] can do is give us an ultimatum so we can force our pupils to study hard. Then they'll be able to work all over the Federation when it becomes a 'New Nigeria.'" M. Zarami is not so much angry at the change in leadership which resulted from the political coup of January 1966 as he is concerned that the "New Nigeria" or "One Nigeria" mentioned so often these days will place the northerner, because of his past unwillingness to press for Western education, at a permanent disadvantage relative to the southern tribes.

## YA AMINA

If Ya Amina cannot trace her ancestry as far back as her husband, her family is, nonetheless, a distinguished one. Her uncle, in whose house she spent her late childhood, was the Imam at the Shehu's mosque (the one Ahmed Kura attended for congregational prayers), and all six of her brothers became *gonis.* She was born in a village located north of Maiduguri and brought to be raised in her uncle's house when she was eight. Four years later her uncle arranged her marriage to M. Zarami. She is now twenty-eight (M. Zarami is thirty-five) and has never had another husband. "You know," she explains, "he didn't spend any money for me. Most of the ritual activities were performed by my family so if he mistreats me people will say he has no respect for his religious gift, that he's treating her as if he married her for money. Sometimes we wrong each other, but remembering the relationship of our families we neither quarrel nor divorce."

Although her own life is set squarely within the best Kanuri tradition—an arranged marriage at puberty and a religious education to enable her to say prayers —she is willing to countenance a different style of living for Bintu. "Some people ask why I allow my girl to remain in school," says Ya Amina. "At first I didn't agree. I fought with her father when he sent her. My uncles and brothers don't worry themselves about girls' education so they supported me. But day by day he made me understand the whole thing. That if she studies and becomes somebody important, she'll come home with gifts for me and my neighbors. Then people will say, 'If only I had known the importance of schools, I'd have sent my child, too.' As for myself, I learned that a schoolchild is wiser than one who is kept at home. You can see when the children play that Bintu talks diplomatically and what she says is like a big person. Without school she'd be no better than the others, probably worse. What I won't agree to is for my daughter to become educated, start getting a salary, and then for somebody to marry her who won't let her work. Once the girl begins to work, nobody should keep her in the kitchen cooking all the time. Anytime she wants to marry I'll give her to the man of her choice. I'm no longer stuck in the ways of our tradition. I want her to become a teacher or nurse so she can feed me when I'm old."

## BINTU

Bintu's home is at the end of a winding dirt lane which passes by many of her relatives' houses. The visitor entering her lane always sees her old white-bearded uncle sitting outside the small mosque where he teaches his students. Some of his recalcitrant younger students are held in chains in a small mud hut across from the mosque to prevent them from running away. The old mallam explains that the chains are a temporary measure and when the students "come to their senses" they will be freed.

The house of M. Zarami clearly marks him as a man of means. Although lacking electricity and running water, it has the space and furnishings of a person of above-average wealth. The house contains two sections. In the first, off two small court-yards, are M. Zarami's private bathroom and two living rooms; he lounges and receives visitors in one and he sleeps in the other. In the second section, separated from M. Zarami's area by a high wall, are the rooms of his wives and their children built around a larger courtyard.

Bintu's mother, Ya Amina, is the senior wife of her father; Bintu is their only daughter. She has three brothers. At eight years of age she is older than Usman, who is five, and younger than Bulama and Harun, who are fourteen and ten, respectively. She has a one-year-old stepbrother and a newborn stepsister through Ya Fati, her father's junior wife. Bintu and her two older brothers attend primary school.

Since Bintu does not look at adults when they speak to her, she gives the impression of being shy. Perhaps she is trying to hide the rather prominent scar under her left eye, or perhaps she is responding to the expectation that children show respect to their elders. At home Bintu is aggressive and fully capable of holding her own against her brothers, if not physically, then certainly verbally. At school she is equally aggressive, both in and out of the classroom. She delights in comparing her results with those of her neighbors, seldom missing an oppor-tunity to brag or to belittle their work. And advantages not deservedly hers she assumes through boldness and exaggeration.

Bintu is very much her father's daughter: bright, competitive, and somewhat boastful. Teachers know her as the girl who receives the most encouragement to succeed. In fact, she excels only in religion, a not unexpected feat considering her father is a *goni*, and is mediocre in arithmetic and English. Her cumulative scores on recent examinations placed her nineteenth last month and sixteenth this month out of thirty-nine students. More important than these results for predicting her future is her intelligence, so very evident all day at home and school, her concern for achievement, and her parents' support in all educational matters.

Since early morning M. Zarami and other friends and relatives have been mourning the death of his brother's wife.[6] Outside the mosque, the male mourners sit on mats and carpets; the women are inside the dead woman's compound. No children may play nearby and only children of close relatives are even present. The dead woman's husband, the Imam of the local mosque, and her brother sit at the center of the group. A space is kept open at their side so that persons coming for condolences can reach them with their comments of "May God bless her" or "May God grant her paradise." People constantly come and go. They approach from all directions, remove their shoes, recite *fatiha* and the funeral commentary, offer sympathy to the family, and then join the wider circle of men.

---

[6] For additional details on Kanuri funerals, see Cohen 1967:72–73.

A car stops on the main street near the mosque and a tall heavy man wearing an expensively embroidered, flowing big gown gets out, followed by two less conspicuously dressed men. As Alhaji, the tall man, moves toward the mourning husband, there is whispering in the crowd. "Yesterday his brother came here." "Yes, this is the elder brother. He's a groundnut agent." "Both have memorized the Holy Koran and though they're only traders they know more Arabic than many of our Arabic teachers." Alhaji joins the crowd of men and exchanges greetings with them. Then for a moment there is silence broken only by the sound of prayer beads clicking against each other.

"I heard she died in the hospital," says Alhaji.

"About two days ago she fell ill with stomach pains. She was taken to the hospital."

"When there were many Europeans working at the hospital, there were fewer deaths," Alhaji complains. "They loved patients and they were very careful. But today everything is under people who don't treat patients properly. They aren't punctual and because of this people die every day."

"It's true," agrees M. Zarami. "The Europeans are hard-working. We really differ only in religion."

Alhaji continues, "In Lagos and Port Harcourt there are many communal hospitals. People contribute large sums of money and provide doctors, midwives, and nurses who give the best treatment. They'll help you even if you call them at midnight."

"Here we have no such hospitals. This town is large and only one hospital serves the whole place."

"I've seen many people going to Molai."

"They provide better treatment. That's why. You pay money [government services are free] and get the best care. I've seen patients who weren't cured by the hospital doctors get thoroughly cured at Molai."

"I hear it's a mission hospital."

"Yes, but missions are very good for treatment. They're better than the government doctors."

Alhaji looks at his watch and says that it is time to go to work.

Two old men come to condole the brother of the dead woman. After they finish, they sit at the side to converse with M. Zarami.

"Sometime last year," one of them says, "I remember I went to that school for a meeting." He points toward the school compound, which is near the mosque. "A teacher showed me a post that indicates the direction of the wind."

"Yes, I even saw it myself."

"What does it look like?"

"It's just a standing post with some metal pieces sticking out at the top."

"I've never seen it before."

"Europeans are wonderful. If not, how could they do such a thing? This is really great magic."

The people sitting nearby smile at the man's comment even though it is unusual to smile at a death ceremony.

Another man makes his way through the crowd and shakes hands with the men at the center. "Death is very sad. May her soul rest in peace." His words are heard by others who respond with "Amen."

The Imam says, "Now she's dead and her case is left to God. Some people forget about Him and become drunkards, adulterers, and thieves. God has prescribed punishment for every evil doer."

The men are attentive. They appear to be reflecting on these words, much as they do on the admonitions heard at Friday's congregational prayers. A man says to the Imam, "They say a man who's been bad soon learns the grave can't contain him because the moment he's buried his body becomes magnetic and is drawn toward the earth. Then the earth presses down upon his body until he cries with pain."

The Imam confirms this. "Yes, it's true. And soon after a man is buried, the angels give him new life and then the judgment begins. This is merely a preliminary judgment. They ask you to write all the things you've done on earth. You ask them, 'Where is my pen?' and they say, 'What about your finger?' Next you ask them for ink and they say, 'Your saliva.'"

A man interrupts. "What language?"

"Even though there are so many languages in the world, all the questions and the writing and the judgment are in Arabic."

"What about people who don't know Arabic?"

"You're joking! You don't understand the Omnipotent. Through God's power everyone knows Arabic."

The listeners nod in approval at this response.


In M. Zarami's house the children are preparing for school.

"The water in the pot is too cold."

"Don't we have any rainwater from yesterday?"

"Bintu already said she'd bathe in the rainwater," answers Ya Fati, her stepmother.

"Then all of us should have a chance," protests Harun.

"No, only me," says Bintu.

"Why?"

"Because you've got a pump at Mafoni [Harun's school] and in the boarding school there are lots of bathrooms."

"You're right," agrees her mother.

"She isn't right," says Bulama. "We have only one tap at school."

"If you go to the boarding school right now all the bathrooms are open, aren't they?"

"Isn't she right?"

The boys are forced to agree and Bintu has her way. She goes to wash and returns shortly to dress in her mother's room.

"Why are you putting clothes on?" her mother asks disgustedly. "That's why your father says you act like a *karuwa*.[7] You don't care to oil your hair, but you

---

[7] A *karuwa* is a prostitute with the reputation of applying powder to her face and dressing stylishly, but seldom washing or "polishing her body." Sometimes they are called "beautiful

always powder, just like a *karuwa*. Now oil your hair and also put this kohl on your eyes."[8]

Bintu finishes dressing, eats, and joins her friend Zara to walk to school. When they pass some Ibo schoolchildren carrying writing slates and balancing on their heads school boxes made of old kerosene tins, Bintu comments that she likes the "Ibo school." It is not actually an Ibo school but a mission school attended primarily by children from the southern tribes.

"Why do you like it?"

"Because of their uniforms and because they go to school late on cold mornings when the sun is already shining."

"If you like it so much, tell your father to transfer you. Christian school! Who'd teach you Islam? God forbid!"

"No Arabic! God forbid!"

When they reach school each child joins her own class for general clean-up duties. The headmaster talks to some children sweeping near the teachers. "Are you working or playing? Now stop playing and let me see you work properly."

"Hmm, those children don't work when there's nobody shouting at them."

"If they don't work willingly, I know how to make them work. What's the time, Mallama?[9] Ah, it's just about time. Go ring the bell, Hasana."

M. Garba, Bintu's teacher in 2A, spends a few minutes taking the roll before ordering the students to open their English readers to page 28. There is immediate uproar, the noise of students who left their books at home or in the locked cupboard at the back of the room. M. Garba allows those whose books are in the cupboard to go free with a scolding. The others, Bintu among them, each receive three lashes.

Thus the day at Bornu Primary School begins for Bintu with a beating. Other beatings will follow, although in her case, contrary to Maliki Nguru's, it is not merely that she is naughty but that her teacher is unusually short-tempered and punitive. Corporal punishment is the rule in Bornu. Even if M. Garba acts according to the rule, he is not typical of most teachers who also respect the tradition that misbehavior and ignorance must be punished. M. Garba punishes at the least provocation, his beatings tempered by no strain of mercy or justice. His beatings are not particularly effective in deterring either misbehavior or ignorance; their primary value may be to provide an outlet for his frustration at being a teacher, rather than a member of some other department of local government, and/or for being an inept teacher.

M. Garba holds his book in his hand and says "Read," the class saying "Read" after him. Then he says, "John is lifting the hoe," and the class repeats this sentence over and over for two minutes, sounding more like a chant than a reading in English. Next he reads, "Mary is bringing the goat" and "We are looking at our

feathers of a peacock," implying that if you remove the feathers, there is just an ordinary bird underneath.

[8] A black substance, usually antimony, commonly used to darken the rims of the eyes.

[9] "Mallama" is the female form of "mallam" and refers to a female teacher.

*Children arriving at a mission school.*

teacher." The latter sentence is written on the board for the class to locate in their readers. Bedlam follows as the cries of beaten children, who had their fingers in the wrong place, mingle with the shouts of students trying to attract the teacher's attention to their correctly placed fingers.

Now M. Garba faces the class, his angry look signaling that more trouble is to come. "I thought you finished Lesson 28, but there are still foolish children who cannot read it. It is five days since we began this lesson." He throws the neem switch in his hand at a girl who is playing at the back of the room. "See. Look at her. She plays while we learn. Stand up and read," he says in Kanuri. Parts of the English lesson are conducted in English; most of the school day is conducted in Kanuri.

The girl rises and reads the lesson correctly, repeating it three times.

"Oh ho! You understood and memorized the lesson. That's why you were playing. Read, Bintu."

Bintu also rises and reads the lesson twice.

"Very good. Now let's try, 'John is lifting the hoe.'" The class repeats this sentence many times before M. Garba stops them by asking who can show him a picture of John in the book.

Although the picture of John is shown clearly on the page, it may as well be invisible when the request to find it is made in English. Only a few succeed at this ostensibly simple task. They are the bright ones who by virtue of endless repetition[10] can link object and sound in English, having learned, for example,

---

[10] The apparent success of the method with some students precludes teachers from fully appreciating the need to improve their instructional techniques for all students.

that the sound "teacher" refers to the querulous, unpleasant man who instructs them six days a week.

M. Garba notices some boys asleep and wakes them to read. When they fail, he makes them remain standing while he tries to locate a girl who can read and thus further embarrass them. Failing in this, he calls on a boy who does read correctly and is then "rewarded" with an invitation to slap the two "dull boys." M. Garba shouts the boys into silence when they cry. They begin to sweat and after failing to read a second time they shake in anticipation of the punishment to follow. As M. Garba appears to lose all control of himself and the class, he turns over the lesson to two students from the Arabic Teacher Training College who have been coming daily to observe and practice-teach. At the sound of the bell the children run with great relief from the room to prepare for physical education.

M. Garba again takes over his class. First he organizes them for warm-up exercises. Then they are grouped by sex to play their own separate games. M. Garba joins the boys and leads them in a circle game. Tiring of this, he stretches out on the ground, supports his head on the palm of his hand, and watches his students run around.

Bintu and the other girls play a short distance away. Accustomed to playing without guidance they move effortlessly from activity to activity. To begin with, they stand in a U-shape and sing and clap. At some signal one girl separates herself from the group, dances alone, and then flings herself back first at the girls in the base of the U, who fling her back and up as high as they can. The game can go on endlessly with a different girl coming out to be tossed each time. Next they form a circle for a quieter, less merry game. Bintu leads the girls in a song, the girls shouting "yei" after each sentence she simultaneously sings and acts out.

An old man.   Yei!
With a gray beard.   Yei!
Full of gray hair.   Yei!
Throw it to the north.   Yei!
Throw it to the east.   Yei!
Throw it to the west.   Yei!
Throw it to the south.   Yei!
Throw it to the sky.   Yei!
Throw it to the earth.   Yei!
Throw it to Mohammed.   Yei!
Throw it to Falmata.   Yei!

Shortly before the period is over, children from different classes who have been outside for physical education crowd around a tap struggling for a chance to drink. When it is Bintu's turn, she cleverly clears a space by placing her finger on the tap and squirting water all over. She nonchalantly bends over to drink as the children around her move back to avoid the water, and receives a surprise knock on the head from the big boy behind her. Remaining calm, she steps back to allow him to drink and when his mouth is on the tap she shoves him out of the way, making room for another child to move into his place.

"If your brother wasn't my head boy, I'd beat you."

"Beat me," she taunts him. "I'll tell him and you'll see what happens!"

He lifts her up threatening to drop her in the water, but she is unafraid and simply tells him to release her.

"Your big mouth knows how to say strong words."

Bintu ignores the boy. She soaks her head scarf in the water and walks toward her classroom flicking the wet scarf at passing children.

M. Garba prints on the blackboard, "Arithmetic. Do Exercise 44. Page 62. 1–5."

The children scramble for their materials while M. Garba sits at his desk waiting to correct their completed work. Bintu's wrinkled forehead gives her the appearance of concentration. She absentmindedly sucks her thumb and then counts an answer on her fingers. The second problem puzzles her, so she turns to Mukhtar to borrow his counting stones and eraser. He accuses her of looking for an excuse to copy his work.

"Look at my exercise book," she says in defense. "You see. There are more 'v. goods' than in yours. I am not a thief. I'm better than you. I only want your eraser and stones."

The girl behind Mukhtar whispers to him, "Bintu is better than you. She was higher in the last exam."

"You always ask me for a pencil or stones," Mukhtar says to Bintu. "Here they are, but don't ask me anymore. You bring me nothing from home. When I help Gona with rulers and erasers she brings me candy."

Bintu uses the stones to complete her work, missing those problems whose sum exceeds the number of her counters.

Before the children even appear at his desk for corrections, M. Garba announces that the room is too hot and they should go sit outside to review simple arithmetic.

"Monitor, fetch me a whip.[11] O.K. Now I'm ready. Everybody sit down. Ready. Here's the first problem. Two minus one."

The class grows silent.

"Still you don't know, Madu Bultu?"

Madu, his eyes searching the neem branches for inspiration, timidly says, "One."

"Sit down," is Madu's reward from M. Garba. "O.K. Three minus one."

Five children miss the problem before Bintu gives the correct answer.

"Well done, Bintu. You may please yourself. Slap the face of every pupil who missed."

When she slaps the last child, a girl grumbles, "Because she's your friend you didn't slap her properly."

"I'm very pleased with Bintu. O.K. Four minus two. I know how to catch dull pupils."

He calls on five students, none of whom know the answer. The monitor does, and he slaps the five.

---

[11] Teachers always have a ready supply of whips on hand in the slim branches of the neem tree.

"Aha, aha. Here's a tough one. Two plus two plus three." He asks three children and finally calls on Bintu who proudly calls out, "Seven."

Bintu slaps more vigorously this time.

"Bintu, today you're the star. I want you to keep it up. Don't follow your naughty friend Ya Kyellu. Two plus five. Who knows the answer?"

Only one boy raises his hand. "Ohhh, teacher, ask me please."

"Keep quiet a bit longer. You'll certainly get to exercise your hand."

This time Bintu is among those who are mistaken and the boy, who has been smacking one hand against the other to show how he intends to slap his erring mates, slaps them all, giving Bintu a light tap.

"She's your wife," teases M. Garba, "that's why you didn't slap her so hard."

M. Garba is distracted from the lesson by the arrival of an N.A. Land Rover. The driver greets his friend Garba and they begin to discuss a recent evening spent with prostitutes at the Good Will Bar, clapping their hands in recollection of the evening's pleasure. Just as the driver informs M. Garba that he has come to take Alhaji Isa's daughter to the hospital for treatment, the bell rings announcing the breakfast hour.

Bintu collects her shoes from inside her desk and her broom from the cupboard. On the road outside the school grounds she again meets Zara and they walk home quickly to avoid being beaten for returning late to school.

At home the family has already begun to eat. Bulama, Harun, and another boy are eating from one bowl. Bintu joins her mother who is sitting with Ya Fati. They all eat quickly and the boys play around the compound while Bintu takes paper and pencil and amuses herself by drawing and by writing the alphabet and words from her school lessons.

Ya Amina has been relaxing more than usual this morning because her co-wife has returned to housework for the first time since her baby was born. As Zarami Goni's senior wife, Ya Amina is an important woman in this quarter of the city, and, consequently, throughout the day many female friends pay their respects and stop to visit for a while. During Bintu's breakfast hour she has two visitors.

A very tall woman enters the courtyard accompanied by her young daughter.

"Magaram," Ya Amina warmly greets her, "are you in town?"

"I've been here for a while. What can I do, though, when my husband always worries me, following everywhere I go. If I go out at night to visit friends, he's right behind checking to see whether I've gone to meet a man." She looks at Bintu writing and says, "Nurse. That's what you'll be when you grow up."

"You think I'll become a nurse. What about you? You're already grown up."

"I didn't attend school. If I had, you'd seen me in uniform right now."

"I don't want to be a nurse. I'd rather be an English teacher."

Magaram's little girl is staring with interest at Bintu. "Are you looking at Bintu's writing?" her mother asks her.

"Go to school if you like writing so much," says Ya Amina.

"Don't hurry her. She'll go when she grows up. Nowadays a child without school is like a two-legged donkey. Just a creature who can't do anything. In our day our parents hid us away in pots. Now everybody willingly sends his kids to school."

Ya Amina brings her friend back to marriage talk. "Your husband is so tiring. Why not divorce him?"

"I've tried that. For the sake of love and happiness I'd have left home long ago, but the bond of our marriage isn't broken yet."[12]

"Wonderful! You are patient. Any other woman would have left this man long ago. He always comes home after midnight from his prostitutes, while you remain at home. And if you visit your own relatives, he's always behind you."

Magaram leans closer to Ya Amina saying, "Amina, I want to tell you something," and they whisper to each other until Magaram leaves the compound a few minutes later.

"Ya Amina, is food ready?" M. Zarami shouts from beyond the courtyard wall that separates his quarters from the rest of the family's.

"How do you expect me to finish cooking so early?"

"Stop talking so much. By now all good women have finished cooking," he says jokingly.

"Maybe I'm not a good wife."

"Ya Amina, please don't talk so much. Try and give me food so I can leave quickly."

"Take it yourself from the pot."

"I can't do that. So please, if the food isn't ready, give me a large kolanut."

She selects a kolanut from her basket and gives it to him. "Thank you very much, my wife."

Another woman enters the family courtyard.

"Welcome, Fatima, welcome."

"Don't welcome me, Amina. You haven't seen me for a week, yet you don't ask what happened."

"Let me give you some kolanut to chew." With this offer Fatima's face becomes friendlier. "How upset I was when I saw you frowning," says Ya Amina. "I thought something happened to you that I hadn't heard about."

Fatima smiles broadly. "Not many people have heard." Having offered this bait, she sits back to wait for her friend to urge her on. Then she continues, "Since I've already told you I'm in trouble, I must tell you the rest."

"What kind of trouble? May God protect me from it."

"Such a thing won't occur in your compound. You've stayed with your husband too long and borne him too many children."

"Have you and your husband separated?"

"I'm going to tell you now." Instead of speaking she bites off a piece of kolanut and carefully chews it before saying another word, obviously relishing the

---

[12] She refers here to the fact that in Islamic marital procedure, while a man and woman may reconcile after separations short of divorce innumerable times, they may be divorced no more than three times without breaking the "natural bond" created by the act of marriage. Actually, her response to Ya Amina may be her public explanation, the fact being that she does not care to dissolve her marriage for other more personal reasons.

suspense she believes she is creating. "I've fought with my husband and all my property has been confiscated." Ya Amina raises her hands to her head while uttering sounds of surprise and horror. In fact, she had heard the story before but not from the horse's mouth. "My husband took another wife. I warned him that if he married her I wouldn't live with him. He ignored me and married her. So I went to the Alkali [Islamic judge] and filed a divorce petition."

"What did the Alkali say?"

"He said I must stay with him or else lose all my property. My husband appealed to the court claiming that he still loves me. He won, so the Alkali ordered me to give up all my property. My jewels, my gold bangles, my clothes, everything. They thought the fear of losing my property would make me stay, but I'd sworn I wouldn't live a day with that woman."

Fatima departs, leaving the wives to gossip eagerly for the next ten minutes about their recent visitors. Then Ya Amina gets her large wooden mortar and pestle to pound corn, saying that she must get it done while the sun is hot so it can dry easily. She pours corn and a little water into the mortar and begins to pound, singing over and over to herself as she works the pestle, "In the name of God, God be praised."

Thinking she is late, Bintu grabs a kolanut and runs out the back door to take the shortcut to school. She meets Mairama outside her house and the girls walk to school.

M. Garba's arrival in the classroom helps the monitor to quiet the children in 2A. He goes to the bulletin board to see what subject should be taught next. "God forbid," he says. "It's General Knowledge."

M. Garba makes minimal preparations for teaching the subject. At times he has the children sing songs that are relevant to the topic. For example, when exploration was under discussion the children sang in Kanuri the song about Mungo Park, the famous explorer.

> A young Scottish doctor
> Whose name was Mungo Park
> He came to find the Niger
> But he failed to see the Niger
> Because he died at Bussa.

For the most part, however, a lesson consists of a reading from some story or history book, followed by questions on the reading.

M. Garba moves the class outside and begins to read, intermixing translation and commentary. " 'Some people settled down under Dallah Hill. They were black-smiths who came from the Sahara and were the founders of Kano.' The Sahara is a place with much sand and no rainfall. Blacksmiths are poor people. They make deadly weapons. Kalli, stand up. Your father is a blacksmith, isn't he? 'The first King of Kano was Bagoda but the most powerful one was Mohammed Rumfa.' "

M. Garba pauses in his reading to stare outside at three upper class girls collecting firewood. He calls the tallest girl.

"I always see you at the Premier Cinema with your father even though I've told you several times not to go. Don't you know your father is advertising you? He shows you off at the cinema so that you'll have many suitors. The other night I told your father not to take you there any more."

"Yes, sir. After the night you warned us I never went again."

"Two days ago I saw you even after you changed your seat to avoid me. Next time I catch you I'll report you to the headmaster for a beating."

"Yes, sir."

"Go away."

M. Garba resumes the lesson. "'The first people of Kano were believed to be huge, almighty people. They could easily kill elephants.' One man could kill an elephant? Kai! This isn't true! I can't believe this statement. How could one man kill an elephant without a gun? Even if my whole body became ears I wouldn't believe it."

"What is an elephant, sir?"

"A large animal bigger than cows and camels."

A boy from another class walks over to M. Garba. "Excuse me, sir. I want the whip."

"You want the whip? Good. Lie down."

All the children laugh heartily.

"How can you people ever learn a foreign language if you make such silly mistakes in your own?"

Seeing the Koranic mallam walk toward 2A's classroom, M. Garba knows it is almost time for the next period and he dismisses the children to return to their desks.

"Stand up," orders M. Yusufu, the religion teacher. "Now, take deep breaths and wave your hands. Sit down. We will read *fatiha*. Hadija, you read."

Hadija comes to the front of the class to recite. She is nervous. She looks at the floor and twists her hair around and around, but she manages to finish. M. Yusufu corrects the girl's errors and then praises her, asking the class to applaud her fine performance.

"O.K. Some questions," says M. Yusufu, continuing the lesson. "Bintu. How many Gods are there?"

"One."

"Where does He live?"

"Everywhere."

"How many children does God have?"

"None."

"Sir, what about Jesus Christ?" one child asks.

"Jesus had no father," M. Yusufu explains, "only a mother whose name was Mairama. When she went alone to fetch water from a well she became pregnant just by chance. The way she conceived was by God's spirit through the angel Gabriel. How many wives?" he asks, resuming his questions.

"God has no wives."

"Who cooks for Him?"

"God does not eat or drink."

M. Yusufu glances around the room. He sees one child gazing outside. "Wonderful! You're here to study the Koran, not to look outside. Such behavior won't help in the world hereafter." He touches the boy's head. "I feel pity for you."

M. Yusufu's unexpected gentle comments arouse the class and they turn to look at him and the boy.

"You know what happened to this boy? Listen. His father, Jiddah Abubukar (May his soul rest in peace!), was one of the wealthiest men in town. He rented sewing machines and houses and unfortunately, because he was uneducated, he didn't keep any records. Sometimes the tenants didn't pay him. He also gave people money on credit and forgot their names. Two big men grabbed his wealth after he fell ill and died. They took a large sum of his money for themselves and as a result of this bad deed you all know that already one man died and another lost his job. God has shown them His preliminary judgment. We don't know about His final one."

Throughout M. Yusufu's speech, the children give full attention to his story of two well-known public figures who probably extorted exorbitant death taxes from the estate of Bintu's classmate's father. The fate of the two men was as he described it. When he relates their fate to God's dicta, he is merely doing what teachers often are enjoined to do: associate classroom activities with events happening in their own society outside the school.

"Our main lesson for today," he continues, "is to hear the story about death and paradise. Before anyone dies he must first have a little fever or headache. Two angels interview him after he's been taken to the grave. They ask him to write down his deeds so the pros and cons can be weighed. If his good deeds are greater than his evil ones, the angel's letter is put in his right hand. When other angels appear for the person's final judgment, they go away if they see a letter in his right hand. But if it's in his left hand, they beat him and beat him until they're satisfied."

A boy raises his hand to ask, "How should we be good?"

"A fine question. You must obey your father, mother, and teachers and you must fear God." He looks around and catches a girl sleeping. He shouts at her, "You're sleeping. I know you weren't born free. Because your mother is someone's concubine your case is different from others.[13] You'll be given away without payment [he refers to her marriage] and if you're very loyal to your master and get his blessings, then you may enter paradise."

The next period is the long break, twenty minutes of free time between the fifth and sixth period of the day. The teachers relax in the shade while the children play as they wish. Last night's rain brought a coolness which continued into the early morning. By now the coolness has completely dissipated and any sustained movement causes one to perspire.

As M. Garba enters the classroom the monitor calls out, "Greet." The children

---

[13] See Cohen 1967:41.

answer in chorus, "Good morning, sir." M. Garba reacts angrily. "How many times must you greet me every day?[14] O.K. We're doing nature study. Everybody should quiet down and listen. Most of your parents are farmers. So it's necessary to know more about farming. Who are the strongest people? Chiefs, soldiers, or farmers?"

"Farmers."

"Chiefs."

"Who supports farmers?" He does not wait for an answer. "Now, you've eaten your breakfast. Who supplied the food? Farmers. If you don't eat enough you'll be hungry and if a teacher asks you to multiply two times two you'll say ten. Tafawa Balewa[15] had a farm and the Shehu has a farm. Who produces food?"

"Farmers."

"You'd really die if you went without food for three days. Your eyes would sink in. So eat a lot of food."

"What about water?"

"Without it you last only for a day." He continues with a new point. "Kano was surrounded by walls in the old days and they farmed inside the walls."

"Was there any entrance?"

The question is ignored as M. Garba continues, "Many farmers lived there in luxury, not in poverty like in some places. Today we're also going to learn something about soil. That's the most important thing because we grow all our crops on soil." He walks to the blackboard and draws a picture of a plant's root system with a section of the plant sticking above the surface of the ground. "Roots get food for the plant because the plants have no hands. Roots feed the plants with the food they take from the soil."

All the children are quiet. Bintu looks directly at the drawing on the board. Student teachers from the Arabic Teacher Training College are peering in through the open windows, observing the lesson. M. Garba draws another diagram, similar to the first one, adding some root hairs.

"The plant grows in the air at the top. From here to here is all dirt," he says pointing to a space in his drawing. "Where the root hairs are, this is called 'plant-growing soil.' Repeat what I said, Bukar."

The boy stares at M. Garba.

"Stand up. You're playing. Look here now. Everybody. Who understands what I said?"

Only one boy raises his hand.

"So, the rest of you are deaf! You never say you don't understand if something isn't clear," he scolds the class. "You never ask questions and when you are asked you just stare at the wall. You play all the time. Alhaji, tell me something about these two drawings on the board."

---

[14] The children are expected to rise from their seats and greet every adult visitor to their room, even their own teacher. M. Garba's annoyance will not alter this practice.

[15] This is Sir Abubukar Tafawa Balewa, former prime minister of Nigeria, who was assassinated in the January 1966 coup d'état.

*Vernacular is a required school subject.*

"Flower. No leaves."

The entire class laughs. M. Garba slaps a girl. "You're playing while I talk. Tell something about soil. Bintu, yes, tell me."

Bintu murmurs inaudibly. M. Garba pulls her nose and slaps her. "I didn't hear what you said," she protests.

"You sit in the front row and you didn't hear what I said? Nonsense. Sit down." Bintu sits down, crying.

For teaching vernacular, or Kanuri, the last subject of the day, M. Garba brings the children to the shade outside the classroom and arranges them in a semicircle around his chair. All he does during the period is maintain order, urge another child to speak when one is finished, and eat chocolate candy, despatching a child to buy more for him when he discovers his pocket is empty.

"Everyone must stand up and tell a story. You all know many, so don't say you don't," M. Garba says to get the class started.

A boy volunteers. "I want to tell about a circumcision celebration. My friend Ibrahim came over and when we were warming ourselves before the big fire[16] Ibrahim played with it and a spark caught the zana matting."

The children shout out their displeasure at this story and tell the boy to sit down, not even waiting to hear if he is finished.

Another boy begins. "Yesterday, on the way home from school, we saw a mad woman. She was naked. We called her crazy lady so she began to drive us away

---

[16] On the occasion of a circumcision a big fire is made to roast meat for the celebration. See Cohen 1967:64–65.

and one boy fell into a ditch. The crazy lady threw stones at him but we ran home so I don't know how he got out."

"Who can tell us another?"

"Here I am. Here I am, sir," many children shout.

"Once upon a time a lion gave birth to a baby hen."

"No, no. What we want is true stories. Stories that really happened." M. Garba laughs and laughs so that he can hardly continue speaking. "Wonderful! Lion giving birth to a hen? Very strange. Bintu?"

Bintu says she knows a song and is given permission to sing it.

> A Kanuri boy asked for groundnuts.
> In the market he asked for meat.
> "Give me and give me and give me," he said.
> It is shameful for a Kanuri boy,
> In Bornu, it is shameful for you,
> For you to do this is shameful.
> Next time you can never say, "I am a Kanuri,"
> And be respected by the people.

"A very good song. How shameful for a Kanuri boy to beg for groundnuts and meat!"

The girls have enjoyed the song, whereas the boys sit quiet and sullen, having been bested by Bintu's lyrics.

"Who can repeat the same song?" M. Garba asks. The monitor raises his hand. Instead of singing exactly as Bintu did, he changes the subject from a boy to a girl and now it is the boys' turn to laugh and cheer and throw their caps in the air.

"Settle down now. We have time for just one more story." After looking once around the class, he calls on Suliman.

"One day a farmer planted beans on his farm. A thief came again and again to steal his beans so the man went to his [Koranic] mallam and asked what he could do to catch the thief. The mallam gave him a wonderful doll and said, 'Take this girl and put her on your farm.' The farmer thanked the mallam and went away with the doll. That very day he placed the doll on his farm and the next morning the thief returned for more beans. Seeing the doll he asked, 'Who are you? Talk, or I'll beat you.' The doll was quiet. 'Talk, you beautiful girl, or I'll slap you.' The thief slapped the doll and it held his hand fast. The thief said, 'Let go of my hand or I'll break your leg.' He kicked the doll and his own leg was held fast."

By now the children are jumping with laughter. One boy is trying to act out the story. He hits the wall of the classroom and pretends it has caught him.

"The owner of the farm came and caught the thief and he was put to death by the village head."

Although the bell had rung in the course of the story, the class was too interested to leave. It is now the end of the school day. M. Garba has again finished eating his chocolates while the children have enjoyed their most placid and entertaining period.

Bintu, Zara, and Mairama meet outside on the school grounds. They embrace each other around the neck and depart for home. On the way they pass a group of young schoolboys building mud houses and boasting about their futures.

"I shall build beautiful rooms for my wives, three rooms for them and two for myself. I shall lead a happy life and be the father of many children."

"I shall build a two-story house," announces Kalli, "and welcome strangers. I'll live with one wife like a white man."

"My house will not be destroyed by rains because it"ll be very strong."

"As soon as I've finished my building I shall marry a beautiful woman. Who wants to be a servant? I'll make him rich."

"I want to work for you. I'll become your servant."

"Very nice. Work hard and I'll give you plenty of money." From his pocket he pulls out many empty cigarette packets. "These are five pound notes."

"Shettima will receive a tremendous amount of money. You see how rich Mohammed is."

"They aren't real money. You can't buy things with them," says Kalli.

"What if they're useless. Shettima will work for me and I'll pay him with these packets."

"I'll work for myself."

"I know the reason, Kalli. You have no wrappers of your own."

Kalli, looking furious, stands up and advances toward Shettima. "I'm going to beat you. Your father is a servant and now so are you. I'd never become my friend's servant."

"Touch any part of his body and I'll beat you myself," a bigger boy threatens.

Despite the angry words, Kalli goes to help his friends after he finishes his own house. He is rewarded with three cigarette packets which he is told are worth fifteen pounds. He takes the packets and hands them to an old lady selling groundnuts, one of the many vendors working under the row of neem trees that encompass the school grounds.

"Grandmother, please change my bills," he says respectfully.

As the woman reaches for the empty packets, Kalli seizes a handful of groundnuts and leaps away, leaving the old woman shouting angrily after him, "Thief, thief, thief." A man sitting with her unsuccessfully pursues Kalli in and out of the trees.

Arriving at home Bintu finds her gruel ready to be eaten and she finishes it quickly. Bulama and Harun go away after lunch, leaving an unwilling Bintu to do an errand for her mother. Usman accompanies her. Receiving threepence from Ya Amina, they walk to where some old women sit selling kolanuts, eggplants, and fish.

Bintu greets the fish vendor and hands her threepence saying, "I want dried fish, please." She gets the fish wrapped in old newspaper and the children walk home.

*Two-story houses are found only in cities.*

"Did you see that woman selling kolanuts?" she whispers to Usman. "They say she's a witch. My mother told us not to greet her and whenever we see her we must say 'bismillahi.'"

M. Zarami sees Bintu pass by the entrance to his rooms. He calls out, "Bintu, where did you go?"

"I went to buy something."

"Something with no name?"

"Dried fish."

He jumps up and charges angrily into the family area to berate his wife. "What did I tell you about sending these little ones to shop for you?"

"There was nobody else in the house to send."

"Next time call me if nobody is here. I prefer to go myself than send these children. I just hate for them to do this at their age."

Bintu goes into her mother's room to rest. Her mother pounds a mortarful of millet and goes to lie down in the shade. She dozes off but is soon awakened by her husband reminding her to pray. After praying, she gets a kolanut and tobacco flowers and decorates her teeth. She looks sleepy and begins to nod again. Suddenly she sits up and calls out to Ya Fati, "The muezzin has already called for prayers and look at me, I've put them off just to finish decorating my teeth. [The prayers she completed were the optional ones.] I should know that teeth won't help me in the hereafter."

"Even I've not begun praying, though I did my ablutions at the first call."

"So you heard M. Maaji!" [Maaji is the muezzin at the local mosque.] "Since my first year of marriage he's always called earlier than the others."

"Do I have to do my ablutions again, Ya Amina?"

"You'd better if you have any doubts." The women are careful about their preparations for prayer because if they depart from accepted procedure their prayers will not be effective.

When ablutions are complete, Ya Amina enters her room to pray and returns within minutes to the kitchen to finish her work, making a rapid transition from the tranquil moment of prayer to the sweat-inducing labor of pounding corn.

"It's too hot," says Ya Amina. "I must rest for a few minutes."

"Yes, it's awfully hot today."

"Once I remember working in the sun on a day like this and I became so ill I couldn't recognize anybody for ten days." While she stretches out to relax again, Usman, oblivious to the heat, sings and jumps around the compound. Ya Amina watches him with amazement.

"I guess he'll be a good sportsman," says Ya Fati.

"Yes, he is very active. You know, children who've suffered from sickness usually become famous. This boy was so sick last year he couldn't walk or eat any food, not even the special rice and yams I cooked. Such awful days! I never slept at night. Soon his room grew so smelly that visitors stopped coming to us. His feces were streaked with blood and the poor boy just got sicker and sicker until he became so thin his bones poked out. His father was very worried and bought many different medicines, but we couldn't find out what kind of disease he had. At last Usman told me that he wanted food and my heart leapt with joy. I immediately cooked something and he ate like a starved man. On that very day his father came with his rosary to count beads and pray and the next morning he told four Koranic pupils to read to him from the Koran. By evening when they finished reading their verses he was able to limp around."

"That was strange."

"See that large scar on his kneecap. That won't stop him from becoming a sportsman, will it?" She turns over on her side before continuing. "One time I gave birth to a fat girl; she was really unusual. She died at the age of three months and I heard many rumors about her, even that she was caught by witches. I've given birth to ten children without ever consulting a forecaster. Some women see them as soon as they become pregnant to learn if they're carrying a daughter or a son. They spend much money on this. I'll never do such a thing. If a child of mine dies, I won't ask for the cause.[17] I also heard many rumors when Usman was ill. Some people said the boy was afflicted with *chi kamma*,[18] but I ignore such stories."

Bintu comes out to the courtyard dragging a sizable cardboard carton full of objects she uses for playing house with her dolls. The box is stored under her mother's bed. She is extracting some of its myriad contents when her father calls her to his room.

---

[17] She means that she will not attempt to identify a malefactor by consulting a Koranic mallam or a witch.

[18] *Chi kamma* means "public opinion," and in this context it refers to the belief that a person will suffer from sickness or accident if he is talked about too much, regardless of whether the talk is praise or abuse.

"What did you do in school today, Bintu?"

"We did religion, English, and arithmetic."

"What did you read in religion?"

"We read *fatiha*."

"What did you read in English?"

"We read Lesson 28."

"Did you have any exams?"

"No."

"Or did you fail and that's why you refuse to tell me? Didn't you have examinations last week?"

"Yes, we did."

"What subjects did you pass?"

"I passed English, religion, gardening, vernacular, and hygiene. I failed arithmetic."

"Next time you fail any subject, don't come to my house. Stay in school with your teachers."

With the catechism over, M. Zarami dismisses his daughter. He regularly demonstrates interest, however superficial, in his daughter's schoolwork. Neither the questions nor the answers are particularly meaningful, but the questioning may strengthen Bintu's concern for academic success.

Bulama, Bintu's oldest brother, has returned home and he is sitting against a wall looking at a Koran. Bintu urges him to let her read and when she does read she changes her voice to mimic the young Arabic student who came to practice-teach in her class.

"Even though he reads like that, remember he's still your teacher," Bulama corrects her.

"You always argue against me," Bintu protests.

"Why must you two always fight?" asks their mother.

Bintu begins to read another verse and stops to question Usman, her youngest brother, about what she has read. When he ignores her, she hits him and he runs away. She boasts to Bulama, "Class 2A is very good because M. Garba teaches us what Class 3 is doing. Class 2B is doing what we did in Class 1. In Class 7 I won't sweep anymore, I'll supervise Class 2 children with my whip. If I finish Class 7, I'll rest at home for a while and then go teach little girls. Did you pass your exams?" she asks Bulama, referring to the recent terminal examinations.

"Yes, I passed. I got fifth place. There were twenty failures."

"I didn't pass because the teacher showed favoritism."

In her box of playthings, dolls and their clothes mingle with pages torn from different English readers. She picks one page out. "I know how to read."

"You do nothing in school all day and then you bother us at home."

Ignoring Bulama, she reads, "John is a boy. This is a black book. This is a red book." She throws the page aside, reaching for another. "The teacher is writing. I am going to school." While she is reading, Usman snatches the page from her and tears it up. She threatens to tell her father, but he is away. They hit each other and when Bintu cries, her mother calls out, "Don't fight if you're going to cry all the time. Now shut up and play peacefully."

From deep inside her box she pulls out empty food cartons of different sizes, designating one as a two-story house and another as a garage for her cars. She talks to herself as she handles the toys, asking an imaginary visitor if she has learned Lesson 20 and boasting that her class skipped over Lesson 29 to do Lesson 30. She recites a lesson and then says the entire alphabet in English.

"Who will call Amma for me?" she asks in a cajoling voice. Amma is her six-year-old cousin living in a nearby house.

"I will," answers Usman.

"Very good, my brother."

Amma enters smiling. "You're very happy-looking this afternoon," remarks Ya Amina, "and also beautiful. Stay like this and you'll get a good husband when you grow up." Hearing Ya Amina's kind words, Amma smiles even more.

All these compliments directed elsewhere are more than Bintu can tolerate in silence. "She is not beautiful. She just rubbed powder on herself."

"Bintu, you're an ugly girl. With your scars you'll never get a good husband," says Bulama, ever the reassuring brother.

"No, my girl is beautiful," comforts Ya Amina. "She shall get a good husband."

Bintu and Amma are soon joined by five other little girls from the neighborhood. With seven pairs of hands reaching into the toy box it is quickly emptied and objects are strewn over a sizable portion of the courtyard as the girls dress and undress the dolls, set up little boxes, decorate them as living rooms, and act out situations with the dolls. One box contains "jewelry"—glittering chocolate candy wrappers. After a period of individual play they organize themselves and their dolls for an elaborate mock marriage: a bride and bridegroom play their respective parts, gifts are sent and exclaimed over, a Koranic mallam recites the marriage prayers, the groom is carried to his new house on a horse, and the bride is delivered to her husband's home. All of this entails the dressing and undressing of dolls, the rearrangement of rooms, and the selection of actors who play the different marriage roles as they have repeatedly seen adults play them. In the middle of the marriage ceremony Bintu, hearing her father's radio on the other side of the wall, imitates the announcer. "Radio time, five o'clock. This is Kaduna, Lagos, and Jos."

Cousin Amma stays behind when the other children leave for home. Bintu asks her, "Can you recite the two times table?"

"I don't go to school so how can I know what you know?"

Bintu recites the table while Amma looks wonderingly at her. "The easiest table is ten. At first I thought five was the easiest. Now I found out ten is easier. Amma, why don't you ever go to school?"

"My father won't let me go."

Ya Amina explains, more to her co-wife than to her daughter, "Those mallams [Amma's father is a practicing Koranic mallam] don't send their children to school because they still think it'll hurt their religion."

"Yesterday when the teacher was away we had a competition with group A. In English they beat us but in arithmetic we scored ten over ten and group A scored only four over ten."

"Bintu, do you think Amma understands anything you said?"

"I just hear her talking. How can I understand?" asks Amma.

"You could never understand that. Even I, her mother, don't know anything about ten over ten?"

"We had a group competition," Bintu explains again, speaking deliberately as if this will help to clarify her point. "Group A won in English and our group scored ten over ten and won in arithmetic."

"Bintu, no more over ten. Go get the cooking stuff from your stepmother's room."

"I can't, I'm too busy."

"It's not for washing. Just get them for me. Please go."

She gets the utensils and returns to Amma and her toys. Before Amma leaves for home the girls sing:

> Kyari is a patient man.
> Kyari has a fertile farm.
> He has gone to Mecca,
> To Mecca, to Medina.
> If you're good you go to paradise.

They simultaneously sing and trace zigzag paths in the dirt which signify their road to paradise.

After Bintu finishes putting away her toys, she grinds pepper for dinner. Then she gets a bar of Lux soap from her mother to wash up before eating. She comes out of the bathroom wearing a clean pair of shorts with her chain of charms hanging diagonally across her chest.

"Ya Amina," she calls to her mother, "you promised to give me some new charms."

"Yes, I did."

"I want three charms."

"Be patient, my daughter. I'll get them soon."

"So, Bintu has no charms," comments Kyellu, her mother's friend, who entered the compound while Bintu was bathing.

"I've never given her her own."

"Mother has never given me my own charms to wear."

"What about the ones you've got on?"

"They belong to her. She bought them for herself and I think they aren't good for me. She has different reasons."

"What do you mean 'different reasons?' Aren't they [the Koranic verse each charm contains] all the words of God?"

Bintu touches one of the charms. "Look at this charm. It's for witches."

"True. Wearing that charm a witch can't attack you."

"So for you the charm has little importance?" asks Ya Amina.

"Yes. Wizards attack old people with lots of fat, not young girls like me."

"I've heard a wonderful thing. Don't you know they attack infants as well as adults?"

M. Zarami enters his family's compound and after greeting his wives he says to them, "We're just back from the funeral. It was terribly hot on the road, but the good thing was the ground. It was so soft the diggers easily prepared the grave."

"Everyone's been saying she was a good woman. The ground would've been hard if she'd been bad."

*City girl uses water purchased from waterseller.*

"For a good person God shows his approval in a way everyone can recognize. I've long heard that soft ground means the dead person definitely goes to paradise."

"People don't think so much of that idea, nowadays," says M. Zarami, "but, anyhow, only God knows."

Ya Amina goes to the kitchen area and, seeing that the food is cooked, announces that dinner is ready. After everyone has eaten, Bintu collects the dinner bowls and squats down behind the kitchen to wash them. A lit kerosene lamp is by her side.

After a while Ya Amina calls out to Bintu, "Come here when you've finished."
"I haven't finished."
"She's very lazy," says Harun, Bintu's middle brother. "Hurry up. You should've washed those bowls in two winks of an eye."
"Harun, you always insult me. I'm glad you weren't chosen to play in the football match against Bulabulin [Primary School]."
"I'm sorry to have to listen to a liar. Were you there when we played the match?"
"Just the same, I was told by Karim, your captain."
"I played inside right and scored two goals."
"I heard the results. The score was one-nothing," says Bulama, spoiling Harun's story. He corrects himself when he catches a sign from his brother. "Yes, Harun scored two goals."
"Wasn't there a goalkeeper?" asks Bintu.
"I gave him two hot shots."
"Harun, you really didn't play," says Bulama.
"Ya Amina, do you know how Bulama got his sore?" asks Harun, trying to get even with his brother. "When he was playing football he bumped into another player."
"I'm not interested in all this news. Hurry up, Bintu. We're sitting here in darkness."
Ya Amina needs the lamp because she is preparing to make a visit. She talks to Ya Fati as she changes clothes and rearranges her hair.
"The pilgrims [from Mecca] didn't return so early this year."
"Even now many haven't come back. The transport problem and the new system make the trip terribly difficult."
"There were many changes this year. Yesterday some people told me all about the hardships of their pilgrimage."
"Yes, it's become very hard."
Bintu enters the room where her mother and stepmother are conversing.
"Ya Amina, please do my hair in the WTC [Women's Training College] style."
"What is 'TT?'" asks Ya Fati. "What type of hairdressing is that?"
"She wants the WTC style. That's how the grown-up girls in school do their hair. Bintu, can't you see I'm busy? I can't stop and fix your hair now. Leave it, my daughter. I'll do it tomorrow."
"You haven't enough hair on your head to make the WTC style," shouts Bulama from the courtyard.
"Bulama, don't annoy my daughter."
"Oh, she's your daughter but I'm not your son?"
"Yes, you are my son, but I don't want anybody to annoy either of you." She turns back to Ya Fati. "I've not gone to greet Ya Karu since she came from Mecca."
"You'll meet many women if you go to her."
"Most of them go because they're busybodies. They don't greet her in a real sense. They're just looking for something to talk about."
"They want news for scandal," Ya Fati agrees. "If she got thin, or felt sick, or anything wonderful happened to her—they must know so they can tell their neighbors."

"Everyone around here already has gone to greet her. It's shameful not to go as early as possible."

"It doesn't matter. I explained your situation[19] and told her to accept your greetings and expect you very soon."

"That was good of you. Let me get ready. Do you think she's finished giving presents?"

"Probably not. She brought back a large box filled with them."

Ya Amina rubs cream on her face, puts on a brand new dress, and fixes her silver jewelry in place. She leaves for Ya Karu's house located only a few minutes away.

"Good evening. How are you?" she says to Ya Karu.

"Ah, Ya Amina. Good evening. Since my return I've been asking about you."

"I sent a message."

"When I was going to Mecca you gave me a wonderful gift. I shall never forget it."

"Don't think about that. We've been friends for many years."

"Even my girl Fatima didn't give me as much as you. Here, I brought you some gifts."

Ya Amina eagerly unties a package. Inside are two sticks of scent, some aromatic grains, two bottles of perfume, and a small container of water from Mecca. She looks most pleased with her gifts. "Thank you, mother. Thank you, mother."

"I have no time now to tell you about my trip," says Ya Karu. "I'll come to you sometime and describe everything."

"O.K. Then I'll go now."

Ya Amina is escorted to the front door and on the way Ya Karu disjointedly narrates highpoints from her recent adventure. "There seemed to be millions of people in the courtyard. The Arabs were huge. They said we blacks were too poor, that the money we brought wasn't enough to maintain ourselves. Many people died of the heat. We climbed Mount Arafat. We threw stones and had to run past many places. In the courtyard a man announced, 'Who can raise his head and see the roof above?' No one tried that. If you did you'd die and go to paradise, but no one tried. I must stop here."

Ya Amina, delighted with her gifts, returns home and shows them to Ya Fati.

"That woman is very kind to me. I gave her two pounds before she left for Mecca so I received the largest gifts." She talks to her co-wife as she changes back to her old clothes. Then she joins the children outside in the courtyard.

"Who can tell us a good story?" asks Ya Amina.

"I know a nice one," volunteers Bintu.

"You shut up," replies Harun.

"I can tell a really good one," she insists.

---

[19] Ya Amina's "situation" is that for the past forty days she has had to do all the housework unassisted, as would normally be the case, by her co-wife. Ya Fati was requested by M. Zarami to observe a forty-day, postnatal, nonwork period that is sanctioned by Islam but not accepted as obligatory by the Kanuri. Thus, Ya Fati was unable to do her share of the cooking and cleaning.

"Let's listen to Bintu."

Bintu settles herself comfortably and clears her throat.

"We don't like long, dull stories," warns Bulama.

"Please listen to me. Shut your ears if it isn't a nice story. Once upon a time there lived a man with two wives. The senior wife gave birth to an ugly·daughter; later the junior wife gave birth to a beautiful one named Gaji. The two wives hated each other. The senior wife did much magic to make Gaji die so that her own ugly daughter would be the only heir. But the magic acted on her own daughter instead and made the girl die. Now, the senior wife became so unhappy that she began to talk crazy and her husband had to get her cured by a famous wizard. But he divorced the junior wife because he thought she had bewitched her mate. This left Gaji with her stepmother, a mean and cruel woman who gave her a lot of work to do, like fetching water and firewood and sweeping the house. All the time she cursed the girl, never praising her, so the girl lived in misery.

"One day the king announced that all the beautiful girls should meet at his palace. He was going to hold a big ceremony and pick the most beautiful one as the prince's bride. All the girls began to prepare for the ceremony when they heard the news."

Usman interrupts her. "I'm the prince. Bintu, you're the bride."

"Please let us hear the story so we can tell it to our friends," says Bulama.

"I always criticize you, but today you deserve praise," says Harun. "From the beginning the story has been very interesting."

"I've heard such a story before." This is Amma who returned after dinner.

"Then you finish it."

"Mine is a little different."

"If it's different, why interrupt me? Just sit down and listen like the others."

"Don't bother about her. Continue your story."

"On the day of the ceremony all the girls were at the contest except Gaji, who was too busy to go. Her father gave her specially heavy work that day so she would have no time to attend, and the cruel stepmother gave her a sackful of grain to pound and grind to powder. After she worked for a while she thought to herself that maybe she should escape and try to attend the ceremony. So she did and on the way she heard someone call her name. She looked back and saw a huge monster that frightened her. She was about to go back home because this monster was a big ugly thing. But the monster talked to her in a soft voice saying, 'Do not run away. I am your friend.' And other things like that."

"How did the monster look? Was it like a monkey?"

"No one ever saw anything like it before. It was the only one like it alive, probably from God. Yes, it was sent by God to help the girl."

"Go on, please."

"The monster spoke to Gaji. 'Now I am going to change your shape. I shall make you into a donkey,' and the moment he finished talking, the girl changed into a donkey."

Usman interrupts again. "I'm a donkey. I'm a donkey. Hee haw. Hee haw."

"Please don't disturb the story."

"The monster told her a secret. He said, 'The king will say that anyone who knows the word in his mind should speak it and if you're right you will marry the prince. The word is "kalgum,"' and after this the monster disappeared. Gaji watched the ceremony as a donkey and when the king announced his guessing contest, all the women tried. They said many different words but none got the right one. At last the donkey asked, 'May I be allowed to speak?' The people shouted, 'Wonderful. You are a donkey. You are not human. How can you speak like us?' The king said, 'It surprises me to hear a donkey speak our language. Do you know the word?"

"Is it finished yet?"

"I'm tired," says Bintu.

"Let's hear the end."

"Since you started you must finish."

"Gaji said 'kalgum' and the contest was over. She was tied to a post and given water for drinking and to wash in. A servant of the king spied her cleaning herself and tiptoed over to remove her donkey skin. When he saw her beauty he told his master and the king called her in to see him. He fell in love with her himself and took her as his own wife. In the end he fought with his son and got killed."

After ending on a rather diffident note, Bintu goes to her mother's room, returning to the courtyard with an English reader. She sits down near the lamp and begins to read. "John is a boy. Mary is a girl. John and Mary go to school."

"European!" Ya Amina teases her. "I don't know what she's reading. You children belong to the European's time. Nowadays everything has changed. A child knows what even his great-grandparents didn't know."

Bintu, ignoring her mother's remarks, continues to read page after page until her mother takes the lamp away. Then Bintu puts her head down and falls asleep.

# 6/The Kanuri children in perspective

BEFORE CONTINUING with a discussion of the generalizations that can be drawn from the case studies, it may be useful to reiterate several points. First, the four Kanuri students and their families have been depicted within the format of a single, compositely organized day based on four weeks of intensive observations. Second, the case studies are meant to illuminate the contact between agencies for socialization that, in the context of a traditional society undergoing accelerating social change, theoretically conflict—the "modern" primary school and the "traditional" home. In addition, it may be useful to recapitulate the identity of the central figures in each family.

Aisa lives in the village of Nola with M. Musa, her father, and Ya Falta, her mother. M. Musa is a client of Nola's village head and a small-time grain broker, and Ya Falta sells grain in a small daily market; they are on the verge of divorce. Though M. Musa advocates modern education and medicine, he is traditional in other respects. Ya Falta goes along with her husband in his modern beliefs, but she is not fully convinced that Aisa should be in school. Aisa is a mediocre student whose future success in school is questionable.

In contrast, Buba Nola does very well in school and is preparing to enter a postprimary institution. Although his ailing father, Umar the tanner, is a reluctant supporter of education, his mother, Zara, somehow knows that Western education is important for her son. Perhaps the most distinctive feature of this family is Buba's academic success and the consequences that are likely to follow from this success.

Maliki Nguru is finishing Class 7 in a Maiduguri primary school. His father, Ahmed Kura, soldier, policeman, and petty trader, fully supported Maliki's school-going. Since Maliki's educational and occupational future is uncertain, M. Ahmed now has second thoughts about the wisdom of this support. Ya Jalo, Maliki's mother, does not appear to be involved in such issues. She is a housewife and possibly the most absorbed of all the parents in matters pertaining to witchcraft.

Zarami Goni is a prominent figure in Maiduguri and his daughter, Bintu, shows evidence of being much like her father. He is a Koranic mallam, a grain representative, and a politician; his wife, Ya Amina, is also a devout Muslim, who shares her husband's comparatively extreme views favoring Western education. Bintu is nowhere near the top student in Bornu Primary School's Class 2, but it is easy to believe that she will ably meet all academic hurdles.

It would be intriguing to learn what in fact happened to each child in the next month and next year after the observations for this study were complete. I did not attempt to find out, nor was it necessary for the purpose of this investigation. Case studies with a very limited focus cannot presume to offer such information. However, it is hoped that the data of the case studies, enriched by several years' contact with school and society in Bornu, provide the basis for observations of some merit.

The observations in this chapter often are expressed in general terms, that is, without reference to one of the four children when the data are of an extrapolative nature (see paragraph below regarding social relations, for example). The assurance that an extrapolative statement is warranted may originate in general understandings regarding the impact of schooling in developing societies, but the stimulus for the statement is suggested by the case study material. In effect, this type of observation says that the point being projected has not actually come to pass, but that it could because the basis for it is evident and what has happened in other societies under similar circumstances is known. Other observations differ in that they are more specific and possibly less speculative (see page 131, for example). They, too, may be extrapolative, but they differ from the former type of statement in being more closely related to the facts of one of the children or his parents.

In the next sections I discuss socialization outcomes derived first, from the influence of home and community (but viewed where relevant in relation to the intersecting school experience) and second, from the influence of schooling.

## SOCIALIZATION THROUGH HOME AND COMMUNITY

**Social relations** The four families studied vary among themselves in several aspects (such as age, occupation, and income) and, as mentioned in Chapter 1, they may be distinguished from most of their tribe by their willing cooperation in this study and by their support of primary education. Yet they have inculcated their children with conventional Kanuri norms of conduct regarding proper behavior in personal relationships. During transitional periods, however, customary expressions of respect and deference often appear outmoded to the educated child who may be torn between the attractions of new life chances and the demands of homage to his elders. Although conflict of this kind between young and old was not observed, there is a potential for conflict and discontinuity with traditional social life, first, when schoolchildren recognize the disparity between the prospects of their lives and the realities of their parents and, second, when both schoolchildren and their parents observe the continuing growth of those competencies ("today a child knows what even his great-grandparents didn't know"), the hallmarks of education, that are the student's exclusive and excluding possessions. Thus to be a student in Bornu is to join an elite in the sense of coming to possess relatively unique personal attributes.

A major factor in the generation gap of developing nations, which is actually a subcase of the elite-mass gap, begins with the fundamentals of the prospective elite's education—literacy, number skills, and at least an elementary knowledge of the world beyond kin, village, and tribe—that form the basis of their distinctive life style. The distinctiveness of these achievements is already evident in the lives of children as young as Aisa and Bintu. A generation gap is a relatively recent phenomenon among the Kanuri because during the colonial period social change was limited in scope and they and their Muslim brothers in other tribes repudiated Western education. Accordingly, there was sufficient generational congruence and harmony to ensure no disjunctures of importance between young and old.[1]

Among adults it is the parents of schoolchildren who are most sensitive to the outcomes of schooling that contrast and conflict with accustomed patterns of maturation; they know that their children are growing up to be different in unprecedentedly different times. For the generation or more during which Bornu's primary school children will come mostly from illiterate families, the primary school will help differentiate the elite from the masses, the educated from the uneducated; it cannot do otherwise as long as it eventuates in new aspirations and jobs. The social gaps engendered by these distinctions are not bridged by the mere passage of time. Getting older does not and cannot ensure the educated youth of becoming more like his uneducated parents or peers because of the often profound and persisting attributes that differentiate him.

Other changes in social matters also are associated with education. For example, Bintu will be allowed to choose her own husband rather than have one selected for her. Indeed, in a period of approximately one year (at the time of the study, Bintu was completing the first semester of her second year in school) her mother has adopted unusually Western views: agreeing to Bintu's attending a non-Islamic school, remaining in school past the age of puberty, and working at a salaried and therefore nontraditional job when she leaves school. Ya Amina's consideration of new roles for her daughter occurs at a time when few females in Bornu actually occupy such roles. If a persuasively eloquent husband must be credited with her acceptance of modern ideas, it is nonetheless education's growing relevance for success in Kanuri society that triggered his eloquence. Aisa, raised in the comparatively orthodox environment of rural Bornu, may not be much more "emancipated" than her mother. Were she an able student, with a high probability of completing primary and continuing to postprimary school, a change in role for her could be projected with greater confidence.

Maliki at thirteen is too young for his parents to be concerned with his marriage. This is not true for seventeen-year-old Buba, whose mother not only rejects her husband's fear of Buba marrying an educated girl but also believes that he should marry a girl of his own choice. Zara has further consented to postponing his marriage as long as he remains in school, a view not shared by the many mothers who harass their sons to quit school and get married. There are several points of con-

---

[1] See Cohen 1967:73. "[Y]ounger age groupings are constantly learning the ways of behaving and thinking and almost automatically know how to act as they grow up. By contrast in many western societies interaction between generations is extremely difficult. . . . Because western schooling has not yet separated an entire generation from their parents, there is little room among the Kanuri for many discontinuities in learning. . . ." As is clear from the remainder of this chapter I think that Cohen understates the effect of schooling on the lives of Kanuri families.

flict between old and new marital beliefs, such as whether it is wise to marry an educated girl, who should make the choice of mate, and what is the proper age of marriage. It is only Zara's unaccountably flexible position that prevents conflict on these issues and tends to minimize the disruptive effects of education on marital practice.

Education is related to marriage in still another way. If Aisa and Bintu remain in school for all or most of the primary grades, they are eligible to marry young men of secondary-level education who are reluctant to marry either uneducated girls or girls as well-educated as themselves. Although Bintu, because of the status of her family, probably would have wed an educated man, her education increases the likelihood. Aisa's chances for such a mate are also likely to improve considerably if she can continue in school.

Maliki's poor test scores make his future unpredictable, while Buba's academic success means that his life chances, if only as a primary school teacher, already have surpassed anything his father could attain. His life exemplifies the slow process of nation building at work. Buba's parents are illiterate, unsophisticated, and poor, but he is sent to school and to his intelligence are added the credentials of Western education that qualify him for more education, better jobs, and marriage to an educated woman. His children, accordingly, will grow up in a substantially different milieu than he did, as will his children's children, ad infinitum. Generations of adherence to certain traditions have been broken by Buba's scholastic success and modern Bornu has its first noteworthy recruit from his family. Maliki's school experience is similarly a departure from family tradition, but his poor academic performance means that he will probably join the unemployed school leavers, a group found in many developing nations and which recently has appeared in Bornu. Maliki's life exemplifies a problematic aspect of nation building by underscoring the dysfunctional consequences that result when a society cannot absorb its own educational products in ways that satisfy both individual and society.[2]

As I have reviewed in the opening pages of this chapter, the work experience of the four study fathers differs markedly. Each man has been drawn to the money economy but in jobs with long historical precedents. Furthermore, the rhythm of their work is broken by periods of socializing with friends; nonsalaried jobs support such interludes. The mothers also operate within custom. Zara sells cakes and is kept busy with domestic tasks. Ya Falta, with only Aisa to care for, is free to sell grain and occupy herself with ceremonial obligations. Ya Jalo does her housework, provides meals for her three children, and gads about with her neighbors. Ya Amina, as the senior wife of M. Zarami, manages the household for her large and busy family.

---

[2] Thus, in contrast to Jocano's conclusion that the Malitbog (1969:118–119) are not especially influenced by schooling, the Kanuri child who has completed six to seven or more years of education does not readily "fit into the general pattern of local expectations." Furthermore, the contribution of "modern education" to "social and cultural change" is enhanced both by the discontinuity between school and traditional community and, conversely, by the continuity between school and the modern sectors of community. Among the Malitbog it is perhaps the absence of modern sectors that limits modern education's importance in social change.

The schoolchildren's daily involvement in the classroom complicates the informal learning of their parents' roles and tends to disengage them from the daily round of traditional, pace-setting activities. Schoolboys, though they continue to assist with household and farming chores, may not and need not master their fathers' occupations. To the contrary, their school experiences are a major basis for rejecting their fathers' occupations and for providing a measure of independence that may reduce kinship ties. This is most evident in the case of Buba, whose occupational aspirations understandably do not include tanning, his father's craft. Why select a difficult, smelly, unpredictable, low-prestige job when one's success in school is making one eligible for comparatively superior jobs?

A similar case can be made for schoolgirls—Bintu, for example, speaks of becoming an English teacher. In fact, school life and its concomitant opportunities can so weaken the claims of tradition that parents may be unable to provide guidance acceptable to their children once they have crossed the watershed of primary education. As ever, such observations apply more to the rural than to the urban family. For example, what can ordinary people like Buba's parents offer him by way of meaningful counsel on any but traditional matters? What do they know about jobs acceptable to educated youth? His mother cannot even distinguish an Ibo from a European. The ordinary urban parent, somewhat closer to the modalities of the modern man, is perhaps better equipped to understand and advise his schoolchild.

It is doubtful that the parents are aware of the limits their schoolchild's daily absence from home places on inculcating their own values and beliefs. They are most explicit, however, in expecting their children to fill different, more lucrative and prestigious work roles than they do. The comments of Bintu's parents are most relevant in this respect. M. Zarami envisions his son becoming an important civil servant; Ya Amina hopes Bintu becomes a teacher or a nurse. The job, in their perspective, is intended to be instrumental to traditional goals—enhancing the status of and providing financial support to one's parents. Should their children reject these goals, then, obviously, they would be alarmed. The choice of a nontraditional job does not worry them. But it should. Viewing Western schooling merely as a new, superior means to the attainment of revered ends may mask its other effects, such as individualism and physical mobility, that parents do not bargain for and that may undermine traditional Kanuri life.

Parent-child conflicts stand as future possibilities in that the four study children have not yet left home for further education or jobs and the girls have not yet reached marriageable age. Thus any likely conflict in social relations within the study families should be considered in an anticipatory sense. Cohen's theory in *The Kanuri of Bornu* is that the household is the central social unit among the Kanuri and at the heart of the household are relationships incorporating *bərzum*, or discipline-respect.

> A father gives his son protection, security, food and shelter, a place . . . in the community, an occupation, helps him to arrange a marriage, and represents him in the adjudication of disputes. In his turn the son must be completely loyal, obedient and subservient to his father, and work for him in whatever way the father feels is necessary (1967:46).

Without predicting the disappearance of this relationship, its modification appears highly probable when it involves the *student*-child. If the schoolchild continues to receive and require food, shelter, protection, and security from parents, he also becomes increasingly independent, relatively speaking, in matters of marriage, occupation, and adjudication, and, equally important, in determining his general life style. Consequently, the traditional *quid pro quo* underlying *bərzum* may be vitiated by schooling such that new sets of expectations will be required that take account of changed circumstances in the parent and student-child relationship.

**Religion and the supernatural** At home the children see a wide range of conventional religious behavior and receive sanction only for religious orthodoxy. Their parents perform the daily prayers prescribed by Islam. In quiet moments M. Musa and M. Ahmed count prayers on their beads. Bintu's elders often refer to neighbors and relations on pilgrimage to Mecca. All the families donate food to Koranic students who visit their compounds; Aisa is rebuked when she mocks one. Both city fathers continue to develop their knowledge of Islam. All the families believe in the religious charm, a Koranic verse written on some material and then wrapped and sewn in leather to be fastened somewhere around the body. To prevent disease, accidents, or attacks by witches, M. Musa wears a chestful of charms whenever he goes traveling. Bintu would like her own because she does not think her mother's are appropriate for a young girl. Aisa has one to ward off devils. And the power of Koranic verses to cure sickness or prevent evil is acknowledged by Maliki "drinking a slate" that his mother arranged for him. M. Zarami prepared such drinks as part of his religious work.

At school the children study Islam more than if they simply remained at home; I do not know what their religious posture would be if they attended Koranic school. Meanwhile, there is no apparent erosion of religious sentiment among the children. Aisa's case is somewhat unclear because she is so immature. As for the others, Bintu sings about going to Mecca and recoils at the thought of attending a school which does not teach Islam—"Who'd teach you Islam? God forbid!" "No Arabic! God forbid!" Buba, at seventeen, not surprisingly has the religious habits of an adult, and Maliki, most alert during religious instruction, has shown concern for afterlife in his wish to be the Prophet Mohammed, the one Muslim who is "certain to enter paradise."

Related to religion in terms of supernatural qualities and experiences is an array of beliefs in witchcraft, magic, and old wives' tales. Witchcraft was apparent in M. Ahmed's experience with his jealous namesake, Ya Falta's concern to bury Aisa's fingernails, Ya Amina's advice to Bintu to say *"bismillahi"* when passing a reputed witch, and Zara's fit attributed to a cannibal. Magic in everyday life is exemplified by stories such as Umar's about the man who transformed vultures into chickens and about the district head who matched powers with a thief over a pair of handcuffs. And old wives' tales were heard in Ya Amina's belief that young children who overcome sickness become famous, and Ya Jalo's account of her child's hyperactivity in the womb.

Ya Amina is remarkable in several respects. Though she is religious and duly respectful of the supernatural, she rejects certain commonly accepted ideas such as the desirability of attempting to alter the sex of one's unborn child to assure the preferred male issue and the belief that evil agents cause children to die. These beliefs distinguish her form Maliki's mother, Ya Jalo, whose life is replete with experiences of witches, charms, and spells.

In the case of religion and the supernatural there are no indications of recent syncretic development. Conservatives lament the increasing popularity of non-Koranic schools, viewing enrollment in such institutions as an unreligious if not an antireligious act. Perhaps they would be pleased to learn that the religious practices of schoolchildren appear to be orthodox, as this would be defined in Bornu, unchanged either by urban or educational influences. Indeed the primary school is notable for its reinforcement of religious beliefs and practices; teachers of religion appeared to be better prepared and more effective than most other teachers observed. And since magical powers, witches, and juju are not directly questioned by the school or any other socializing agent in Kanuri society, the children are likely to perpetuate their parents' beliefs in these matters. The qualifier "directly" is added because while it is true that on no occasion were such matters subject to doubt or criticism, perhaps there is some quality that develops with increasing years of schooling that leads one to cast doubt on the existence of empirically nonverifiable phenomena; although according to my experience with primary and secondary students in Bornu, it cannot be assumed that such a quality generally develops.

**Medical practices**   The Kanuri are selective in their choice of medical treatment, preferring Western doctors for some ailments, local doctors for others,[3] and Koranic mallams in addition to or instead of either of the former. For example, M. Ahmed, sick with a swollen body, went first to a mission doctor and then to a Koranic mallam. Umar's unsuccessful confinement in a hospital led him to reject its medicine and for what proved (after this study was complete) to be a terminal disease, he planned to consult a local doctor whose treatment he could understand. Umar's attitude toward medical care, exemplified by the use of perfume and Koranic verses for his wife's fit, contrasts with that of M. Musa, his co-villager and an outspoken proponent of modern medicine. M. Musa pridefully describes the time he kept a catheter inserted longer than necessary by outwitting the hospital doctor. His trust in hospital cures, however, is complemented by his faith in charms. Similarly, Ya Jalo, after returning from the hospital with her sick child, placed a knife under the baby's pillow and burned some substance to counter witchcraft. These illustrations point to a syncretism of modern and traditional medical beliefs among older Kanuri.

There may be changes in the younger generation's, especially schoolchildren's, response to medical practices. In the student culture there is a stigma attached to wearing charms. Hence, while younger children wear them at their parents' as well as their own insistence—Bintu requests three of her own rather than wear her mother's—the older and more independent ones do so much less often. Moreover, the local government's sanction of Western medicine is seen in its estab-

---

[3] For example, the Kanuri claim that peculiar to them is a disease which causes a very stiff neck and severe head pains. It is cured by a local doctor who places his fingers on the patient's palate, thereby making him vomit a thick black mixture of blood and pus.

lishment of Nola's dispensary. On some mornings almost half of Aisa's class is there being treated for bilharzia. Bornu Primary School has its own government-stocked dispensary, and all its provisions, however modest, are products of modern science. Finally, education authorities assist their public health counterparts in arranging smallpox inoculations for all students while in school.

Modern medical treatment may contribute more to social mobilization than formal science instruction of the type available in Bornu's schools. Students receive "scientific" explanations of the body's organs and instructions for purifying water and eliminating malaria-bearing mosquitoes. Such explanations are applicable for school examination purposes, but they are difficult to internalize. Indeed, interviews with recent graduates from Maiduguri's secondary school suggest that they reject classroom knowledge that conflicts with traditional knowledge. When asked about their five years of science instruction, the graduates claimed they knew the "correct" answers for examination purposes but could not accept them as fact. Similarly, Ward tells of African students who disputed the appearance of adult mosquitoes which the day before were in pupal form, believing that their "teacher had come by night and made the exchange" (Ward 1959:74).

Europeans[4] and the urban environment  The village child occasionally sees visitors from the city and enjoys goods brought from outside Bornu. He may even observe planes, trains, and cars. But obviously both modern people and products concentrate in urban areas, so that the city child is exposed to significantly more experiences that may induce social mobilization.

The studies of our city children contain events peculiar to the urban scene such as Bintu's plans for her doll that involve a two-story house and a garage. These buildings are nowhere available in Nola and still uncommon in Maiduguri. She watches schoolboys at play in the mud, their fantasies derived from models of rich city persons; one boy imagines "living with only one wife like a European." Maliki speaks of marrying either a European or an Indian woman; compared to village children, he often sees foreign women. Nola students gather interestedly around the bicycle owner who arrived during the games period. Maliki's arrival on a bicycle at his urban school attracts no attention; the city boy admires the Honda and aspires to own one. Each day on their way to school Bintu and Maliki are exposed to the dramatic machinery used for building Maiduguri's new drainage system.

Because they often require only money, and not a major adjustment in life style, material objects are the simplest innovations to adopt. Thus the wealthier Maiduguri fathers own "urban" possessions such as bicycles, watches, and radios, items that village persons of comparable wealth might not own. Their wives ignite cooking fires with the aid of kerosene, carry food in plastic containers, and wear nylon as well as cotton shawls. At one time M. Zarami even had a phonograph, which he sold when his children scratched all of his records.

Through frequent cinema attendance both city fathers have contact with three societies, English, American, and Indian. They see a brief sequence of foreign news

---

[4] "Europeans" include North Americans as well as persons from England and the Continent.

with each film, receive practice in English (there are no Nigerian vernacular subtitles; none are necessary for the melodramatic Indian film), and are presented with European models for identification in regard to material goods. Furthermore, they listen regularly to news broadcasts and have access to Nigerian and foreign magazines and newspapers. Their children are heirs to these opportunities. M. Zarami's knowledge fully reflects the breadth of information made possible by the communication media and the comparatively rich intellectual milieu of Maiduguri. This is not true of any of the other parents.

While local reactions to Europeans are varied, there appears to be no resentment against them as former colonialists. Nola's village head watches in wonder the "indignity" of a European repairing a flat tire, more shocked than insulted when the man departs without paying the customary respects. Zara and Umar fear for the safety of schoolchildren if Europeans leave Bornu, mistakenly believing that extreme corporal punishment has been eliminated by their control of education. On a more abstract level, Ya Amina sees her daughter as a child of European times, and Buba's parents pridefully accuse him of receiving "too much brain" from the white man.

Many Europeans live in Northern Nigeria's towns and cities, usually doing technical work that Nigerians for the time being are unavailable to do. They are obviously wealthy and culturally different and they seem to be associated with agencies for change in Nigerian society. For decades they have been active merchants and traders in Maiduguri. Together the Nigerian urban elite and the Europeans provide attractive models for students in Maiduguri; such models are seldom available to students in Nola.

There is less apprehension about the European's role in effecting change (he is not blamed for changes attributable to his influence) than there is about change itself, specific changes, such as the "white man's school" with its concomitant opportunities and dislocations, and the general, more far-reaching change in "our times." This latter phenomenon may produce mixed feelings—of anticipation for acquiring the goods and services which are products of the West, and of dismay at the confusion and conflict associated with European-instigated "changing times."

Viewing Kanuri society through the microcosm of Buba, Aisa, Maliki, and Bintu, I discern moderate shifts in values and beliefs as well as areas of stability. Religion remains firm in the children's lives. Yet certain behaviors presumed to be sanctioned by Islam are rejected, such as preferring Western over Koranic education and allowing girls to remain in school past the age of puberty. Marriage is no less esteemed than formerly, but some of today's schoolchildren may have a voice in selecting their mates. While parental authority remains substantially intact,[5] a child's life at school is quite independent of his parents. The schoolboy may be led far from his father's occupation by his experience of five or more

---

[5] A questionnaire from another study on the Kanuri asked high school-aged students and high school-aged nonstudents if they agreed that a twenty-two-year-old man should take a job away from home against his father's advice. Of the former group, 75 percent disagreed; and of the latter, 80 percent disagreed.

hours a day at school. And the schoolgirl has less opportunity to master her mother's domestic skills. Children are exposed to both modern and traditional systems of medicine, often simultaneously as in the case of Ya Jalo's sick baby. Finally, socialization in the city includes contact with many modern objects and individuals which may stimulate and reinforce departures from tradition.

## SOCIALIZATION THROUGH SCHOOLING

Our study parents vary in their estimations of education. Buba's father unhappily recollects that Buba cannot work in the tannery or earn any income because of school. He tolerates Buba's school going because of the boy's success. M. Zarami enthusiastically supports education for Bintu and her brothers because he sees its advantages; his coterie includes successful, educated persons. In contrast, Buba's mother is a simple village woman whose endorsement of education is genuinely audacious since village boys like hers, with neither political nor economic connections nor a family tradition of Koranic or Western scholarship, are most often its victims. Somehow she has become convinced that education is a prerequisite for success in the world of the "new people." Such conviction is uncommon. Ya Falta originally consented to Aisa's admission to school but now is unhappy in the belief that Aisa's misbehavior is due to education. M. Ahmed, contemplating Maliki's future, wonders whether Koranic education would not have been a wiser choice. For it is reasonably definite that Maliki, not wishing to farm, may face long periods of unemployment and/or low-prestige employment. Few acceptable options are open to a thirteen-year-old boy with only a primary education. A girl in the same circumstances can be married without facing hardship or embarrassment. Whether a parent is strongly proeducation, as Ya Amina, indifferent, as Ya Jalo, or uneasy in feeling that it causes the misbehavior of her daughter, as Ya Falta, they all hold to the local tradition of children supporting their parents.

Aside from the feelings and expectations parents have for education, what are its effects on their children? The next section on cultural transmission considers how primary education reinforces community norms, and the section that follows discusses how it contributes to social mobilization.

**Education and cultural transmission** Policy statements from both the colonial and independence periods contain recommendations for Africanizing or adapting primary school curricula to local conditions.[6] Adaptation characteristically requires that indigenous rather than foreign (European) languages, history, and geography be taught, that examples in arithmetic textbooks contain local objects and situations, that poetry and literature draw upon local traditions and writers, and that agriculture or gardening and indigenous crafts be emphasized.[7] These practices, often resisted by Africans in the colonial era as a plot to keep Africans

---

[6] See, for example, Jones 1922; Great Britain 1925; Nuffield Foundation 1953; and UNESCO 1963.

[7] The desirability of adaptation at the university level is discussed in *The Development of Higher Education in Africa*, Report of the Conference on the Development of Higher Education in Africa, Tananarive, 3–12 September, 1962 (Paris; UNESCO 1963). See especially Chapter V.

in their place, are viewed differently after independence when it becomes axiomatic that schools serve national ends by mirroring the best that is past and present in society. Adaptation thus becomes desired cultural transmission.

The adaptation of education to local conditions and needs has a long history in Northern Nigeria, beginning with Lugard's policies (Lugard 1925) restricting missionary educational activity in Muslim areas and implemented in the N.A. schools built in subsequent years. A 1932 government report states that "in matters of dress, correct practice in the form of salutations and courtesies to chiefs and those in authority . . . the schoolboys were required to conform to the best traditions of local society" (Bittinger 1941:214). Instruction was in a Nigerian vernacular, and Islam and Arabic were emphasized in the curriculum. Official colonial documents relating to all of British Africa[8] contain much of the essence of Lugard's educational policy. Accordingly, Nigerian educators, especially at the ministry level, work within a tradition of adaptation that is evident formally, both by the fact of offering particular courses (vernacular, religion, nature study) and by the content of some courses (history, physical education), and informally, by several of the school's nonacademic practices and routines.

In speaking of adaptation the examples below apply equally to both Nola and Maiduguri. Such variations in classroom practice as one sees in the two schools investigated owe more to the fortuitous presence of certain teachers and head-masters than to any single factor inhering in their location. Both schools must follow the same course of studies and their teachers are prepared in the same type of training college. The city school neither tempers nor modifies the experience of living in the city nor produces noticeably different outcomes from the village school.

To begin with, the Kanuri's customary concern for cleanliness is reflected in school inspections and in early morning clean-up activities. While no fetish is made of cleanliness, the children can see standards supported comparable to those of their homes.

It was noted previously that in the early grades Kanuri is the language of instruction. As the children's language competency increases, English should gradu-ally replace Kanuri. In practice, though the better-trained teachers (those with Grade II qualifications who composed only 16 percent of all primary school teachers in 1966) frequently teach in English, perhaps a majority of all teachers have not adequately mastered English to do so. Consequently, instruction in the vernacular prevails in most classes and even Buba's conscientious teacher reverts to Kanuri at the end of a tiring day despite a scheduled English grammar lesson. And Buba's class continues speaking Kanuri as they turn to telling riddles rather than studying during their after-school prep period. The overuse of vernacular in terms of official expectations helps to establish a comfortable linguistic environ-ment for both students and teachers; it also represents an unintended form of adaptation since English, not Kanuri, is the language to be mastered in school.

In the lower grades English and arithmetic cover nearly half the total lessons,

---

[8] See footnote 6 above.

and in the upper grades half or more of the total for each week.[9] Comparable time and effort are not given to the other subjects, which tend to be taught indifferently (religion excepted) and to be replete with adaptive elements. For example, vernacular lessons usually are periods of games, songs, riddles, and stories, similar to what Bintu's family might arrange after dinner or what Maliki and his friends might do at night under the nearby house light. Oral activities are one part of the vernacular scheme of work set forth in the official syllabus (see Northern Nigeria 1959); however, the two other parts, reading and writing, are neglected. Physical education, especially if not taught by a recent training college graduate, frequently consists of indigenous games, songs, and dancing, particularly for the girls. Soccer provides variety for the boys. In the lower grades, general knowledge and history/geography emphasize the contemporary market, tribe, and village, and the history of the tribe and locality; in the upper grades, the average teacher's knowledge is inadequate to meet the syllabus requirements of teaching about national and international events at more than a superficial level. Finally, during rural science or nature study children usually labor in the school garden using techniques like those they already know; by offering these courses, so the questionable rationalization argues, the school best acknowledges the agrarian nature of society. The courses seldom are taken seriously by student or teacher. Agriculture, generally, is not profitable or prestigious, and no amount of classroom instruction will change the prevailing consensus that it is something to avoid.

Not only has the school curriculum been "indigenized" in the ways mentioned above, it also has incorporated elements from Islamic tradition. Most of these are relatively minor practices of the school. Teachers are called "mallam," an address formerly applied only to those knowledgeable in religious scholarship. As in the mosque, children cover their heads (a normal part of the school uniform is a cap for the boys and a small head scarf for the girls) and remove their shoes before entering a classroom. Like the Koranic student who must work for his mallam, the primary school student fills his teacher's water pots, cultivates his crops, occasionally washes and irons his clothes, and even cooks his chickens.

More central to Islamic tradition is the school's six periods per week of religious instruction during which students learn Arabic and theology (the nature of God, angels, and paradise), memorize verses from the Koran, and practice correct procedures for praying and performing other religious acts. In addition, they receive continual encouragement for moral behavior (supported by the threat of hellfire) and practical advice on everyday matters (as in the reply to Maliki's question about the man with two wives, one of whom received fancy gifts from her relatives). Student interest in and concern for religious learning are often greater than in other subjects, none of them relating so directly to what students know are important issues, such as how to have good relations with one's spouse and how to enter paradise. Religious instruction, unequivocably sanctioned by the community, is an instance of the school doing the bidding of all groups in Kanuri

---

[9] Newer English textbooks have been specially prepared for Nigeria, and at least reflect African rather than European culture; arithmetic textbooks have not been Africanized, although texts specially prepared for Nigeria were in process.

society; no other subject can as readily utilize both internal and external incentives for learning.

In emphasizing adaptation I do not mean to suggest that the primary school perpetrates either unique or unsound procedures. In fact, since this still alien institution arouses parental anxiety, perhaps it should contain an abundance of familiar and therefore nonthreatening experiences. At any rate, many aspects of primary education represent an extension of Kanuri tradition into the classroom. They derive both from ministry-established instructions and courses of study and, I imagine, from teachers naturally adjusting the tasks of teaching to their own experiences and strengths and weaknesses.

**Education and social mobilization**  Teachers in Bornu are unwitting agents of social mobilization,[10] that is, they do not consciously lead students to disrespect their elders, to question authority, to doubt conventional norms, or to aspire to urban living—all behaviors that would signify the erosion of old commitments. Trained teachers, however, having spent from three to five years in the usually urban setting of a teacher training college, often get accustomed to modern ways. At college they experience for the first time in their lives a relatively cosmopolitan environment that includes daily contact with expatriates and with an intellectually select group of classmates from varied ethnic backgrounds. And in striking contrast to their own homes, they live in cement-block houses supplied with electricity and running water. Teachers face a village assignment with predictable displeasure after their training is complete, anticipating a life less varied and exciting and more physically uncomfortable than that of their training college years. Thus it can be easily understood why teachers may communicate negative attitudes toward village life to their students— "[I]n Nola there are the same round huts everywhere," observes M. Zannah, Buba's teacher, "so there's little to see and little to do. In towns, though, some people are walking . . . some are selling in shops, and some are rushing about. There is much to do."

If economic and political development in Bornu continues and more teachers acquire higher professional qualifications, then schools may provide a more definite thrust for social change than is implied by social mobilization. At the time of this study the political leadership of Northern Nigeria was cautious and hesitant in respect to social change, encouraging economic innovation but protective of tradition in its other institutions. In apparent accord with the dominant cultural values of their society, the teachers I observed waved no revolutionary banners (and none were apparent from other sources). Ostensibly their daily lessons were innocuous. Clearly, students did not rush home exclaiming over what they had learned in school. In light of these facts, *social mobilization* is not too conservative a term to describe the effect of Western schooling in Bornu. The term does not convey the impression of cataclysmic or revolutionary change. The facts do not warrant such a conclusion. It is meant to convey the feeling that primary students are being opened to the possibility of "new patterns of socialization and

---

[10] It is no surprise to learn that schooling contributes to social mobilization. The potential for it is high whenever children in the new nations learn to read and there is little or no restriction on reading matter in their society. My intention here is to note the full range of its development from primary schooling in Bornu.

behavior." At this time it is unclear what these "new patterns" will be and what elements of the traditional and modern they will incorporate.

If the study children learn nothing that alarms their parents, they do nonetheless manifest nontraditional behavior that originated in school. In this regard Maliki was seen modeling in clay, disobeying his father and breaking the Islamic injunction that prohibits man from depicting living things. Maliki's education uncovered his talent in arts and crafts and may have revealed the most promising, and otherwise unknown, direction for his life work. In like fashion Buba has assumed leadership roles in the school's structure. Aisa, as well as the other children, is an actual member of a youth subculture so large and socially diverse as to be without equal outside the school. And Bintu's cleverness receives new channels of expression from her schooling. The children are continually differentiated both by level (in terms of marks and class) and area (in terms of subjects and activities) of achievement. In short, the maximization of human achievement which underlies the specialization and complexity of modern society (Eisenstadt 1966:*passim*) is promoted by the routine operation of the school.

Aisa informs her mother that she thinks of school "as home," this positive response signifying the capability of the school to join the home as a socializing agency. Much to the amazement of Ya Falta, Aisa draws pictures and sings and counts in English. To Aisa's mother these are singular achievements. Those of us who investigate the effects of schooling must so perceive them if we are to appreciate the disjunction that schooling may create between tradition-oriented parents and their first generation schoolchildren. This is true especially if Western schooling has been introduced relatively recently and the language of the school is the language of an elite. Our lives are shaped by our aspirations, and if those of seven-year-old Aisa cannot be taken seriously, it is noteworthy that her desire to be a nurse is justifiably held only by the educated. How different from the aspirations reasonably held by women like her mother, a seller of grain in one of Nola's small markets! Aisa is a long way from becoming a nurse. Though the school for the present is no more than a pleasant place for her to interact with friends and to learn things that impress her mother, the beginnings of social mobilization are nonetheless evident in her life.

Buba and a younger school friend are observed reviewing a hygiene lesson that involves the relationship between disease and untreated water. To Buba's mother this scene is hilarious—when one is thirsty one should drink whatever water is available. Buba's parents take for granted his constant reading and his prominence in Nola Primary School. Umar, never completely reconciled to Buba's unavailability for work, can still appreciate Buba's clever comments and good-naturedly accept his wife's observation that "schoolboys have been given too much brain by the white man." While Buba realistically appraises the opportunities associated with each type of postprimary school, his hope is to return home after completing his education. Since he holds to his parents' values, except possibly regarding personal cleanliness, Buba's case indicates that all students are not wrenched from their traditional moorings. Since it is also known that primary education has potential for social mobilization, Buba will probably never live again in his village after he enters secondary school in Maiduguri, notwithstanding his intentions to the contrary.

Little Bintu, with a scar under her eye and a devastating verbal attack, receives exceptional parental support to excel in school. Though not at the top of her class, she will probably be among the fortunate few who advance from primary to secondary school. She definitely carries home her scholastic experiences, frequently reading and reciting from an English reader and relating school events to her mother and friends, still too young to appreciate the bewildering effect her tales of "ten over ten" and "group A against group B" have on them. After one of Bintu's "John is a boy. Mary is a girl," performances, Ya Amina jocularly chides her for behaving like a European and for belonging to the European's time. "As for myself," says Ya Amina, "I learned that a schoolchild is wiser than one who is kept at home."

Thus, with each child education has "taken" in some definite ways. That children have learned to read, to write, and to calculate *in English* and, in addition, to aspire to higher education and professional occupations, signifies that social mobilization is occurring, even though from day to day there is little that is noticeably disruptive to traditional life. Other ways that schooling may have "taken" can be inferred from the subjects taught and from other characteristics of school life.

To begin with, geography and history could expand the students' perceptive and cognitive horizons by leading them to become aware of realities far beyond village and city life in Bornu. If it is doubtful that the subjects as taught in the two schools produce such important results to any appreciable extent, the fact cannot be dismissed that some broadening occurs when Buba learns about South America and Maliki learns about the commonwealth countries. To be sure, though geography and history are taught in a desultory fashion, the schoolchild certainly has experiences that represent a beginning for developing empathy. The nonschool child is much less likely to have comparable experiences.

Sound explanations in nature study and hygiene regarding how plants get food, why there is night and day, or how the heart uses oxygen could predispose children to scientific rationality in accounting for natural phenomena. Meanwhile, Bintu's lesson on plant roots and "plant-growing soil" is more punishment than instruction. Maliki responds with a barely audible *No* to his teacher's inadequate account of a round earth. His headmaster's superficial discussion of the heart is equally ineffective. A round earth is a difficult idea to accept, as are the notions that the earth moves or that the heart pumps blood throughout the body. To begin to be credible they require lucid and cogent explanations from teachers who comprehend the explanations themselves. At worst, the students' classroom encounter with natural phenomena may demonstrate that schools are absurd institutions; at best, it may provide groundwork that is built on further by later schooling. Children entering school from a prescientific milieu[11] are not substantially advanced in their understanding when taught by unsophisticated teachers like the Bornu Primary School headmaster or the one Ward mentions who faithfully described the life history of the malaria parasite without believing a word of it (Ward

---

[11] The Kanuri are not unscientific. Indeed their traditional methods of farming and medical treatment suggest a wise response to prevailing conditions and materials. Their tradition is prescientific in a Western, experimental sense, that is, in regard to the application of modern technologies and theories to the understanding and control of biological and physical phenomena.

1959:75). Is it not incredible that a tiny mosquito conveys the dreaded malaria! Perhaps if subjects dealing with natural phenomena were offered in as many periods as English and arithmetic and were as central to success on the Common Entrance Examination, more of their potential would be realized.

Furthermore, a mastery of arithmetic and English may lead to a breach of traditional expectations. Arithmetic locates right and wrong in conventions and processes which, when learned, give children the means to identify teacher error. When they master reading they gain access to the teacher's sources of information, which are relatively unprotected from the special pleading of esoteric interpretation and experiential requirements. Students are compelled to think always in terms of right and wrong, admittedly with the teacher as arbiter, but with books that they can read and understand available as ultimate judge. Hence in the Western-type school, more than in any other area of Kanuri life, it is easier for the young to be aware of the errors of adult authority and to acquire in consequence both the intellectual means and the inclination for independence from adult authority, beginning with their teacher.

However limited the school's prestige and authority, its teaching often stands as a conflicting alternative to what children already know and believe. The school also teaches much that is new. From these facts a presumptive case can be made for social mobilization resulting from the experience of schooling; moreover, there are many classroom experiences that establish the basis for more than a presumptive case, as I attempt to demonstrate in the following paragraphs.

The bastions of traditional authority—the family, religion, the polity—are not directly undermined at school. However, from Class 2 throughout their school life children are tested and ranked three times a year. There are no comparable events outside the school. The characteristic striving for marks, rank, and honors in school makes it a very competitive affair. On a lesser scale is the daily contest for grades and recognition, if not for the sadistic pleasure of slapping one's classmates. School competition is unique because it proceeds by universalistic and achievement criteria. First, females are as likely to be "winners" as males ("Bintu, today you're the star. I want you to keep it up."); there is no sex barrier to success and no separate demands or expectations based upon sex. Second, high economic status, while bestowing the usual advantages, does not predetermine the outcomes of school competition. The poorer Buba outshines the wealthier Maliki. Third, the child with ability may win regardless of his family's social rank, thus giving credence to the notion that children may attain rewards commensurate with their demonstrable ability. Schools offer children from ordinary families a route to success other than the traditional client-patron system that defines the relationship between M. Musa and Lawan Abba. This boost to achievement is a latent dysfunction in terms of customary procedure for social mobility. In terms of the requirements of economic and political modernization it is decidedly a latent function.[12]

---

[12] For an excellent discussion of the consequences of schooling that develop from the operation of the school rather than from the content of instruction, see Dreeben 1968. According to Dreeben, American schools provide norms that are different from those of the home but are required to get along in American society. Bornu's schools also develop such norms, but they are not endorsed by the home.

Finally, throughout a child's school career new standards are inculcated and old standards are applied to new areas. In regular classroom activities he experiences accuracy rewarded and inaccuracy punished; possibly no other behaviors are more persistently reinforced. He receives warnings that points will be lost if his examination paper is carelessly written. And unlike traditional life outside the classroom, time is handled in the inflexible manner characteristic of modern institutions. Although infractions of the school's time regulations are common, children are subjected to unique constraints. They are expected to reach school on time, to complete their work on time, to sit in class for specified periods of time, and to leave school on time. The school's timetable extends to the student's home, determining when he is available for meals and other household activities.

Standards regarding accuracy and time are omnipresent aspects of educational institutions. Though they may be enforced with some indifference (and we are uncertain of the degree to which they are adopted and become part of adult life styles), they are accepted school norms. Through their enforcement children are prepared for modes of work and living which are nontraditional in nature.[13]

There is no record of the study children rejecting family tradition. Their parents, however, justifiably fear that this is or could be happening as a result of schooling. Ya Falta is concerned that as an *educated* young lady Aisa will bring shame upon the family. M. Ahmed, worried that Maliki's failure at school will bring him to join the city's young ne'er-do-wells, urges his wife to detain the boy after dinner and tell him folktales. Even M. Zarami, the advocate of Western education, has reservations about school, fearing that it may lead Bintu to reject Islam, the one unaltered pillar of orthodoxy in his life.[14] I hazard the conclusion that however much an educated child may come to feel apart from family tradition,

---

[13] The pertinence of schooling to work in modernized institutions was noted by McLaren in Australia: "In a word, their [the workers'] total output was very small not merely because of the difficulty they found in handling tools or equipment, but because all their attitudes and behaviors were attuned to a mode of life utterly different from that of an industrialized people. They had not learned the disciplines and habits, the self-control, the time-consciousness, the drives which our own babies pick up from their parents or our youngsters learn in the elementary schools" (Hall 1954:23).

[14] A paradox of primary school is that even though it provides a thoroughgoing Islamic education, it is still suspect as a place that not only does not offer genuine Islamic studies but, worse yet, weakens religiosity. However it happens, I would guess that there are more doubters and disbelievers among an educated than an uneducated population. Some verification for this is provided by the responses of a sample of 15-to-26-year-olds indicated in the table below.

| Influence of religion should: | School | | | | Nonschool | | | |
|---|---|---|---|---|---|---|---|---|
| | Male | | Female | | Male | | Female | |
| | % | N | % | N | % | N | % | N |
| Increase | 80 | 204 | 87 | 156 | 96 | 71 | 96 | 69 |
| Remain the same | 6 | 16 | 11 | 19 | 3 | 2 | 4 | 3 |
| Decrease | 13 | 33 | 3 | 5 | 1 | 1 | 0 | 0 |

The findings are from questionnaires I administered for another study.

it is uneducated children and adults who soon may feel most profoundly alienated. Remaining closer to tradition, they may be less able to understand and participate in the inevitably predominant "new world" for which Buba's mother is happy he is being prepared.

The social mobilization outcomes discussed in this section result not so much from any direct effort or intent of the primary school to cast doubt on traditional beliefs, values, and roles as from the fact that schoolchildren acquire new skills, knowledge, and standards, and learn to compete in a new arena on unconventional terms. These achievements pave the way to more education and to new jobs that promise economic and status rewards greater on the average than those available from Koranic education and the old jobs; in addition, they are links to the attractive, nontraditional life styles of the European and new Nigerian urban elite.

These outcomes of schooling may be promoted most in schools with able teachers and headmasters, but it must be noted that to some degree they occur regardless of the quality of the school. The simple fact of a school acting as a school is conducive to these consequences. And except for those students present in every classroom in no more than a physical sense, they more or less affect all students.[15]

## SCHOOL AND SOCIETY IN BORNU

The primary schools of Bornu bear a relatively light cultural burden. They transmit valued religious ideas and some aspects of tribal history and local administration. They also reinforce community norms—recall the teacher's reaction to the song of a shameful Kanuri boy who begged for groundnuts. Such contributions may help to make education in a non-Koranic institution more acceptable to the local community; they are not part of the intended consequences of education. In fact, schoolchildren and their parents do not expect the primary school to transmit the core values and beliefs of Kanuri society. As Cohen ably demonstrates, the household and other institutions exist for this purpose. They do expect the school to promote personal gain through the new educational and vocational opportunities mentioned above. Furthermore, from a societal perspective, government in Bornu holds the same view. If government, like our study parents and others, is fearful of undesirable change resulting from schooling, it is fully cognizant of Western education's relationship to the economic and political requirements of the emerging modern Bornu. Merely to stay abreast of social change in Nigeria, as well as in Africa and the rest of the world, leaves Bornu no choice but to support and extend Western education.

As agents of cultural transmission, schools may teach what is not or cannot be efficiently and effectively learned elsewhere. Religion in Bornu is a case in point. Koranic schools are necessary in order to meet several of the community's role requirements. For most of the Kanuri a similar assertion cannot be made for

---

[15] The universality of marks, subjects, grade levels, competition, time constraints, and the like in all Western-type schools throughout the world suggests that whatever other differences may characterize schools, there are sufficient structural similarities to hypothesize a convergence of some effects.

Western education. Unlike primary schools in Western societies, those in Bornu are not meant to prepare children to live like the adults whose children are in school. That is, growing up to become a Kanuri adult is not yet linked to the Western system of education; the traditional passage-in-being from childhood to adulthood is not abetted and, more important, is not expected to be abetted, by the primary school. The modern passage-in-becoming is another matter altogether. It is shaped and defined as society changes and as school attendance increases. What part the school, with public approval, will play in this modern passage will remain unclear until many more educated parents are available to place their children in school. Consequently, the adaptation efforts, most of the subjects taught, the games period, and the pep talks are mere formalities and can be taken lightly. But if the payoff of primary education is desired, due regard must be given to whatever happens to be its specific requirements—memorizing nonsense syllables, tying knots, sketching chimera, or, as is in fact the case, mastering English and arithmetic.[16] Students, teachers, and parents can perceive the functional relevance of English and arithmetic to academic and occupational success and the functional relevance of academic and occupational success to the aforementioned traditional goals of enhancing one's status and providing financial support for parents.[17] The other subjects, religion possibly excepted, are not *perceived* as functional in any way.

The elements of primary schooling that relate to adaptation and to social mobilization are unplanned by those who work in the school. The adaptive elements, many of them inspired by Ministry of Education directives, are also derived from the teacher's own experience as a student and reinforced by the character of the schools in which he teaches, *without his awareness of a rationale relating to adaptation.* Similarly, the teacher grades and ranks students, enforces standards, and creates a competitive environment, unaware that the results may be at odds with traditional behavior. There is no evidence that teachers knowingly create and perpetuate a school environment either to harmonize or to clash with local values in Bornu. That is, I have no evidence to this effect. Perhaps some particularly sophisticated primary school teachers consciously teach from a philosophy of adaptation (I met none in two years of association with primary schools in Bornu), and some, like M. Zannah, digress from the prescribed syllabi to discuss the good life of the city or adopting some of the European's ways. I doubt if there are many, or that such teaching is done systematically.

By Western standards schools suffer from financial and pedagogical shortcomings. In a more profound sense they suffer as newly introduced institutions that are necessary if Kanuri society is to modernize but that are still obtrusively situated at the periphery of that society, their mandate weak, their constituency limited. In the present transitional stage of Nigerian development they do not reflect the

---

[16] For purposes other than success in school the mastery of English and arithmetic is translatable into desired behavior outside the school, as when a child reads a letter for his parents or does some financial computations for them.

[17] These do not exclude the reasonable possibility of other goals existing and being important. Data from another study show that Bornu adults expect the primary school to help children adapt to changing times. And the students themselves may aspire to goals that have no bearing on family or personal status and financial support.

richness and complexity of either Western or Kanuri society. Instruction in the primary school will become more fully meaningful to the populace when the requirements of Kanuri culture preclude its satisfactory transmission by other agencies, that is, when their contribution is considered germane to growing up to be a Kanuri adult.[18]

The lives of the four Kanuri schoolchildren suggest that Kanuri society in terms of values and beliefs is relatively stable and intact. How long this impression will conform to reality is uncertain since modernization already has begun in Bornu. For example, new schools have been built and enrollments are increasing. All-season roads have been constructed, a railroad link established with major cities in Northern Nigeria, exports expanded, and agricultural improvement schemes implemented. These changes do have the potential for undermining tradition; education is an ally in this process.

Not until the introduction of Western education did children enroll in a type of school which tended to separate them physically and culturally from their family and community. Although traditional Koranic education occasionally involved long periods of absence from the family—periods of itinerancy with one's teacher for the few training to become mallams—the Koranic student seldom rejected his culture. This is not true for the Western-educated student whose school upon close examination appears as a syncretic institution, simultaneously reflecting characteristics and requirements of both traditional and modern Bornu. Aspects of the latter open new opportunities that can usually be seized only at the cost of disregarding some traditional obligations.

The study parents are aware of these new opportunities and value them. They are essentially economic in nature, and it is their financial promise rather than a weakening of religious spirit, a rejection of traditional norms, or a sensitivity to manpower needs that explains the attraction of Western education. This conclusion is supported by the parents' common expectation that schooling will enhance their child's earning capabilities.[19]

The several general effects of schooling may be summarized as follows. If a

---

[18] The above argument is pertinent to understanding the limitations of curricular reform. The quality of instruction can be improved and concern for currently neglected subjects can be increased. All that is required is to include them on the Common Entrance Examination. But as long as the content of education does not appear important either for everyday life outside the school, for academic or occupational success, or for identification with some elite group, it will be neglected if it is not a factor in examination success or learned by rote if it is. This observation applies equally to school learning anywhere in the world. Since more variables than have been investigated bear on the issue of how a subject is received by students, further conjecture would be unwise.

[19] It is misleading to focus exclusively on the economic nature of the opportunities created by schooling. There is also a status aspect, difficult to separate from the economic. When the Kanuri speak of becoming a "big man," they refer to a position that includes status and power as well as wealth. With the exception of M. Zarami, who imagined his son (not a study child) as a government officer and, therefore, definitely a big man, none of the parents spoke of their expectations from education except in fairly modest economic terms. However, the ubiquity of the term "big man" in everyday conversation in Bornu suggests that the parents of the study children probably view economic achievement as integrally linked to status achievement.

child does well in school, succeeds in getting a good job, and maintains his kinship ties, then, as this matter is perceived in Bornu, a family has realized education's maximum good at a minimum cost. Under other circumstances the cost may be quite high. A child may fail in school but have attended long enough to reject traditional alternatives regarding where to live and work; he may succeed in school but become a drifter after failing to find a satisfactory job; or he may succeed both academically and vocationally and in doing so become a stranger to his parents and their way of life.

For the time being, schools do at least what Bornu supports them to do, albeit not as well and not as efficiently as desired: they develop the language and number skills of those children who survive the challenges of schooling and pass them on, some prematurely to the economy, others to the next level of schooling for more instruction and hopefully for more development. These are the manifest and desired consequences of primary schooling. In contrast schooling has latent and often undesired consequences that are summarized in the concept of social mobilization. Depending on the values of the viewer, these latent consequences may represent either the costs or the benefits of children in a non-Western traditional society being socialized by Western-type schooling.

With less than 10 percent of Bornu Province literate and less than 10 percent of all school-age youngsters in school, education's fullest potential for supporting discontinuities with the past remains unrealized. Consider the force of 30, 40, or 50 percent of the school-aged population attending school in a society that has continuously modernized its institutions!

Clearly, the impact of primary education is fully appreciated only when seen within the perspective of "aggregate effects of small-scale changes" over time (Moore 1963:71). For example, 8,822 girls attended Bornu's primary schools in 1966, more than twice the enrollment of five years earlier. Thus, a proper consideration of societal change through education must view the impact of educating females in magnitudes greater than those suggested by Aisa's and Bintu's case studies. In short, there were thousands of girls undergoing social mobilization, becoming eligible for postprimary education, and preparing to fill new roles as well as old roles in new ways. There were almost 19,000 Bubas and Malikis learning to speak English and developing a self-image which sharply differentiates them from their elders. Each year the enrollment of both sexes steadily increases.

In the northern provinces of Nigeria the primary school cannot be regarded as an alien institution as it was during decades of colonial rule. No longer does a colonial government control education, moving with reservation and restraint to expand school facilities. Independent, Muslim-controlled local governments are in power and they have become aware that survival in the modern world is irrevocably tied to Western education. Consequently, now it is Muslim leaders who forcibly urge Muslim parents to send their children to school. While the expansion of education is certain, it will be many years before parents are comfortable with the "white man's school," their hesitancy existing as long as adult society is essentially illiterate.

The study parents know that admitting a child to school is like opening Pandora's box. Emerging from the school experience may be a future civil servant or an unemployed malcontent, a respectful son or an errant daughter. In Bornu, opening the school's door to a child is tantamount to gambling with his future. Keeping the door closed, however, and trusting his future to the seemingly tranquil and stable alternatives of either no education or Koranic education is equally a gamble in that he may be permanently precluded from all but peripheral participation in modern Bornu society.

# Appendix

EDUCATION IN BORNU AND IN NORTHERN NIGERIA

TABLE 1
PERCENTAGE LITERATE IN BORNU AND NORTHERN NIGERIA, 1952

|  | % Literate in English | % Literate in Arabic |
|---|---|---|
| Bornu | 1 | 2.2 |
| Northern Nigeria | 1.9 | 5.4 |

SOURCE: Figures taken from Northern Nigeria 1965, *Statistical Yearbook 1964*. Kaduna: The Government Printer.

TABLE 2
PRIMARY SCHOOL ENROLLMENTS IN NORTHERN NIGERIA BY SEX, 1959–1966

| Year | Male | Female | Total |
|---|---|---|---|
| 1959 | 184,522 | 66,390 | 250,912 |
| 1960 | 206,443 | 76,405 | 282,848 |
| 1961 | 230,500 | 85,764 | 316,264 |
| 1962 | 262,083 | 97,851 | 359,934 |
| 1963 | 295,644 | 115,062 | 410,706 |
| 1964 | 323,399 | 128,920 | 452,319 |
| 1965 | — | — | 492,510 |
| 1966 | 367,776 | 151,088 | 518,864 |

SOURCE: This table is compiled from two Ministry of Education Publications: Northern Nigeria 1965, *Steps on the Path of Progress*. Kaduna: The Government Printer; and Northern Nigeria 1966, *Classes, Enrollments and Teachers in the Primary Schools of Northern Nigeria in 1966*. Kaduna: The Government Printer.

TABLE 3

QUALIFICATIONS OF PRIMARY SCHOOL TEACHERS IN BORNU AND
NORTHERN NIGERIA, 1966

| | Qualifications (by percentage) | | | | | Number of Teachers | | |
|---|---|---|---|---|---|---|---|---|
| | Grade 2 | Grade 3 | Grade 4 | Un-trained | Religion Teachers | Male | Female | Total |
| Bornu | 14 | 33 | 4 | 35 | 14 | 799 | 99 | 898 |
| Northern Nigeria | 24.2 | 35.1 | 4.1 | 27.7 | 8.9 | 13,559 | 2,147 | 15,706 |

SOURCE: Figures taken from tables in Northern Nigeria 1966, *Classes, Enrollments and Teachers in the Primary Schools of Northern Nigeria in 1966.* Kaduna: The Government Printer, pp. 21–22. The amount of education associated with each qualification is: grade 2— 7 + 5; grade 3—7 + 3; grade 4—7 + 1; untrained—7 + 0.

TABLE 4

NUMBER AND PERCENTAGE OF CHILDREN IN SCHOOL COMPARED TO THEIR AGE COHORTS IN BORNU AND NORTHERN NIGERIA, 1960

| | 1960 Population | Age-group 6–7 Years | Enrollment in Class 1 | %age Age-Group in Class 1 | Age-Group 10–11 Years | Enrollment in Class 4 | %age Age-Group in Class 4 | Age-Group 12–13 Years | Enrollment in Class 7 | %age Age-Group in Class 7 |
|---|---|---|---|---|---|---|---|---|---|---|
| Bornu | 1,559,353* | 31,187 | 2,769 | 8.9 | 28,068 | 2,201 | 7.9 | 26,610 | 314 | 1.2 |
| Northern Nigeria | 19,737,041 | 394,468 | 74,281 | 19 | 357,355 | 26,492 | 13.0 | 336,810 | 13,426 | 4.0 |

SOURCE: This table is adapted from Northern Nigeria n.d., *The Administration of Primary Education (Oldman Report)*. Kaduna: The Government Printer, *passim*.

* All figures are estimates. It should be noted that Bornu showed the highest percentage increase in primary school enrollments in 1962 and the second highest in 1963, thereby reducing the disparity in enrollment ratios between Bornu Province and the Region.

TABLE 5

PERCENTAGE OF PRIMARY SCHOOL PUPILS IN BORNU AND NORTHERN NIGERIA, BY PROVINCE, BY CLASS AND BY SEX IN 1966

| | Percentage of Pupils | | | | | | | | | | | | | Number in All Classes | | |
|---|---|---|---|---|---|---|---|---|---|---|---|---|---|---|---|---|
| | Class 1 | | Class 2 | | Class 3 | | Class 4 | | Class 5 | | Class 6 | | Class 7 | | M | F | Total |
| | M | F | M | F | M | F | M | F | M | F | M | F | M | F | | | |
| Bornu | 12 | 6.4 | 12.6 | 5.5 | 11.8 | 5.2 | 9.9 | 4.4 | 8.1 | 4.7 | 7.0 | 4.3 | 5.8 | 2.2 | 18,791 (67.2%) | 8,822 (32.7%) | 27,613 |
| Northern Nigeria | 12.5 | 6.0 | 11.7 | 5.3 | 11.3 | 4.6 | 10.6 | 4.4 | 9.1 | 3.5 | 8.0 | 2.9 | 7.3 | 2.2 | 367,776 (70.5%) | 151,088 (28.9%) | 518,864 |

SOURCE: This table is a modified version of Northern Nigeria 1966, *Classes, Enrollments and Teachers in the Primary Schools of Northern Nigeria in 1966*. Kaduna: The Government Printer, p. 3.

# References

BITTINGER, D. W., 1941, "An Educational Experiment in Northern Nigeria in Its Cultural Setting." Unpublished doctoral dissertation, University of Pennsylvania.

BUCKERFIELD, M. J., AND J. W. V. CHAMBERLAIN, 1963, *A Handbook for Inspectors.* Kaduna: The Government Printer.

COHEN, R., 1967, *The Kanuri of Bornu.* New York: Holt, Rinehart and Winston.

COLEMAN, J., 1958, *Nigeria.* Berkeley: University of California Press.

DEUTSCH, K. W., 1961, "Social Mobilization and Political Development." *The American Political Science Review*, LV, September 1961, 493–514.

DREEBEN, R., 1968, *On What I Learned in School.* Reading, Mass.: Addison-Wesley Publishing Company.

EISENSTADT, S. N., 1966, *Modernization: Protest and Change.* Englewood Cliffs, N.J.: Prentice-Hall, Inc.

GREAT BRITAIN, 1925, *Memorandum on Education Policy in British Tropical Africa.* London: H.M.S.O.

HALL, R. K., ET AL. 1954, "Education and the Transformation of Societies." In R. K. Hall et al., *The Yearbook of Education.* New York: World Book Company.

HOUTSMA, M. TH., ET AL. (eds.), 1927, *The Encyclopedia of Islam.* Leyden: E. J. Brill, Ltd.

IBRAHIM, SIR KASHIM, 1965, "Speech by His Excellency the Governor of Northern Nigeria on the Occasion of the Second Anniversary of National Day."

IWANSKA, A., 1965, "New Knowledge: The Impact of School upon Traditional Structure of a Mexican Village," *Sociologus*, **13**, 2, 1965, 137–149.

JOCANO, F. L., 1969, *Growing Up in a Philippine Barrio.* New York: Holt, Rinehart and Winston.

JONES, J., 1922, *Education in Africa: A Study of West, South and Equatorial Africa by the African Education Commission.* New York: Phelps-Stokes Fund.

LEVY, S. J., 1968, "Kanuri Personality, Marriage, and Divorce." (Mimeographed.)

LEWIS, O., 1962, *Five Families.* New York: Science Editions, Inc.

LUGARD, F. D., 1925, *Education in Tropical Africa.* London: Longmans, Green and Company.

MEAD, M., 1953, *Growing Up in New Guinea.* New York: The New American Library.

MOORE, W. E., 1963, *Social Change.* Englewood Cliffs, N.J.: Prentice-Hall, Inc.

NNTEP, 1965, "Program Development Conference Proceedings," Zaria, Northern Nigeria, April 19–22, 1965.

NORTHERN NIGERIA, 1959, *English, Vernacular and Writing Syllabus.* Zaria: Gaskiya Corporation.

NORTHERN NIGERIA, 1961, "White Paper on Education Development in Northern Nigeria." Kaduna: The Government Printer.

NORTHERN NIGERIA, 1964, *Education Law of Northern Nigeria.* Kaduna: The Government Printer.

NORTHERN NIGERIA, 1965, *Statistical Yearbook 1964*, Kaduna: The Government Printer.

NORTHERN NIGERIA, 1965, *Steps on the Paths of Progress*. Kaduna: The Government Printer.

NORTHERN NIGERIA, 1966, *Classes, Enrollments and Teachers in the Primary Schools of Northern Nigeria in 1966*. Kaduna: The Government Printer.

NORTHERN NIGERIA, n.d., *The Administration of Primary Education (Oldman Report)*. Kaduna: The Government Printer.

THE NUFFIELD FOUNDATION, 1953, *African Education*. London: Oxford University Press.

PESHKIN, A., 1967, "Education and National Integration in Nigeria," *The Journal of Modern African Studies*, 5, 323–334.

TRIMINGHAM, J. S., 1959, *Islam in West Africa*. London: Oxford at the Clarendon Press.

UNESCO, 1963, *The Development of Higher Education in Africa*, Report of the Conference on the Development of Higher Education in Africa, Tananarive, 3–12 September 1962, Paris: UNESCO.

WARD, W. E. F., 1959, *Educating Young Nations*. London: George Allen and Unwin Ltd.

CASE STUDIES IN EDUCATION AND CULTURE

GENERAL EDITORS
George and Louise Spindler

*Related Series Edited by George and Louise Spindler*
*CASE STUDIES IN CULTURAL ANTHROPOLOGY*
*STUDIES IN ANTHROPOLOGICAL METHOD*

HOLT, RINEHART AND WINSTON, INC.
383 Madison Avenue, New York, N.Y. 10017